The Social Life of Achievement

Wyse Series in Social Anthropology

Editors:
Maryon McDonald, Fellow and Director of Studies, Robinson College, University of Cambridge
Joel Robbins, Sigrid Rausing Professor of Social Anthropology, University of Cambridge, and Fellow of Trinity College, Cambridge

Social Anthropology is a vibrant discipline of relevance to many areas – economics, politics, business, humanities, health and public policy. This series, published in association with the Cambridge William Wyse Chair in Social Anthropology, focuses on key interventions in Social Anthropology, based on innovative theory and research of relevance to contemporary social issues and debates. Former holders of the William Wyse Chair have included Meyer Fortes, Jack Goody, Ernest Gellner and Marilyn Strathern, all of whom have advanced the frontiers of the discipline. This series intends to develop and foster that tradition.

Volume 1
Sociality: New Directions
Edited by Nicholas J. Long and Henrietta L. Moore

Volume 2
The Social Life of Achievement
Edited by Nicholas J. Long and Henrietta L. Moore

Volume 3
The State We're In: Reflecting on Democracy's Troubles
Edited by Joanna Cook, Nicholas J. Long and Henrietta L. Moore

The Social Life of Achievement

Edited by

Nicholas J. Long and Henrietta L. Moore

berghahn
NEW YORK • OXFORD
www.berghahnbooks.com

Published in 2013 by

Berghahn Books

www.berghahnbooks.com

First paperback edition published in 2016

Library of Congress Cataloging-in-Publication Data

A C.I.P. cataloging record is available from the Library of Congress.

British Library Cataloguing in Publication Data

A catalogue record for this book is available from the British Library.

ISBN 978-1-78238-220-1 (hardback)
ISBN 978-1-78533-215-9 (paperback)
ISBN 978-1-78238-221-8 (ebook)

Contents

Figures

Acknowledgements

This book has grown out of a series of conversations with scholars from a range of disciplines on the nature and consequences of achievement. Although only eleven of us are represented in the present volume, we are very grateful for the support, interest and ideas of our interlocutors in those discussions, most notably Steven Borish, Amy Brown, Matei Candea, Andrei Cimpian, Merve Demircioglu, Vanessa Fong, Jessica Gerrard, John Herzog, Kristin Kostick, James Laidlaw, Robert LeVine, Claire Loussouarn, Jonathan Mair, Ros McLellan, Laura McMahon, Mark de Rond, Renata Salecl, Mitchell Sedgwick, Nikolai Ssorin-Chaikov and Joachim Stoeber. Their work, perspectives, and critiques have greatly enriched the present volume. We would also like to offer our very warmest thanks to the Wenner-Gren Foundation for Anthropological Research who generously helped us bring the authors of the present volume together to refine their arguments in the light of each other's work, as well as to the staff and students of the Division of Social Anthropology at the University of Cambridge for putting up with more 'achievement'-related activities and discussions than they had ever expected or wanted. In this regard, particular thanks are due to Jan-Jonathan Bock, Su Ford, James Hale, Paolo Heywood, Julia Leijola, Marlene Schafers, Madeline Watt, Louis Wenham and Anna Zavyalova for their enthusiastic support of the project.

It has been a pleasure to work with the editorial team at Berghahn whilst putting together this volume, and we would like to thank Adam Capitanio, Ann Przyzycki DeVita, Charlotte Mosedale, Megan Palmer, Ben Parker, Melissa Spinelli and Lauren Weiss for their tireless hard work on getting the manuscript into production. A team of anonymous peer reviewers gave invaluable comments on individual chapters, and we would like to thank them for their help. Finally, we are grateful to the Wyse Fund of Trinity College, Cambridge, for their financial assistance in preparing the volume for publication.

Introduction
Achievement and Its Social Life

Nicholas J. Long

and

Henrietta L. Moore

It's a rainy winter's day in Atlanta, Georgia, and a weary anthropologist is heading for his flight. The subway train is lit a sickly yellow, and the figures in the carriage huddle into the corners of their seats, hands in their pockets and coats zipped up to the neck. It's the kind of journey on which even a quick, friendly smile could make all the difference. At first no one looks back. They focus their eyes on their knees, the floor, a point somewhere just outside the window. Then somebody meets his gaze – not exactly a reciprocation; a scowl. He turns away.

The journey drags on. But throughout, there is one person who is ready to lock eyes with him. She takes this train every day. She's a smiling, confident, attractive middle-aged woman and she's up there, on the wall. She's written a book – it's about how to unlock the secrets of success and how to be 'a winner' every single moment of every single day. She'd love the people on the train to read it. It could help them. They could unlock they potential. But, for today at least, none of the other passengers seem able to bring themselves to look at her.

He changes trains. A preacher is on the platform. The crowd needs to be warned – they might think we know what it means to 'achieve' – having a great job, a great salary, a great house, a great relationship. But these are earthly pleasures, these aren't 'true success'. True success means getting into the Kingdom of Heaven. They must repent, renounce their worldly ways and live good Christian lives. Then they will be true successes on Earth.

A few minutes later, at Hartfield-Jackson Airport, a billboard offers another perspective (Figure 0.1). Advertising the philanthropic clothing company Geoffrey Beene, it proudly declares that 'we measure success by how much we give away'. The slogan is a testimony to the millions of dollars raised by the company to fund charitable causes. But it is offset by a picture of an improbably thin woman in an open-backed black dress, averting her gaze from the attentions

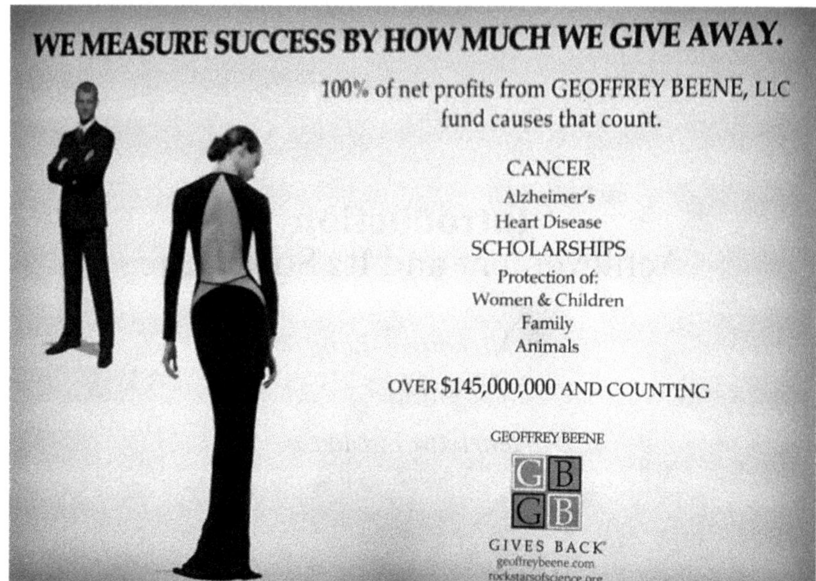

Figure 0.1 A billboard at Atlanta's Hartfield-Jackson Airport.

of a handsome blond man. The advert is arresting, but also unsettling. Are we meant to think that this woman is a success because of how much she is able to 'give away'? And what exactly is she 'giving away'? The skin her sylph-like figure is allowing her to reveal? Or something else…?

One journey in Atlanta. Thirty minutes. And yet a trip saturated by images, injunctions and appeals to 'achieve' and find 'success'. A trip filled with differing visions of what 'success' might actually comprise, but with a clear consensus that it is something that one should want to obtain. In some ways, of course, the journey is exceptional – a strange confluence of achievement-related incidents that befell an academic who just happened to be editing a volume on the social life of achievement. Yet it is a journey that any of us could have taken, and the sort of journey that many of us have probably been on, whether or not we were aware of it at the time.

The language of 'achievement', in fact, has become one of the defining features of the contemporary moment. As people are faced with the pressures of neoliberal exhortations to become ideal worker-citizens on the one hand, and on the other are obliged to navigate an increasingly austere economic situation following a devastating global financial crisis, achievement can seem to be the perfect solution, guaranteeing both the security and the worth of themselves and their loved ones. Such a perception is backed up by both the authority of a sizeable and globally circulating academic discourse on 'achievement' from within the social sciences (notably the discipline of psychology, but also anthropology and sociology to a lesser degree), and a burgeoning international self-help industry. Indeed, the British media notes that during the recent economic downturn, self-help book sales increased by 25 per cent at a time when overall book sales were falling.[1] Yet despite this, achievement is so often not the solution that people hope it will be – a realisation that prompts us to consider in more detail how, why and when achievement both manages and fails to live up to its promise, and the ways in which such an enquiry might not only illuminate contemporary times, but also enrich the notions of efficacy, agency, motivation and selfhood implicit in current social science.

The Social Life of Achievement

One of the challenges in writing about achievement is that the central object of the enquiry proves remarkably resistant to definition. For what is 'an achievement'? Much of the literature is quick to take such phenomena as academic attainment, sporting prowess or business success as synonymous with 'achievement', but as anthropologists we know that this may not always be how they are experienced by people on the ground. Moreover, we know that often the things that are seen as 'achievements' for some people might seem entirely trivial, ridiculous or even horrific to those around them. For a serial insomniac, getting to sleep without medication could be a remarkable achievement yet it is something that most of us take for granted. Seemingly 'inconsequential' events, such as giant vegetable contests or winning a local domino drive, can be incredibly significant for those involved in them. A company turning around its fortunes and boosting shareholder profits can be seen as an achievement from one point of view, but as the ruthless exploitation of its workers on the other: nothing to be proud of.

In this volume, then, we are not interested in developing any normative definitions about what is, or is not, an achievement. Rather we see achievements as emerging through affective and evaluative engagement with things that have been done in the world, either by oneself or by others. Such assessments, and what is at stake in them, are necessarily contingent on the particular historical and geographic circumstances in which they take place. Thus, although a present-anchored reading of the past might suggest that human beings have always counted 'achievement' amongst their primary concerns, it is important to remember that what was at stake in such arenas as the Roman gladiatorial ring, the medieval tournament or the Renaissance quest for learning was distinct, if not unrelated, to what achievements in the fields of sports, science or combat might signify today.[2] Equally, as this volume will make clear, the significance and implications of 'achievement' in contemporary societies are highly variable – not only between more 'individualistic' and more 'communitarian' settings (the distinction most popular within social psychology) but, more strikingly still, between populations in former imperial metropoles and those in the former colonies, those whose ancestors were slaves, and those who were or are a subordinated proletariat.

Achievement's contingent and socially embedded character is one reason why we choose to write of 'the social life of achievement'. But there is much more at stake in that phrase than simply alluding to different definitions and contestations that the term 'achievement' might attract. Rather, we are seeking to ground our enquiry into achievement and its effects in a deep and nuanced understanding of human sociality. As we have argued elsewhere (Long and Moore 2013; Long forthcoming), human beings are always already emplaced in a dynamic matrix of relations with other humans, non-humans and an environing world. These relations are necessarily ones of interdependence, co-production and co-constitution: they are formative of the subject but they are also something upon which the subject can reflect and which he or she may subsequently transform through his or her own creative and ethical endeavours. Processes of self-making and self-stylisation, of which both striving and managing to achieve are a part, thus need to be understood in relation to the specific ways in which subjects at particular historical moments understand themselves, the entities with which they share the world, and the relations between them.

Thus even in a setting where everyone subscribes to the same cultural definition of achievement – as, say, a high mark in a school exam – the ways in which achievement is lived out and experienced will vary widely between a pupil who feels compelled to prove that she is the top of her class, a pupil hoping that a high mark will secure him a scholarship at the university of his choice, or a pupil desperate to please his teachers. Given this, however, a second point becomes relevant. As Moore (2011: 76) has emphasised, 'you can never completely know yourself and nor can you completely know the other'. As such, the relations between self and others that subjects seek to cultivate and transform through achievement are 'set up in fantasy, based on a series of identifications and their circulations ... [and] shot through with social imaginaries and relays of power' (ibid.: 76).

It is important to emphasise that these fantasised relations exist at all temporalities and scales. When a student hopes that a high-scoring degree might earn the approval of a cold, expectant parent, it is clear that the anticipated future relationship between parent and child is a fantasised one, but the present 'cold' relationship, based on a long history of identifications, projections and introjections, is no less fantasmatic in character. Moreover, self–other relations are scalable, which is to say that whilst some of them might be 'premised on detailed empirical knowledge of shared intimacies and spaces, ... others are mediated by more distant institutions, structures and imaginaries' (ibid.: 78). The others with whom the self is in relation might be those close to hand, but they can equally be very far flung, as when Guyanese men of low socio-economic standing train songbirds in pursuit of a 'reputation' that will affirm their worth relative to the national elite (Mentore, this volume), or Indonesians take part in competitions hoping this will equip them with the skills needed to be 'globally competitive' (Long, this volume). Indeed, as noted above, the contemporary moment seems to be marked very widely by cases of people whose relations to their own achievement are partially or wholly set up in messianic fantasies of attracting wealth or acquiring a sense of personal worth; expectations that find their roots in discourses of the self-made man and the American Dream, that can help to explain achievement's powerful appeal, but also illuminate the potential for disillusionment and frustration when it eventually occurs. An enquiry into the social life of achievement thus demands that we interrogate the factors and processes that underpin the specific ways in which achievement has become an aspect of particular human subjects' imaginative and fantasmatic engagements with self and others. Doing so demands an in-depth and ethnographically grounded understanding of the matrix of relations within which a human subject is emplaced: a matrix which includes but cannot be reduced to the cultural traditions, institutionalised discourses and political-economic regimes that have preoccupied previous anthropologies of achievement.

The second reason we are drawn to the terminology of 'the social life of achievement' is that it reminds us that individuals' relations with achievement have, as it were, lives of their own that are worthy of being documented and scrutinised. The social life of achievement is an ongoing trajectory that rolls forward over time, as the self comes to be understood in new ways, as new relations are forged, and as old relations transform in character. And amongst the many events that can contribute to this ongoing process of recasting achievement's place in the subject's imaginative engagement with the world, one stands out for its empirical and theoretical interest: actually achieving.

The things that happen when someone achieves are often not what anyone would expect, opening up unforeseen ways of imagining the self, both in its own right and in relation to others. Norman, the retired miner in Alecky Blythe's 2012 documentary play about a talent show in the economically depressed British town of Stoke-on-Trent, is so moved by reaching the semi-finals and the applause that his performance receives that he skips about the stage and asks out loud the question that Blythe chose as the title of her work: 'Where have I been all my life?'[3] Testimonials for college courses and life-coaching point to similar new horizons of, as well as structural opportunities for, self-making – as in the case of Nathan Keen, a student enrolled in the 'Achieving Together' programme at a vocational college in Walsall:

> The best moment at College was when I received my first qualification and seeing the 'pass' on the certificate. This gave me the confidence to go further and take even more qualifications ... My achievements at College gave me the idea to help others in a similar situation to do the same. I am now due to start a job as a Classroom Assistant ... I'm nowhere near where I want to be yet, I've now got the determination to go that extra step further and see what else I can achieve.[4]

In other cases, the new understandings of self and sociality that achievement engenders can prove rather more painful. The American playwright Tennessee Williams found that, after years of struggling to 'make it' as a writer, his eventual

Broadway success with *The Glass Menagerie* plunged him into a deep depression. He described himself as suffering a sense of 'spiritual dislocation', becoming sick at the sight of his Manhattan hotel room, and feeling so removed from the world that he could no longer taste the difference between the chocolate sauce and the gravy on his room-service tray (Williams [1945] 2009: 33). 'A well of cynicism rose in me', he wrote, 'conversations all sounded like they had been recorded years ago and were being played back on a turntable. Sincerity and kindliness seemed to have gone out of my friends' voices. I suspected them of hypocrisy. I stopped calling them, stopped seeing them' (ibid.: 33). Such experiences, which Williams (ibid.: 34–35) attributed to being tyrannised by his 'public self', prompted him to designate success 'a catastrophe'.

It is obvious from these examples that achieving can engender new forms of imaginative engagement with self and others that are transformative, profoundly affecting and highly diverse. Yet to date, the social sciences have failed to develop a satisfactory comparative framework that can illuminate how and why achieving might have such diverse effects, or that can account for the differences between specific cases. That is precisely what this volume sets out to do.

We therefore begin this introduction by outlining the most dominant theoretical approaches that have hitherto characterised the anthropological study of achievement, with a view to examining why they proved unable to account for the extreme variation in human subjects' experiences of achieving. We then explain how the limitations of these previous approaches might be overcome by turning to our notion of the social life of achievement, grounded in the understanding of human sociality as a dynamic relational matrix that human beings navigate through ethical endeavour. To understand how the social life of achievement rolls forward, we argue, requires a theorisation of the specific character of achievements as events: events that give rise to particular forms of affective, linguistic and social knowledge which in turn underpin transformations in the ways in which human subjects conceptualise themselves and exist alongside others in the world.

Early and Current Anthropologies of Achievement: A Critical Review

The Need for Achievement

In the 1930s, Harvard psychologist Henry Murray ([1938] 2008) initiated a bold and influential attempt to develop a psychology of personality that would allow him to explain why individual participants in his experiments would either follow or stand apart from the general trends in the group under study. Concerned that conventional methods could not explain the causal mechanisms underpinning concrete events, he attempted to develop a new approach, investigating the ways in which research participants pre- or sub-consciously apprehended the world, so that their behaviour in experiments could be interpreted in the context of their personalities. Murray did this by tracing the relative balance of each participant's viscerogenic and psychogenic needs, drawing from a long (and supposedly exhaustive) list including the need for sex, the need for order, the need for abasement and the need for achievement.

Murray described the need for achievement as a need 'to overcome obstacles, to exercise power, to strive to do something difficult as well and as quickly as possible', and singled it out for special status as 'an elementary Ego need which alone may prompt any action or be fused with any other need' (ibid.: 81). This approach was to have lasting ramifications for how achievement would be conceptualised within the social sciences, suggesting it was something that was needed by human subjects, albeit to varying degrees, and thus as something that one could be more or less oriented towards, and more or less motivated to obtain. Reading Murray today, we can see that his model did also allow for a theory of why achievement might affect people differently when it occurred, since those with a high need for achievement would presumably experience pleasure, calm or relief upon achieving, whilst those whose need for achievement was relatively low would be more likely to be unmoved by their accomplishments. They might even experience a decrease in well-being if their achievements meant that other psychogenic needs (such as a need for abasement) were going unmet.

For those researchers taking their cue from Murray, however, the elaboration and testing of such hypotheses seemed a less pressing concern than trying to develop more rigorous causal mechanisms of how and why human beings came to have different levels of the various psychogenic needs Murray and his associates had identified. As we will explain below, the consequences of this particular intellectual problematisation were twofold. Firstly, a host of new ideas about what made somebody 'achievement oriented' were generated in the academy, from where they then travelled outwards into various domains of public life, forever transforming the ways in which people would conceptualise their own relationships with achievement. Secondly, achievement's analytical status as a 'need object' was implicitly sustained, along with an associated set of assumptions about how achievement affected people when it occurred.[5]

Culture, Achievement and Anthropology

Murray's *Explorations in Personality* was a book largely concerned with the classification of personality and its constituent psychogenic needs. Reviewing it in *American Anthropologist*, John Dollard (1941) praised this as a useful 'first step' but pointed to two 'painful' gaps in Murray's account. Not only had Murray failed to provide a detailed account of how psychogenic needs were learned (or otherwise acquired), he had also ignored the question of 'social structure', much to the dismay of Dollard who imagined that 'some very interesting correlations between specific needs and class background, mobility, and the like might have been forthcoming' (ibid.: 120). Although Dollard himself never launched a detailed enquiry into this possibility, his remarks foreshadowed the most significant way in which anthropologists and social psychologists would think about the problem of achievement for much of the twentieth century.

Ten years after Dollard's review was published, the question of how social and cultural circumstances might influence one's need for achievement was taken up in earnest by Harvard psychologist David McClelland. Writing at the heyday of modernisation theory, he argued in his seminal work *The Achieving Society* (1961), that the economic development of nations could be attributed to the levels of the 'need for Achievement' (which he labelled *n* Achievement, sometimes abbreviated to *nAch*) amongst their populations. For McClelland, *n* Achievement was believed to engender a self-reliant, risk-taking entrepreneurial character – exactly the kind of mindset that modernisation theorists (e.g., Rostow 1960) considered to be essential for economic growth in the developing world. 'Achievement motivation' was thus recast within his work as something that was not just an individual characteristic but an attribute of entire groups of people, a move that naturally led to the question of why some populations appeared to have higher average levels of *n* Achievement than others. Rejecting the tendency (prevalent at the time) to attribute these apparent differences to racial, genetic or climatic differences, McClelland sought to develop explanations at the level of 'national culture', suggesting that particular forms of child-rearing and religious practice (particularly those marked by individualism and 'positive mysticism') encouraged the kind of psychological dispositions needed to be self-reliant and entrepreneurial. Thus, even as McClelland's work marked a new interest in the topic of cultural difference, it did so within a framework in which the ideal 'achieving society' was strikingly Anglo-American.[6]

Although McClelland is usually thought of as somebody who wrote about achievement motivation rather than the consequences of achievement, the latter concern in fact lay at the heart of the causal mechanism by which he believed subjects actually acquired the achievement motive:

> All motives are learned, and develop out of repeated affective experiences connected with certain types of situations and types of behaviour. In the case of achievement motivation, the situations should involve 'standards of excellence', presumably impressed on the child by the culture ... Behaviour should involve either competition with those standards of excellence or attempts to meet them which, if successful, produce positive affect or, if unsuccessful, negative affect. (McClelland et al. 1953: 275)

As Izard et al. (1966: 5) note, positive and negative affect in McClelland's work are 'inexorably identified with subjective pleasure and pain ... [experienced as a] diffuse autonomic reaction'. In other words, McClelland thought that there was something intrinsically pleasurable about meeting cultural standards, and that this pleasure would instigate 'approach' behaviour (a desire to experience achievement again). By contrast, the unpleasantness of failure would spur the subject to avoid repeating such an experience – by striving for achievement. This pleasure/pain approach to motivation, widely referred to in psychological literature as the 'hedonic principle', might seem crude and generalising as an explanation for how someone comes to acquire a 'need' for achievement. Nevertheless, there is something exciting and provocative about McClelland's ambitions in seeking to take seriously the developmental role that intense individual affective and embodied experiences might play in shaping behaviour and broader social trends, especially in the light of current anthropological theory, which invites us to pay more attention to moments of visceral and affective experience in our understanding of social forms. Certainly McClelland raises some intriguing possibilities that could have given rise to a more nuanced and modest theory of how experiences of achieving transform social life.

For many of his readers at the time, however – and certainly those within the discipline of anthropology – the questions of whether (and how) meeting a 'standard of excellence' really did engender positive affect, and whether such affect really did lead to the acquisition of a motive, were largely overlooked in favour of investigating whether 'a culture' was effective at impressing standards of excellence upon its children in the first place. Reboussin and Goldstein (1966: 740), for example, described their study of the Haskell Institute in Kansas as 'compar[ing] the scores of Navaho [sic] Indians and White university students on an established measure of *n* achievement in order to verify previous statements that achievement motivation is not emphasised in Navaho [sic] culture'. (The Navajo actually turned out to have higher *n* Achievement scores than the White students – but rather than revoking their hypothesis, the authors instead concluded that their Navajo sample was 'probably not representative' [ibid.: 744].) In a similar vein, LeVine's (1968) study of 'dreams and deeds' in Nigeria sought to test the hypothesis that the high status mobility of Ibo might lead to forms of child-raising that fostered *n* Achievement, in contrast to the feudal Hausa. Soon large numbers of researchers were taking up the idea that particular cultural arrangements might give rise to greater or lesser degrees of achievement motivation, and policy makers and intellectuals in both the developed and developing world drew on McClelland's ideas to devise ways in which they might be able to press 'standards of excellence' upon, and raise achievement orientation amongst, their youth (see, e.g., Nandy 1987; Ford and Thomas 1997; Long, this volume).[7]

As research in the field intensified, both the monolithic portraits of 'culture' that had dominated McClelland's work and the assumptions of a stable set of 'needs' and 'drives' that composed a subject's 'personality' came under increasing critical scrutiny, with achievement motivation increasingly being understood not as a 'personality trait' but as the ongoing processual outcome of how any given human being interacts with and interprets the changing world around him or her (Weiner 1990: 620–21; Maehr 2008). This resulted in numerous sophisticated ethnographic studies of the evolving relationships between achievement motivation and the power relations, social imaginaries and structural barriers with which people were faced at various stages of their lives (e.g., Ogbu 1987; Wilson 1991; Suárez-Orozco and Suárez-Orozco 1995). With Signithia Fordham's work (discussed below) standing out as a notable exception, however, such studies of achievement usually placed a heavy emphasis on the question of motivation, underplaying the question of what particular individuals – and those around them – actually experienced upon achieving, let alone the diverse ways in which that experience might transform their lives.

The Problematisation of Achievement

A similar charge could be levelled against the most recent theoretical development in anthropological studies of achievement and motivation, which has been to investigate how individual engagements with achievement are shaped by the specific ways in which it has been problematised for them by particular constellations of power and knowledge. This approach is heavily indebted to the work of Michel Foucault, and his concept of problematisation, which refers to the process by which a 'domain of acts, practices and thoughts' comes to 'stand out from the general terrain of human life and experience', and 'emerge as an object of thought', prompting people to reflect on it and thereby develop 'a specific politics, a form of government of the self, and the elaboration of an ethics in regard to oneself' (Foucault 2000: 114; Moore 2011: 19). It is certainly true that this characterisation seems pertinent for the study of achievement in the late twentieth and early twenty-first centuries, a period in which achievement appears to have been very widely problematised, standing out from the terrain of human life more, perhaps, than ever before. This trend, though neither unique nor universal to contemporary times, can be linked to two factors that have caused achievement to 'lose its familiarity' and 'provoked difficulties around it' (Foucault 2000: 118). The first is the rise of broadly neoliberal forms of statecraft and governance, which place a growing burden on individuals, especially the young, to achieve so as to demonstrate their employability and thereby safeguard their own economic security. The second has been the global circulation of discourses of achievement psychology, many of which can be traced back to the influence of Murray, McClelland and other social scientists writing on the topic, which suggest that success – however defined – is intimately connected with one's attitude, mentality, mindset or culture.

Such discourses, and the common language they provide, establish achievement as a problem for both the work of government and the work of the self,[8] as has been revealed by studies focusing on everything from the 'competitiveness' policies that states have developed to ensure their population's market relevance (Krugman 1994; Bayly, Long, this volume), to the highly elaborated forms of self-government and self-regulation exhibited by individuals hoping to achieve (Demerath 2009, this volume; Davidson 2011). Moreover, it is clear that discourses of achievement can play a significant role in the constitution of ethical life, a domain which encompasses the 'experiences we have of ourselves', 'how we are constituted as subjects of our own knowledge' and 'the kinds of selves we are for ourselves and others' (Moore 2011: 19). To see how deeply implicated achievement can be in both one's self-understanding and the question of how to relate to others, one need look no further than the section of de Rond's (2009) ethnography of a male rowing team at Cambridge University in which Jake, a 22-year-old American student hoping to row in the prestigious annual Oxford–Cambridge Boat Race, has suffered a setback in his training. Jake explains that:

> Having lost my seat-race was like finding out something about myself – something I didn't like seeing – I felt guilty – I felt guilty because I'd let my team-mates down, my friends, it's this incredible feeling of loss ...
>
> I had to ask myself all sorts of questions like 'Can I really do this?' and 'How good am I really?' and 'What am I worth?' – and did I really want the answers to those questions? What if I were to discover that I wasn't good enough, is that something I could live with? ...
>
> I like Colin and Oli and feel sad about having to compete with them for a place in the Blue Boat ... The fact that they were my friends meant that I knew things about them that could be conceived as insecurities that could work to my advantage, but I really didn't want to exploit them – I mean even in my own thoughts – but the mind games I played with myself were so intense and I wanted so badly to get inside their heads and let them know I was the alpha male – it's so confusing to mentally attack your friends – it drives you insane but sanity seemed like a small price to pay for something that I wanted so badly. (ibid.: 143–49)

Given that, as Jake's candid remarks underscore, achievement can play such a crucial role in how people think of themselves and their relations to others, it is perhaps surprising that anthropologists working on achievement from a broadly Foucauldian perspective have placed their emphasis on questions of aspiration, anticipation and the imagination of achievement that is yet to come, rather than investigating what actually happens when this deeply wished-for achievement occurs. This is not to dismiss or trivialise the importance of achievement-related aspirations and desires (or indeed, earlier decades' interest in 'motivation'), which are without doubt a crucial dimension of contemporary subjectivity. However, we argue that their detailed investigation has been at the expense of a related but distinct problem. This is the *experience* of achievement: something that is both material and semiotic; concretely embodied and affectively charged, yet also known and elaborated through the work of fantasy and the imagination. It incorporates the question of whether expectations, hopes and desires are thwarted or met – but is not limited to this. It is an experience which can serve to reinforce (or challenge) definitions of achievement whilst also inflecting them with meanings that might form the basis of new interpretive beliefs. It is an experience that can have profound ramifications for the questions of aspiration and motivation but also for much more besides. The question we are now faced with is how to study it.

Achievement as a Context of Cultural Invention

Although the McClellandian approach that set the course of much scholarship on achievement in the late twentieth century had a clearly articulated theory of achievement's consequences, its simplistic assumptions of success generating 'positive affect' do not stand up to close anthropological scrutiny. Not only does the evidence speak to the contrary, there is a regrettable conceptual blindness to the significance of context for determining achievement's affective (and other) outcomes. Building on the important work that has been done by applying Foucauldian notions of problematisation, self-formation and ethics to the question of aspiration, we might therefore advance an initial proposition that the consequences of achievement must themselves be understood in relation to the specific ways in which achievement has been problematised for a particular subject, and the specific forms of ethical self-formation to which that problematisation has given rise. Such processes have been integral in crafting the self that is now experiencing achievement, and thereby determine just what is at stake in any instance of success or failure.

Persuasive evidence to this effect can be found in Fordham's (1996) landmark study of the existential burdens and psychic trauma afflicting high-achieving Black schoolchildren at Capital High, a secondary school in Washington D.C. These pupils, Fordham explains, sought to parallel and even surpass the academic achievement of their White peers in an attempt to elevate and transform the meanings of African American humanness (ibid.: 236). In doing so, however, they had to conform (at least partly) to the practices and behaviours of dominant groups, and so risked being accused of 'acting White' and even of losing membership in the Black fictive kinship system (ibid.: 252). They had to navigate the contradictions between ideologies that valorised academic success, and those that saw 'authentic' Blackness as an achievement in itself, or being Black as something at which it was easy to fail (see also Phoenix 1998: 863). As a result, school success was both desirable and dangerous; and high-achievers' psyches were riddled with ambivalence, self-imposed conflict and self-doubt (Fordham 1996: 246–48). The point that merits underscoring here is that such dissonance proved so deeply troubling precisely because of how important academic achievement was to the students in their 'unswerving desire to reclaim and reconfigure their African humanness' (ibid.: 327). It was because 'pursuing academic success [was] a form of warfare' for them (ibid.: 235) that they became its casualties. Reading Fordham's ethnography from the theoretical position we are developing in this volume, one can see that the way the social life of achievement rolled forwards for these pupils has to be understood in terms of the distinctive ways in which achievement stood out as a problem for them.

Nevertheless, a focus on problematisation is not in itself enough to explain all of achievement's possible consequences, since it offers no tools through which to understand why the experience of achieving should so often prove unexpected and counterintuitive, even by the parameters of subjects' own political and ethical reasoning. These are cases that are much more difficult to unravel than those in which self-evidently unrealistic expectations go (traumatically, but unsurprisingly) unmet. We might think of such examples as when competitiveness policies prove successful, but the newly competitive population feels underwhelmed (Sweeney 2003: 140), a schizophrenia patient who reports that his condition makes him feel numb at all times is taken aback by the unexpected boost of energy and sense of accomplishment he feels having scored highly in a quiz (Perivoliotis and Cather 2009: 824), or a pupil who proudly brings a trophy to school discovers she will henceforth be pilloried by her peers (Fordham 1996: 323). What all these cases reveal is that the way in which the social life of achievement rolls forward is always contingent on how the environing world – including one's own body and mind – responds to achievement, whether or not that is what one expects. What follows in achievement's wake affords opportunities for individuals to have new experiences of themselves, and to become a new object of knowledge for themselves and others. In short, it can serve to *reproblematise* achievement – and the social sciences need to develop a framework for how and why this should be the case.

When an achievement takes place, new knowledge is created about the achiever in relation to him- or herself: at a minimum the realisation that he or she has accomplished a certain feat within the world, and that he or she has the capacity to do so. It may also generate new knowledge in relation to those around him or her who either have or have not enjoyed the same achievement, either in the present instance or in the past. Following on from this, it can be seen that achievements should be understood as 'events' with the potential to rupture or entrench previous knowledges through their witnessing and acclamation – as per Caroline Humphrey's (2008) anthropological restyling of Alain Badiou (2006). In other words, achievements offer an opportunity for cultural invention, in which both subjectivity and sociality might be recast.

While human subjects always exist in a dynamic relational matrix, one of the most important features of human subjectivity is the human capacity for virtuality – for reflecting on the state of things as they are, and envisaging how they might be otherwise (Moore 2012). Henrietta Moore (2011: 16) has developed the concept of 'the ethical imagination' to describe these 'forms and means ... through which individuals imagine relationships to themselves and to others', arguing that the ethical imagination is a primary site of cultural invention because although ethical practices are proposed, suggested and imposed upon individuals by their social environs, and forms of subjectification are linked to the normative and with distributions of power, these are not, and cannot be, absolutely determining processes. The sharply variable and often unexpected affective responses to achievement are precisely evidence of this. Instead, she writes, 'what remains open, unforeclosed, unfinished is present in its active possibility' (ibid.: 16) and 'it is a feature of human subjectivity that we are born into and make ourselves under conditions that we may then choose to transform' (ibid.: 18).

Two points warrant particular emphasis at this juncture. The first concerns the multifaceted character of the ethical imagination and the precise nature of the 'choice' to transform or maintain the conditions of one's being in the world. As Moore argues, although conscious thought, linguistic reasoning and decision-making are crucial elements of the ethical imagination, so are affect, performance and the placement and use of the body; identification and fantasy even proceed through forms of unknowing and incomprehensibility (ibid.: 16; see also Long 2012). Thus, staying true to Moore's expansive definition of the ethical imagination, contributors to this volume examine how achievement builds, sustains or dissolves attachments to an energetic, affective and material world, even to the point where an attachment might be perpetuated that is actively doing the subject harm, as in Aronofsky's (2010) Hollywood melodrama, *Black Swan*.[9] Contributors also explore the forms of ethical, imaginative and interpretive reasoning that achievement can prompt, and the implications of the language in which it is expressed – all of which are themselves embodied processes with their own distinct affectivities (Long 2012: 92). These are all factors that shape the subject's conceptualisation of, and imaginative engagement with the self, others and the very social world in which he or she inheres.

Secondly, achievement events are not just events for the achiever. This is a point that has already been highlighted by researchers in the field of psychological anthropology, who have argued that the witnessing and identification of something that 'some group of humans ... [have] agreed ... will count as an achievement' establishes cognitive schemas of 'achievement' that might then be internalised by achievers and those around them, instigating future action, and functioning as a goal (D'Andrade 1992: 35; see also Strauss 1992a, 1992b). However, such an emphasis on the cognitive domain at the expense of questions of affect, feeling, attachment and investment, let alone the relational matrix within which these schemas were learned and subsequently redeployed, leaves us with an incomplete understanding of achievement events. Grounding achievement in a theory of human sociality underscores that those around the achiever, who now comes to be viewed as 'an achiever', have also found their matrix of relations to have been recast, and their ethical imaginations will guide how they come to reconceptualise their relations to themselves and those around them – including their relationship with the achiever. Whilst being identified as an achiever affords a subject the possibility of imagining a new way in which he or she relates to others, it equally renders him or her open to being imagined and fantasised differently by others – a situation that appears to underlie many cases of ambivalence or guilt in the wake of achievement (e.g., Spurlock 1985; Suárez-Orozco and Suárez-Orozco 1995: 74–79; Williams 2009), but which can also be responsible for the joy and delight that achievers take in their success (Long 2007: 96–98). As such, and as all our contributors seek to highlight, achieving is at once intensely personal, relational and intersubjective, and can have ramifications on one's life and the matrix of relations one inhabits, both in the short-to-medium term and over the course of one's entire life.

At the core of these processes of cultural invention, however, are the various new forms of knowledge and understanding that achievement elicits. In order to develop a more systematic framework for studying the social life of achievement, we have ordered the chapters of this book so as to understand more deeply the nature and effects of the three principal forms of knowing that we have identified as unfolding in achievement's wake. The first is the affective, physical, embodied forms of experience that arise in the immediate aftermath of achievement; the second is the linguistic knowledge that transmits information about the achievement of oneself and others; and the third is the knowledge of how one's relations in the world have been maintained or transformed by achieving. By doing so, and by putting the ethnographic contributions highlighted by our contributors into a critical dialogue with emergent approaches in the sociology and psychology of achievement, we hope not only to shed light on how to explain the striking diversity of achievement experiences documented within the volume, we also seek to develop a fresh conceptual and methodological framework for researching 'achievement' within the social sciences.

The Sense of Achievement

The affective pleasure of achievement is supposed to be one of its most intoxicating properties. The idea that meeting standards of excellence engenders positive affect – pleasure, satisfaction or a 'feel-good factor' – has been one of the most prevalent assumptions underpinning diverse theories of achievement and motivation (see, e.g., Kruger 1933; McClelland 1961; Paul 1990: 439; D'Andrade 1992: 23). Indeed, even psychologists who have noted that achieving can very quickly give rise to feelings of anxiety, ambivalence or depression are willing to concede that, at the moment of achieving, it probably felt good (Clance and Imes 1978: 244; Dweck 1999: 112). Whether achievement always involves such immediate positive affect, whether that affect is always of the same variety, and why achieving feels good or bad are thus all questions that warrant closer attention.

Anthropology's contribution is particularly exciting given that psychologists' own re-evaluations of the hedonic principle (the idea that people are driven towards the pleasures of achievement and away from the pain of failure) have tended to focus on internal mental processes rather than the interactions between subjects and the social world around them. Higgins (1997), for example, encourages his readers to focus on the different forms of 'regulatory focus', 'regulatory anticipation' and 'regulatory reference' that underpin diverse instances of motivated striving, noting that the pleasure of securing a success which is valued for its own sake may be qualitatively different to the pleasure elicited by avoiding failure through having been successful. But Higgins's approach, like those to which it is responding, radically decontextualises the subject experiencing this pleasure.[10] What is left out of view is that which is immediately apparent to any anthropologist observing the joys or woes of achievement on even an individual scale: its embodiment, its emplacement and its materiality.

Quite the opposite perspective to Higgins's can be found in contemporary discussions of affect in cultural theory (e.g., Clough 2008; Venn 2010). These exhort us to view the human body as 'matter in-formation', and to analyse the ways in which affective energies are transmitted between it and other materials in the world – an approach which frames the question of why achievement feels good (or not) in an entirely different way. As elaborated elsewhere (Long and Moore 2013), we would caution against the tendency to view affect as autonomous or pre-social, advocating instead an ethnographic attention to how it is anticipated, channelled and comes to attach to particular bodies with 'structured precision' (Hemmings 2005: 562). Thinking about how, why and when achieving bodies are affected in certain – and perhaps unexpected – ways contributes to such an endeavour whilst also foregrounding the value of material-semiotic approaches towards the question of how the social life of achievement rolls forward. Equally, by examining how attachments to living – and imagined relations to the self and others – are sustained by the circulation of affect and attunement to atmospheres within a world that is at once material and social, we are able to open up nuanced questions about what exactly we recognise as an achievement, and the repercussions it can come to have over the course of an entire life.

Kathleen Stewart's chapter offers precisely such an analysis, developing a cartography of her mother Claire's existence in the world. Unlike conventional anthropological approaches to achievement, which she intimates may often be too quick to draw theoretically informed connections between thinking subjects, concepts and the world, Stewart advocates a slowing of theory, which allows for a compositional approach in which the anthropologist can create 'descriptive eddies' and 'speculative attunement[s] that at least aspir[e] to align with the commonplace labours of becoming sentient to whatever is happening'. This proves to be a highly productive way of thinking about achievement. It foregrounds the question of how circulating forces (of which the pleasures of the hedonic principle are but one) come to 'take on forms', in Stewart's words, 'animat[ing] a life but also incit[ing] the labours of its production'. By then charting these worldings over the course of a single life, she draws our attention to their patterns and regularities – as well as their disjunctures and displacements – and the way these lines of a life might become prismatic, and scored onto forms of attunement. In particular, Stewart highlights the pain of ageing, illness and dying – in which the world that a subject has made matter slowly abandons her or him, an element of the social life of achievement's relentless trajectory that is only made crueller by the subject's attachment to his or her efficacy, and which Stewart both identifies and evokes as unspeakably sad.

Stewart thus shows how the sense of achievement emerges through participation in a world that is both energetic and material: as Stewart remarks, a life's elements 'have a radical materiality that literally matters', and anthropologists are especially well-placed to attend to this and, by examining how and why it matters, broaden the horizons of what has hitherto been conceptualised as 'achievement psychology'. Rebecca Cassidy's account of Brian, a British gambling professional does just this, by studying how externally generated shifts in the material and political economic circumstances of betting can transform the affective experience – and motivational force – of achievement. In the late 1990s, Brian made his money by laying bets at racecourses. At the time he emphasised that this was a strictly professional pursuit – and that success was a result of knowledge, hard work and dispassionate rational calculations. There was thus no place for him, in his own self-representations, for the affective thrills that McClelland thought made achievement so motivationally compelling.

Cassidy compares Brian's behaviour on the racecourse with his betting activity in the late 2000s, which was conducted at home using the online betting exchange Betfair. While Brian made comparable amounts of money using Betfair as he did at the racecourse, working on a computer and never having any days where he could celebrate a 'big win' made it 'less exciting' for him – so much so that he eventually retired. As Cassidy argues, this illustrates starkly the difference between 'winning' and 'achievement'; the sense of the latter hinged not on financial outcomes but on a distinctive temporality of success, emplacement on the race course, and a bodily affect of 'excitement' – even as this was something that he sought to suppress or deny. Thus, just as Appadurai (1986) argued that the value and identity of an object could be entirely transformed as it moved through different contexts, or 'regimes of value', Cassidy urges us to think of how people relate differently to outcomes – such as winning £1,000 by gambling – when they take place within discrete 'regimes of achievement' to which one is variably attached and attuned.

Such affective attachments and attunements are far from divorceable from the historically specific social imaginaries and relays of power that pervade particular contests, as emphasised by Laura Mentore's analysis of Guyanese 'birdsport'. Birdsport is an activity in which two finches are pitted against each other in a 'race' to complete a certain number of songs in the fastest time possible. Victory in the races between the birds is largely attributed to luck, thereby allowing birdsport to serve as an egalitarian space in which any participant is able to win, and assert their integrity and worth. Moreover, birdsport affords multiple avenues for men to cultivate their 'reputation' – a concept that developed under conditions of colonial rule, and which emphasises creative individualism within contexts that are equally accessible to all men. Passion, and in particular the robust and passionate use of the human voice, is thus a prime component of 'reputation'; so too is the skilful maintenance of relations and connections. Sourcing finches from indigenous communities (and 'passionately' fathering children in the process), smuggling them to the city, or building such a relationship with them during training that they sing with energy and zeal during races, are all ways in which reputation can be achieved through birdsport.

For Mentore, however, what ultimately makes birdsport so popular is the passionate aurality of the bird race, and the relational transmission of affect that it involves. This allows participants to 'embody such passion as an aspect of their own social being that transcends the more restrictive categories of person to which they are bound in other facets of life', and so plays an important role in postcolonial practices of self-making. Once again the world's radical materiality, and the attachments and attunements that this materiality engenders, come to the fore, but within the context of a world of affective resonance and cultural meaning that has its own deep history in colonial and postcolonial power relations and the identifications, fantasies and desires to which those have given rise. These are factors that anthropologists can highlight to explain more comprehensive understandings of how achievement events make people feel. But those instant feelings are only the start of the story, and it is to achievement's impacts on forms of semantic knowledge regarding self and sociality that we now turn.

Putting Achievement into Words

However palpably achievement is felt, the moment at which it is recognised as 'achievement' is by definition one of narrativisation – even if it is only a narrative that one tells oneself. This, of course, was the point D'Andrade (1992) was making when he wrote of achievement as a cognitive schema – but in contrast to his view that this is foremost a cognitive process, the contributors to this volume are interested in exploring such recognition and narrativisation in the context of dynamic matrices of relations, imaginative and ethical engagement with the world, and the fantasmatic processes of intersubjectivity. This is because the act of recognising and narrating 'achievement' is not only informed by subjects' previous experiences of the social world (D'Andrade's 'cultural models'), but also highly consequential for the social world because, as the next three chapters argue, both deliberate and unthinking practices of narrating and recognising achievement can profoundly transform one's imaginative engagement with the self and others.

One of the most fundamental narratives within mainstream discourses of achievement is that of praise – a practice often assumed by educationalists, policy makers and the public to engender positive affect, and thereby boost an achiever's self-esteem and motivate them to continue on a cycle of success (see, for example, the comments of the teachers cited in Demerath, this volume). Although the ethnographic record throws up cases of situations in which praise is a source of discomfort, misery or shame (e.g., Harkins 1990), in recent years a growing body of work within social and developmental psychology has indicated that, even in contexts where praise is normatively desirable, matters may be less straightforward than praise-givers might assume. In such settings, while praise of any kind usually leads to an immediate burst of pleasure and pride, there are striking differences in the long-term consequences of praise focused on an outcome (the achievement itself), the process by which that outcome was achieved, or the qualities of the person responsible (Corpus and Lepper 2007). Significantly, this is not simply a case of individuals experiencing affective overstimulation from their success (cf. Hultberg 1985), but is related directly to the semantic content of praise language. Each distinct form of praise – particularly when foisted upon young children – can introduce implicit theories and social imaginaries of causality and ability that then prove formative for how the achiever imaginatively engages with the world around him or her.

Such distinctions in language use can be remarkably subtle. For example, Cimpian et al. (2007) chart the differential effects of praising children's artwork in ways that are generic of the child in question ('You're a good drawer!') and non-generic commentaries on process ('You did a good job drawing!'). The children that were praised generically displayed more extreme emotional reactions in the face of criticism because, the authors argue, generic praise implies performance is underpinned by a stable ability; subsequent mistakes are thus thought to reflect upon this and so lead to a significant decrease in motivation (see also Mueller and Dweck 1998; Dweck 1999; Kamins and Dweck 1999). Further studies have suggested that a similar effect occurs when children hear the achievements of others being talked about in generic terms such as 'math whiz' (Heyman 2008), and that, when exposed to a mixture of praise types, as little as 25 per cent generic praise can lead to demotivation in the face of difficulty (Zentall and Morris 2010). Such studies thus suggest that the semantic terms in which achievement is described have a major effect on the way in which the social life of achievement rolls forward, a point which in turn informs the long-standing interest in questions of 'achievement motivation' and 'achievement orientation'.

To date, most of the research conducted in this field has been experimental in nature, asking children to role-play with puppets or imagine how they might react in hypothetical situations. The danger of this approach is that it extracts experimental subjects from the dynamic relational matrices within which achievements, praise and theories of ability come to acquire meaning in daily life. Observational and ethnographic studies therefore offer an important complement to laboratory-based work on cognitive development. Their full potential, however, can only be realised through a deep and rich investigation into how an ethically imaginative subject engages with the context in which he or she is found.

Nicholas Long's contribution to this volume moves in this direction. Working in the recently created Indonesian province of Kepri, he shows how the theories of self, confidence and behaviour of the province's young achievers are constantly evanescent and transforming as they engage with heavily politicised discourses of a regional 'human resources crisis'. While government policies rely on a theory of achievement and its consequences that is directly inspired by McClelland, believing that high achievers will be motivated go-getters who go on to live prosperous and exemplary lives, thereby solving the human resources crisis, the reality is often more complex, with high achievers displaying extreme anxiety and self-doubt in the face of further challenges. Long argues that although such people's achievement is often praised in processual rather than generic terms – focusing on their hard work, discipline and religious devotion – the more consequential theory of self is one of constitution through relations, in which the inadequacies of Kepri's human and material resources are believed to be transferred to children who grow up in the region. As such, the very rhetoric of a human resources crisis which underpins provincial achievement policies inadvertently serves to terrify those who achieve within the context of Kepri about their latent inadequacies, whilst achievement in wider contexts (such as at national level) can lead to surprising re-evaluations of the region's quality through the accomplishments of the self it created. Long thus highlights how deploying various academic models of achievement and motivation within the field of policy might lead to unanticipated responses. Ultimately, as he shows, these come to include a stretching of the very parameters of what counts as achievement, engendering new experiences of attachment, attunement and alienation towards the world.

Whilst the *post hoc* narration of achievement can be responsible for transmitting implicit beliefs and knowledges in the way Long describes, it can also open up spaces for reflexivity and ethical practice – as argued by Joanna Cook in her analysis of a Thai meditation monastery in which attaining 'non-self' is the pinnacle of achievement. Cook notes that achievements are conventionally seen as objects – events, states or statuses – that can be pursued by a subject, and that such an assumption underpins cognitive anthropologists' accounts of goal schemas and their capacity to provide directive force (e.g. D'Andrade 1992). But when the telos of achievement is the very negation of the subject itself, a different frame of analysis is required. Building on Strauss's (1992b) analysis of the different ways in which goal schemas can be internalised, Cook suggests that there can come a point where a schema is so fully internalised that it is not only directive and motivational but constitutive or definitional. Thus rather than being seen as a cultural value which has directive force on action from without, Cook invites us to see 'non-self' as creatively recast in the relationships in which it is iterated.

These relationships include those between renouncers giving narrative accounts of their achievement of non-self, and the meditators who listen to them. Hagiographic narratives, which bespeak the spiritual attainment of the narrator, are crafted in such a way that it is impossible to distinguish between formulaic tropes of the genre and personal details relating to the speaker. Narrators therefore circumvent the paradox that they are appearing to give a 'personal' testimony of achieving 'non-self', and their accounts afford experiential insights into non-self by allowing listeners to be placed in the story and be marked by its impression. Their narratives, Cook argues, are both communicative and constitutive, their meanings dialogic and emergent in practice, and their tropes intrinsic to the way in which those who employ them perceive and organise their experience within the world: '"cultural schema" intersect with transformative processes of person-making'. As such, she argues that the internalisation of certain narratives of achievement is not just a cognitive process but also an ethical one.

A complementary perspective on the issue of achievement narratives is offered by Olga Solomon, whose chapter explores how Southern Californian families in which a child has been diagnosed with an Autism Spectrum Disorder (ASD) engage with the life histories of high-achieving autistic individuals. As Solomon explains, the hegemonic notions of work, occupation and market value that circulate in American society have historically led to pessimistic prospects for autistic children. Given such a context, Solomon argues that the writings of high-functioning adults with ASD, as well as their music, artworks and cinematic accounts of their lives, have changed the existential landscape of possibilities for children diagnosed with autism and their families by suggesting that achievement can occur despite, or perhaps even because of, their autism. Such narratives engender affordances – opportunities for action provided by a particular object in the environment – in which achievement is a possible outcome, and Solomon thus traces how children and their families work to make the narratives relevant to their circumstances and thereby craft a particular kind of achieving self going into the future.

A similar principle underpinned the use of imagery (both verbal and visual) of achievement within the U.S. civil rights movement. Campaigners hoped to use images of Black achievers and heroes to instil racial pride and self-esteem amongst African Americans whilst also overturning negative stereotypes held by Whites (Hughes 1941; Berger 2010).[11] The affordances described by Solomon are more complex because of the imputation that achievement may not just be despite, but also because of autism. Of course, such reasoning constitutes exactly the kind of generic statement about who achieves and who doesn't achieve that have been argued by developmental psychologists to have counterproductive and demotivating effects for both achievers and their peers (Heyman 2008; Cimpian 2010). What Solomon's material suggests, however, is that even if such narratives propagate problematic understandings of the self as having fixed traits, these problems are outweighed by their capacity to redefine the implications of autism (often already understood as a fixed trait of the self), thereby creating spaces for hope, motivation and empowerment for autistic children and their families. The psychological and social effects of generic achievement talk might thus be much more positive for people occupying marginal subject positions.

Achievement and Social Knowledge

If the chapters by Long, Cook and Solomon place their focus on how the semantic knowledge that unfolds in the wake of achievement shapes the subject's imaginative engagement with the self, the final four chapters in the volume place an emphasis on how the achieving subject imaginatively engages with others, and is in turn imaginatively engaged with by them. This field of outcomes, which we bracket under the term 'social knowledge', is very diverse: it can include affect and narrative, as well as deliberate and conscious projects of ethical reasoning, but it often unfolds simply through the performance and practice of everyday interactions. These might not only lead to new ways in which relations with others are imagined or fantasised; events can occur in such a way that structural opportunities to participate in social worlds are opened up or closed down. When this happens, the way in which the social life of achievement rolls forward through time can become something over which the ethically imaginative subject has limited if any control. One thinks, for example, of the British singer Susan Boyle, who experienced a nervous breakdown after – and seemingly as a consequence of – her audition on the television show *Britain's Got Talent* catapulted her unexpectedly into the public eye: her audition received over 186 million views on YouTube in just nineteen days, and her personality and life story was intimately probed by national and international media (Enli 2009: 487–89). Conversely, for all that the South Korean workers studied by Joseph Park (2011) strove to boost their job prospects by improving the quality of their English language, they found that every time they had reached a certain standard, the expectations of the job market became correspondingly higher and the monetary recognition of their achievements (for which they had so desperately hoped) was endlessly deferred. Such processes can, as these examples show, have tremendous implications for subjects' imaginative engagement with the self and others, and with the notion of achievement itself.

Sarah Green's account of the men who developed the private equity sector in the U.K. shows how central the issue of continuing participation in a particular social world can be, even in a context that is often portrayed as fundamentally self-interested. Private equity has led to many of its practitioners becoming incredibly wealthy, but also being pilloried in the mass media as morally suspect. However, neither of these factors plays a significant role in explaining why practitioners continue or cease to remain involved in private equity; nor is money-making taken as a primary index of one's achievement. Instead, Green argues that the field of private equity is construed as a fun but high-risk game that carries distinct pleasures and has its own moral valence, participation in which is predicated upon skill and integrity in the management of both numbers and social relations. Given this, practitioners were not only impervious to the moral critique of their financial activities; they were also unfazed by the prospect of massive drops in their net worth. Having already made amounts of money that they described as being 'beyond any sane logic', practitioners would not consider a loss to be painful on its own terms: what the money represented was not an achievement in itself, but rather an index of the skill that one had in playing the game – a skill that, given the brutal firing rates, needed to be demonstrated repeatedly if one wished to keep playing it. It was this skill, Green emphasises, that was the achievement. Of course, being a highly skilled and effective economic actor is itself something that is heavily incentivised within the cultural logic of neoliberalism. What stands out when reading Green's account, however, is how little her interviewees described the pleasures of this achievement in terms of fulfilling broader social norms, and instead the importance that they placed on sustaining their attachments to the world of private equity that they had created: to the beauty of the calculations, and to the intricacies of managing the social relationships. Achievement was not important because it allowed them to become a particular kind of person so much as because it allowed them to inhere – psychologically and structurally – within a distinctive, highly exclusive and incredibly pleasurable social world.

The question of full participation in a desired and fantasised social world is also a central concern for the Vietnamese citizens discussed by Susan Bayly in her study of how Vietnam's marketisation has transformed experiences of and attitudes towards achievement since high-socialist times. There have been continuities: achieving is still widely felt to be seen as something that is done for the collectivities of family, community and nation to which one belongs, rather than personal gain, and establishing the strong position of Vietnam within a world of global others has long been a crucial ethical and political problem. Yet the parameters of how this could be done are transforming, giving rise to emergent new notions of achievement. No longer does achievement involve Vietnamese citizens being sent to other socialist countries in order to acquire or share expertise. Patriotic achievement in Vietnam now involves constituting oneself as a high-quality human resource, who is able to propel the nation up global human development rankings, and who does so whilst maintaining his or her distinctive Vietnameseness.

Bayly reveals that, although these recent problematisations of achievement have engendered new dilemmas for contemporary Vietnamese – from anxieties over stature to the fear that they are creating an epidemic of 'achievement disease' – historic formulations of what it is to be an achiever continue to inform present-day ideas about what it is to live an ethical and virtuous life. Moreover, far from simply defaulting to the dominant ideas of human resource quality associated with globalisation and neoliberalism, the current interest in 'human resources' is leading to creative new possibilities. Not least amongst these is the emergence of credentialised psychics as a new (albeit controversial) category of achiever. This serves to recast the matrix of relations between Vietnamese and global others because the psychic arts are construed as a form of human capital that is uniquely advanced in Vietnam, to a degree and of which richer and more powerful nations could only dream. As such, Bayly shows how the social life of achievement rolls forward over time in an ongoing process of cultural invention, giving rise to novel and powerful social imaginaries of how achievers might know and be known by others, which operate on domestic, national and global scales.

Whether or not one actually is known by others in the way that one hopes, however, is a crucial determinant of the way in which achievement affects persons and collectivities, as the final two chapters in this volume reveal. Peter Demerath's chapter focuses on a high-achieving school in 'Wilton', in the American Midwest, where pressure to achieve is inculcated as a means of helping pupils to safeguard their class status in an uncertain future. Demerath's analysis thus takes the school itself as a dynamic relational matrix, showing how the social life of achievement rolls forward in ways that teach an 'unwritten curriculum' for being an employable worker-citizen: competitive, confident, highly directed, able to advocate for oneself (for example in negotiating grades) and prepared to cheat or lie when necessary. Key elements of this process include what Demerath calls 'hypercredentialing' – a veritable proliferation of achievements, designed to give pupils the confidence (and the CV) required to achieve life-long success – and intensive parental involvement in their children's work. However, as Demerath, argues, achievements in Wilton are fetishised as individual, despite having largely been generated systemically, ideologically and relationally: it is the presence of this fetish that allows pupils to claim achievements as their own, and thereby derive from them the pleasure, self-belief and confidence required for an imaginative engagement with the world that will prove effective in neoliberal times.

Demerath's analysis thereby implicitly highlights the vulnerabilities that can be associated with coming to know oneself as an achiever – for what would happen if the fetish slipped? It is such vulnerability, and the potential it opens up for structural and symbolic violence, that lies at the heart of Signithia Fordham's study of a high school in the upstate New York city of 'Rodman' in which she explores the dilemmas presented by achievement for two Black girls, as well as for women (of colour) more generally, in a world where achievement of various kinds is frequently presented as both desirable and illegitimate, and the narration of others' achievement can thus become an immensely powerful weapon of aggression, competition and bullying.

Keyshia, one of Fordham's two focal students, is extremely talented academically, yet she seeks to downplay this – sitting her college admission exams out of state and disclosing her results only to selected friends, swearing them to secrecy. This, Fordham explains, is the result of Keyshia's painful experiences when studying in Maryland, where her results led her to be shunned by her Black peers for 'acting White', but also be envied and rejected by her White peers, who cruelly attributed her success to affirmative action policies. This led to Keyshia harbouring enormous insecurities that she is 'not Black enough', prompting her to latch onto other Black girls at her new school as a means of support. Fordham thus shows how achievement – because of its capacity to be narrated to and known about by others – can render the achiever vulnerable within her matrix of relations, and prompt new, defensive, strategies of sociality. The issue is exacerbated in Keyshia's case by the question of gender. While her parents want Keyshia to be academically successful, her own standard of achievement conforms to the dominant templates of femininity that circulate in her school: she wants to marry and have children. Where such norms prevail, as Fordham argues with reference to the U.S. more widely, female success in school or the workplace can actually be experienced as a form of loss.

Secondly, Fordham suggests that patriarchal contexts of this kind structurally induce women to 'compete to lose' – a concept she illustrates by analysing a fight between Nadine, Keyshia's former best friend, and Kristen, a White cheerleader at the school. When Kristen calls Nadine a 'nigger bitch', Nadine hits back. She wins the fight – but by crying and presenting herself as a victim, Kristen is able to ensure that Nadine is excluded from school shortly before her final exams. Within this competitive and highly gendered school environment, Kristen is able to manipulate her status as the fight's 'loser' in order to shape the social life of achievement that Nadine must go on to endure. Fordham's chapter thus highlights that achievement frequently has an inherent bifocality – because what looks like 'winning' from one perspective can be contested as 'losing' from another – and that the study of this bifocality must be integral to any study of the social life of achievement. This partly involves attending to the fact that such bifocality can be and is manipulated deliberately and inadvertently, in ways that assure the dominance of some, whilst trapping other seeming 'achievers' in a subjectivity of 'social defeat' (Luhrmann 2006). It also demands sustained attention to the ways in which the appropriateness of various forms of achievement varies according to such categories as sexuality, gender, class, nationality and race.

Conclusion

While Jan Malloch (2009) promised her readers that 'no matter what you achieve in life ... you will feel such a wonderful sense of achievement', and Tennessee Williams ([1945] 2009: 36) suggested that if you 'ask anyone who has experienced the kind of success I am talking about – What good is it? ... [T]he word he will finally groan is unprintable in genteel publications', the consequences of achieving are by no means as straightforward or as predictable as either of these writers would have us believe. Nor can such differential outcomes as they experienced be readily predicted. However, they can be understood, and it is in this regard that the notion of the social life of achievement that we have developed in this volume offers a distinctive contribution to the social sciences.

Dominant anthropological and psychological approaches to achievement, which primarily conceptualise achievement practices in relation to 'culture', cognition or regimes of governmentality, struggle to provide a framework which can account for the striking differences in how particular subjects are affected by achievement in particular situations. This, we have argued, is because their approach operates on too broad and generalising a scale, failing to pay sufficient attention to the specific dynamic relational matrices in which human subjects exist, or to the fantasmatic character of intersubjectivity. By contrast, studying the entire social life of achievement allows us to develop sharper and more insightful ways as to how subjects imaginatively engage with the world both before and after achievement occurs.

Secondly, as our contributors demonstrate, the forms of affective, semantic and social knowledge that are generated through achievement events pay a critical role in re-problematising achievement for subjects, leading to diverse new forms of understanding of the self and its relations with others, new forms of attachment to the world, new endeavours of ethical imagination, and, as such, practices of cultural invention ranging from the benign and pleasurable to the masochistic or destructive. The way in which the social life of achievement rolls forward is thus contingent on the event of achievement itself. On the one hand, this means that any overarching theory seeking to predict how the social life of achievement will roll forward in advance of it occurring is doomed to be frustrated by the complexity of events as they actually unfold. On the other, though, a more careful assessment of factors and circumstances may offer some capacity for predicting how specific individuals are likely to be affected by achieving; and at the very least may help to ward off some of the most destructive forms of damage that can be wreaked in achievement's name. But exploring the potential applications of the framework we have developed is a task that lies beyond the present volume. For now, we simply hope that the diverse analyses proffered by our contributors will provide a stimulating conceptual toolkit for our readers – both as they investigate 'achievement' within their research, and as they grapple with it as an ethical and political problem in their professional and personal lives.

Acknowledgements

Many thanks to Andrei Cimpian, Dawson Price and Olivia Steinberg for invaluable input on the latest research in developmental psychology. Nicholas Long's work on this introduction was generously supported by a British Academy Postdoctoral Fellowship, a Junior Research Fellowship at St Catharine's College, Cambridge, and funding from the ESRC (grant number RES–000–22–4632).

Notes

1. See, e.g., a report in the *Daily Mail*: <http://www.dailymail.co.uk/femail/article-2026001/self-help-books-ruin-life-they-promise-sell-millions.html> (accessed 13 February 2013).
2. Indeed, intense as current interest in achievement and success can be, these very terms are in fact a relatively recent introduction to the popular consciousness: literary critic George Parsons saw the European preoccupation with 'success' as having its origins in the

nineteenth century, writing in 1888 that 'To succeed! – this word, *unknown a century since*, is to-day the sovereign ruler of all lives' (Parsons 1888: xv, our emphasis). Moreover, several observers have commented on the difficulty of translating the term (and concept of) 'achievement', even into such languages as French, a fact which suggests that the term's resonance, although increasingly widespread, is not yet universal (Hofstede 1980: 21; Clement 1988).

3. Blythe's play *Where Have I Been All My Life?* (dir. T. Heskins) premiered at the New Vic Theatre, Newcastle-under-Lyme, 7–28 April 2012.
4. Quoted from the website of Walsall College: <http://www.walsallcollege.ac.uk/mmlib/includes/sendfile.php?id=3912> (accessed 5 June 2012).
5. Of course, there were many authors writing during the twentieth century who were far from blind to the ambivalent outcomes of 'achievement'. Anthropologists writing on witchcraft showed how excessive success could easily lead to suspicion and ostracism (Kuper 1983: 78), while the works of such writers as F. Scott Fitzgerald and Tennessee Williams did much to highlight the empty promises of 'success' and the American Dream. Despite this, however, the ambivalent outcomes of achievement rarely became an explicit point of reflection or investigation within the social science disciplines more broadly.
6. See also the critiques of McClelland developed by De Vos (1973), Graves (1974) and Owens and Nandy (1978).
7. This was an impact that had been anticipated by McClelland himself, who had argued that his work was 'of more than academic interest because so many countries consciously want to develop rapidly at the present time. They might ... be willing to grant that ... *n* Achievement is somehow needed for economic growth, but then they would naturally want to know how to produce more of it. A whole new perspective is opened up – the possibility of social planning in terms of its psychological effects' (McClelland 1961: 336–37).
8. Of course, the precise implications of this language is contingent on how it intersects with other ethical and political concerns in any given context. Moreover, as Foucault underscores, social, economic and political influences are necessary but not sufficient conditions for something to stand out as a problem: they 'instigate' the process, but the ultimate form of the problematisation is original, specific and determined by individuals' own processes of thought (Foucault 2000: 118).
9. Ballerina Nina, the protagonist of this film, is presented as a character so desperate to achieve her dream of being cast in the lead role in Tchaikovsky's ballet *Swan Lake* that she subjects herself not only to a punishing physical and dietary regime, she slowly descends into madness, a process which culminates in a brilliant but suicidal performance on stage. In the closing scene, as her co-stars rush to her dying body, we hear her final words: 'It was perfect'. Unsubtle as the film's narrative might be, it finds such chilling parallels in this volume as Peter Demerath's portrait of an American schoolgirl so driven to achieve that she disrupts her own hormonal balance, or the Vietnamese discourses of 'achievement disease' traced by Susan Bayly.
10. Higgins's later work (e.g., Higgins 2011) places more emphasis on the apprehension of the social world; but the self is still fundamentally presented as a perceiving and interpreting monad rather than as physically present within, or dynamically co-productive of, that world.
11. In addition to Berger (2010), see also the 2012 exhibition *For All the World to See: Visual Culture and the Struggle for Civil Rights* (curator M. Berger). The exhibition was organised by the CADVC, University of Maryland, in partnership with the Smithsonian National Museum of African American History and Culture, and viewed at the National Civil Rights Museum, Memphis, TN, 28 March 2012.

References

Appadurai, A. 1986. Introduction: Commodities and the Politics of Value. In *The Social Life of Things: Commodities in Cultural Perspective* (ed.) A. Appadurai, 3–63. Cambridge: Cambridge University Press.

Aronofsky, D. (dir.). 2010. *Black Swan*. Fox Searchlight Pictures.

Badiou, A. 2006. *Logiques des mondes: l'être et l'événement*, vol. 2. Paris: Seuil.

Berger, M. 2010. *For All the World to See: Visual Culture and the Struggle for Civil Rights*. New Haven: Yale University Press.

Cimpian, A. 2010. The Impact of Generic Language About Ability on Children's Achievement Motivation. *Developmental Psychology* 46, no. 5: 1333–1340.

Cimpian, A., H.-M.C. Arce, E.M. Markman and C.S. Dweck. 2007. Subtle Linguistic Cues Affect Children's Motivation. *Psychological Science* 18, no. 4: 314–316.

Clance, P.R., and S.A. Imes. 1978. The Impostor Phenomenon in High Achieving Women: Dynamics and Therapeutic Intervention. *Psychotherapy: Theory, Research and Practice* 15, no. 3: 241–247.

Clement, R. W. 1988. Management Development in the 1980s: A Field in Transition. *Journal of Management Development* 7, no. 1: 45-55.

Clough, P.T. 2008. The Affective Turn: Political Economy, Biomedia and Bodies. *Theory, Culture and Society* 25, no. 1: 1–22.

Corpus, J.H., and M.R. Lepper. 2007. The Effects of Person Versus Performance Praise on Children's Motivation: Gender and Age as Moderating Factors. *Educational Psychology* 27, no. 4: 487–508.

D'Andrade, R.G. 1992. Schemas and Motivation. In *Human Motives and Cultural Models*, (eds) R.G. D'Andrade and C. Strauss, 23-44. Cambridge: Cambridge University Press.

Davidson, E. 2011. *The Burdens of Aspiration: Schools, Youth, and Success in the Divided Worlds of Silicon Valley*. New York: NYU Press.

De Rond, M. 2009. *The Last Amateurs: To Hell and Back with the Cambridge Boat Race Crew*. London: Icon.

De Vos, G.A. 1973. *Socialization for Achievement: Essays on the Cultural Psychology of the Japanese*. Berkeley: University of California Press.

Demerath, P. 2009. *Producing Success: The Culture of Personal Advancement in an American High School*. Chicago: University of Chicago Press.

Dollard, J. 1941. Review of *Explorations in Personality*. *American Anthropologist* 43, no. 1: 118–120.

Dweck, C.S. 1999. *Self-Theories: Their Role in Motivation, Personality and Development*. Philadelphia: Psychology Press.

Enli, G.S. 2009. Mass Communication Tapping into Participatory Culture: Exploring *Strictly Come Dancing* and *Britain's Got Talent*. *European Journal of Communication* 24, no. 4: 481–493.

Ford, D.Y., and A. Thomas. 1997. *Underachievement among Gifted Minority Students: Problems and Promises*. Reston: ERIC Clearinghouse on Disabilities and Gifted Education.

Fordham, S. 1996. *Blacked Out: Dilemmas of Race, Identity and Success at Capital High*. Chicago: University of Chicago Press.

Foucault, M. 2000. Polemics, Politics and Problematizations. In *Essential Works of Foucault 1954–1984*, Vol 1: *Ethics* (ed.) P. Rabinow, 111–119. London: Penguin.

Graves, T.D. 1974. Urban Indian Personality and the 'Culture of Poverty'. *American Ethnologist* 1, no. 1: 65–86.

Harkins, J. 1990. Shame and Shyness in the Aboriginal Classroom: A Case For 'Practical Semantics'. *Australian Journal of Linguistics* 10, no. 2: 293–306.

Hemmings, C. 2005. Invoking Affect: Cultural Theory and the Ontological Turn. *Cultural Studies* 19, no. 5: 548–567.

Heyman, G.D. 2008. Talking About Success: Implications for Achievement Motivation. *Journal of Applied Developmental Psychology* 29, no. 5: 361-370.

Higgins, E.T. 1997. Beyond Pleasure and Pain. *American Psychologist* 52, no. 12: 1280–1300.

——— 2011. *Beyond Pleasure and Pain: How Motivation Works*. Oxford: Oxford University Press.

Hofstede, G. H. 2001. *Culture's Consequences: Comparing Values, Behaviors, Institutions, and Organizations across Nations* (2nd edn). Thousand Oaks: Sage.

Hughes, L. 1941. The Need for Heroes. *The Crisis* 48, no. 6: 184–206.

Hultberg, P. 1985. Success, Retreat, Panic: Over-Stimulation and Depressive Defence. *Journal of Analytical Psychology* 30, no. 1: 73–93.

Humphrey, C. 2008. Reassembling Individual Subjects: Events and Decisions in Troubled Times. *Anthropological Theory* 8, no. 4: 357–380.

Izard, C.E., G.M. Wehmer, W. Livsey and J.R. Jennings. 1966. Affect, Awareness, and Performance. In *Affect, Cognition, and Personality: Empirical Studies* (eds) S.S. Tomkins and C.E. Izard, 2–41. London: Tavistock.

Kamins, M.L., and C.S. Dweck. 1999. Person Versus Process Praise and Criticism: Implications for Contingent Self-Worth and Coping. *Developmental Psychology* 35, no. 3: 835–847.

Kruger, M.S. 1933. Pleasure and Pain and the Emotions. *British Journal of Medical Psychology* 13, no. 1: 51–62.

Krugman, P. 1994. Competitiveness: A Dangerous Obsession. *Foreign Affairs* 73, no. 2: 28–44.

Kuper, A. 1983. *Anthropology and Anthropologists: The Modern British School* (rev. edn). London: Routledge and Kegan Paul.

LeVine, R.A. 1968. *Dreams and Deeds: Achievement Motivation in Nigeria*. Chicago: University of Chicago Press.

Long, N.J. 2007. How to Win a Beauty Contest in Tanjung Pinang. *Review of Indonesian and Malaysian Affairs* 41, no. 1: 91–117.

——— 2012. Utopian Sociality. Online. *Cambridge Anthropology* 30, no. 1: 80–94.

——— forthcoming. Sociality, in Anthropology. In *International Encyclopedia of the Social and Behavioral Sciences* (2nd edn), (ed.) J.D. Wright. Oxford: Elsevier.

Long, N.J., and H.L. Moore. 2013. Introduction: Sociality's New Directions. In *Sociality: New Directions* (eds) N.J. Long and H.L. Moore, 1–24. Oxford: Berghahn.

Luhrmann, T. 2006. Subjectivity. *Anthropological Theory* 6, no. 3: 345–361.

Maehr, M.L. 2008. Culture and Achievement Motivation. *International Journal of Psychology* 43, no. 5: 917–918.

Malloch, J. 2009. Achievement and the 7 Benefits of the Feel Good Factor. <http://www.selfgrowth.com/articles/achievement_and_7_benefits_feel_good_factor.html> (accessed 5 May 2012).

McClelland, D.C. 1961. *The Achieving Society*. Princeton: van Nostrand.

McClelland, D.C., J.W. Atkinson, R.A. Clark and E.L. Lowell. 1953. *The Achievement Motive*. New York: Appleton-Century-Crofts.

Moore, H.L. 2011. *Still Life: Hopes, Desires and Satisfactions*. Cambridge: Polity Press.

——— 2012. Avatars and Robots: The Imaginary Present and the Socialities of the Inorganic. *Cambridge Anthropology* 30, no. 1: 48–63.

Mueller, C.M., and C.S. Dweck. 1998. Praise for Intelligence Can Undermine Children's Motivation and Performance. *Journal of Personality and Social Psychology* 75, no. 1: 33–52.

Murray, H.A. [1938] 2008. *Explorations in Personality*. Oxford: Oxford University Press.

Nandy, A. 1987. *Tradition, Tyranny and Utopias: Essays in the Politics of Awareness*. Delhi: Oxford University Press.

Ogbu, J.U. 1987. Variability in Minority School Performance: A Problem in Search of an Explanation. *Anthropology and Education Quarterly* 18, no. 4: 312–334.

Owens, R.L., and A. Nandy. 1978. *The New Vaisyas: Entrepreneurial Opportunity and Response in an Indian City*. Durham, NC: Carolina Academic Press.

Park, J.S.-Y. 2011. The Promise of English: Linguistic Capital and the Neoliberal Worker in the South Korean Job Market. *International Journal of Bilingual Education and Bilingualism* 14, no. 4: 443–455.

Parsons, G. F. 1888. Introduction. In *The Magic Skin*, H. de Balzac, i-xliii. London: Routledge.

Paul, R.A. 1990. What Does Anybody Want? Desire, Purpose, and the Acting Subject in the Study of Culture. *Cultural Anthropology* 5, no. 4: 431–451.

Perivoliotis, D., and C. Cather. 2009. Cognitive Behavioral Therapy of Negative Symptoms. *Journal of Clinical Psychology* 65, no. 8: 815–830.

Phoenix, A. 1998. Dealing with Difference: The Recursive and the New. *Ethnic and Racial Studies* 21, no. 5: 859–880.

Reboussin, R., and J.W. Goldstein. 1966. Achievement Motivation in Navaho and White Students. *American Anthropologist* 68, no. 3: 740–745.

Rostow, W.W. 1960. *The Stages of Economic Growth: A Non-Communist Manifesto*. Cambridge: Cambridge University Press.

Spurlock, J. 1985. Survival Guilt and the Afro-American of Achievement. *Journal of the National Medical Association* 77, no. 1: 29–32.

Strauss, C. 1992a. Models and Motives. In *Human Motives and Cultural Models* (eds) R.G. D'Andrade and C. Strauss, 1-20. Cambridge: Cambridge University Press.

——— 1992b. What Makes Tony Run? Schemas as Motives Reconsidered. In *Human Motives and Cultural Models* (eds) R.G. D'Andrade and C. Strauss, 197–224. Cambridge: Cambridge University Press.

Suárez-Orozco, C., and M. Suárez-Orozco. 1995. *Transformations: Immigration, Family Life, and Achievement Motivation Amongst Latino Adolescents*. Stanford: Stanford University Press.

Sweeney, J. 2003. Is That It? Questioning Economic Success. *Ethical Perspectives* 10, no. 2: 138–150.

Venn, C. 2010. Individuation, Relationality, Affect: Rethinking the Human in Relation to the Living. *Body and Society* 16, no. 1: 129–161.

Weiner, B. 1990. History of Motivational Research in Education. *Journal of Educational Psychology* 82, no. 4: 616–622.

Williams, T. [1945] 2009. The Catastrophe of Success. In *Tennessee Williams' New Selected Essays: Where I Live* (ed.) J.S. Bak, 32–36. New York: New Directions.

Wilson, P. 1991. Trauma of Sioux Indian High School Students. *Anthropology and Education Quarterly* 22, no. 4: 367–383.

Zentall, S.R., and B.J. Morris. 2010. 'Good Job, You're So Smart': The Effects of Inconsistency of Praise Type on Young Children's Motivation. *Journal of Experimental Child Psychology* 107, no. 2: 155–163.

1

The Achievement of a Life, a List, a Line

Kathleen Stewart

The social life of achievement is a phantasm of attachment and dream circulating across bodies of all kinds – human bodies, bodies of thought, plant and animal bodies, bodies of pain and pleasure, assemblages of histories and politics, forms of caring and abuse solidified into models of what counts for the family or the social. Every word in the phrase – social, life, achievement – tweaks labours, attachments, judgements, sacrifices, generations; worlds of finance, education, health, luck and hope; forms of compulsion, addiction and accumulation; and pieced together modes of daily existence of all kinds. The force of the phrase, and all it catches up in situations and circumstances, indexes a prismatic ecology of self, world, attachment, attainment, attunement, animation and desire.

Finding ways to approach the live density of the social life of achievement, then, raises basic questions of theory and description. This is because its subjects and objects are not prefixed entities easy to name in an ether of prefabulated knowledge. Their forms, moves and scenes are left out of the equation that hopes to simply name some direct determinants of an achievement proper. Instead of the short-hand language of opportunities taken or lost, constraints overcome or not, motivations, ideals and representations that obscure possibilities or become themselves conditions of possibility, I wonder, here, how circulating forces spawn worlds, animate forms of attachment and attunement, and become the air and ground of living in and living through the things that happen. I wonder how individuation itself happens and how a self achieves whatever counts as 'a life'. I wonder how forces take on forms, how they come to reside in experiences, conditions, objects, dreams, landscapes, imaginaries and lived sensory moments, how they not only animate what we call a life but incite its actual labours of production.

My writing and thinking here is aligned with forms of non-representational theory (Thrift 2007) including weak, or reparative, theory (Sedgwick 1997), fictocriticism (Muecke 2008) and the material semiotics of actor-network theory (Latour 2007). I suggest the need to slow theory – to give pause to the quick, naturalised relationship between thinking subject, concept and world, in order to create descriptive eddies that wonder what the object of analysis might be, to create a speculative attunement that at least aspires to align with the commonplace labours of becoming sentient to whatever is happening. I take ordinary labours of attunement to be the sometimes banal, sometimes eventful, sometimes buoyant, sometimes endured, sometimes so sad, enactments of what Heidegger (1975) called 'worlding' – an intimate, compositional process of dwelling in spaces that bears, gestures, gestates worlds. In the labours of worlding, things matter not because of how they are represented but because they have qualities, textures, tracks and rhythms (Lefebvre 2004).

Here I take one approach among almost countless possibilities that might open the social life of achievement to slow description and questions of how worlds emerge. I evoke some of the phantasmatic labours and lived dream worlds of a single life.

I am suggesting here that we might now think of a life – a collective life or an individual life – as a series of worldings that have laid down tracks of reaction, etched habits and of composition onto identities, desires, objects, scenes and ways of living. These dense and textured worldings are not the bloodless effects of distant systems but the lived affects of countless big and small efforts to acclimatise to whatever is happening, or to fashion something inhabitable out of it. Or they are the lived affects of someone spinning out of control, or deflating, or shouldering tasks and identities in the effort to succeed, or to survive, or to find something.

The Line of a Life

In the line of a life, a worlding is both a promissory note and an imperative that demands a response: an imperial promise that shows up in ordinary sensibilities and situations. A worlding might become a life; it might be shouldered as an all-consuming identity, something to pour yourself into, something devotional or required. Or it might be temporarily adopted and then abandoned, or ignored, or used for some purpose, or held at arm's length as an object of sarcasm or good-natured humour.

So many things happen in a life, with or without the deliberative, self-constructing kind of agency we imagine as the generative force of a life. Latour (2007) asks how all of these other things that happen are themselves agents. The effects of what happens are not all that predictable. It can be surprising how the composition of a life amplifies them in forms, directions and tempos; which forms of a life end up being gripping, which don't end up mattering much; which ones set off lines; which ones remain ungathered, yet turn out to matter more than anything else; how things matter differently in the positing of scenes, atmospheres, sentiments, causes. From the longitudinal view of a life, then, a person is a nexus of a great pile of things: the fierce and febrile attachments, the sedimented habits, the flights of fancy, the events of all kinds, the stubborn plans and their roadblocks and abductions, the sheer weight of things, or a stance to the world that remains as a residue – a distillate cooked down.

Writing a life means writing strands of cohabitation with the things of the world. There are buildings to be considered, family lines, institutions, roads, registers and genres somehow set in motion, the unrelenting too-muchness of things coupled, cruelly, with the felt lack at the heart of a life. The great piles of things distributed across fields of worldings: objects, events, plans, roadblocks, abductions, the dullness of everything, the threat of an outside, the rote agencies, the great pile of scenes of living that are not exactly memories but can pop up, the elongated fingers of an old hand wavering over the body, floating aimlessly into the now permanently darkened world that blindness brings.

What follows here is a cartography of a life written through lists and lines. A distributed biography tracing a self-worlding across a field of intensities, durations and compelling puzzles.

My mother is running in the dark across the fields, toward the burning house. A lightning strike, the thunder and rain that crashed through the night. Ten bedrooms, the silver that melted on the dining room credenza, the Irish linen, the Irish lace, there must have been some money from somewhere. Aunt Irene was still living there at the time, the smell of smoke saturating her skin, a bad smell.

The house was in her father's mother's family: Ellen Pendergast, from Ireland, from Philadelphia with a dozen sisters, the row houses – they swept the steps everyday, they visited the farm in the summer, the great aunts, the laughing outright, the pond, the fields, the attic. Claire was the one with all the personality, the smiling one who told stories and watched everything enrapt, the one whose baby picture won a beauty contest in the 1920s and was published in the Lawrence paper – she looked just like the Gerber baby. The great aunts favoured her over the next sister who grew up resentful and strange and Republican in a sea of Democrats.

People watched Claire, followed her around. As a child, she had the Shirley Temple curls and the spring in her step. People passing on the street would take a double take. The men at the market would lift her onto the counter to dance 'The Good Ship Lollipop.' By ten she was driving her father's farm truck; by fourteen, she was driving it all over town. When she bought a cabin in New Hampshire others did too. When she walked downtown people would cluster around her. They called her for all kinds of reasons. When she moved to assisted living, a network of women pulled their antennae into attention in that direction.

She came from a line of people started when Ellen Pendergast attached herself to Michael Driscoll, who never worked another day in his life, and with him came a long and broad line of men who drank and fought with fists and knives and beat their families and left a stain as if in the blood. Michael would sit in the kitchen of the big house with his feet in a pot of water. He had a helper (another drinker) who lived in the barn. There was a currant field where the blackcurrants grew.

Nine kids – all the boys drank – grew up to live within a quarter of a mile of one another on the edges of the fields. Bill, Mary, Parkie (he was killed by a car when he was young, walking home drunk), Helen, John, Francis, Irene, Jack, Winnie died young. Mary was pregnant with her fifth child when her husband died of a heart attack while carrying a bathtub over his head. Then she ran the plumbing business and her own big house became a boarding house full of working men. She'd feed them all, and the five kids, at a long dining-room table. A stern, competent, adventurous line of women who loved children but not necessarily their own. Aunt Mary showed some meanness to hers but she'd take the cousins – my mother – all the way to Boston Harbour in her 1930s wooden Beach Buggy to ride the boats and sing songs.

Jack Driscoll was handsome; he had the curly black hair and the blue, blue eyes, and he and my mother's mother, Bea, both liked to dance. She could sing and play any tune on the piano by ear. She never had lessons. She'd memorise the poems in the Sunday paper. 'Paul Revere's Ride', 'The Wreck of the Hesperus'. She knew all the lyrics of all the country music songs, 'You Are My Sunshine'. Everyone liked her. She was friendly and liked to talk. She was so cute and nice. But crabby too. Her mother was a mean drunk. Bea and all her sisters started work in the mills when they were still children; Bea was a dyer. Jack and his brothers were bricklayers and contractors; they had a superior attitude about mill work. He was a good worker when he wasn't drinking. And very popular – everyone liked him. Silver-tongued. The Driscoll men built the Holy Rosary School, the Musgrow building, churches in Massachusetts and Maine, the high school. John built a mansion across the street with Italian marble. He went back to Ireland a lot. His son, Diamond Jack, flashed it. He drove a Cadillac. There were times when my mother's father, Jack, would be home for dinner for a while and things would be kind of normal. And then the night he didn't show up you'd know. He'd get the DTs. He'd get so sick he couldn't hold his peas. He'd cry to my mother, maybe because she was the oldest.

Bea slept with a board under her bed in case he came at her in one of his drunken rages. She was determined that her kids would have as normal a young life as possible. She made their clothes. She'd help them sneak out to go to dances, putting pillows in the beds to make it look like they were in them asleep. She would say, 'Go up and pick some green beans for supper'. She would can tomatoes. My mother loved that. Bea'd say, 'Don't tell anyone we only had potato soup for supper'. But it didn't bother my mother at all; she loved potatoes. They would go down to the back fields. Bea'd say, 'Get me some blueberries and I'll make a pie'. She didn't like making pies. Claire grew up terrified of the workhorses she walked behind, their massive haunches pulling the plough. Once the girls went to a dance without their father's permission. He was sitting on the porch with a shotgun when they got back. They ran to Aunt Nunna's and stayed with her. Nunna once threw a milk bottle at Parkie. She'd come down and milk the cows when Jack was off drinking. Finally, at age eighty-three, my mother says to me, 'My father was not a person I was fond of'. Another time, I finally tell my elderly mother, 'You have brain damage'. She says, 'Is it because of my father?' I say, 'What, the drinking?' She nods. I say, 'No. No. It's the episodes'.

She feels she has been stained by her father's violent drinking. You would never know it to meet her. People like to get around her. When she was still able to get out to go to wakes, she would hold court in a corner surrounded by a line of people who wanted to speak to her. People say she's a saint, she has something not quite articulable but noticed – an impersonal pleasure in people and what comes out of their mouths. A habitual spark of response lodged in her body, a kind of timing without exception or lapse. She can't understand why people see her this way – the saint. She thinks maybe it's her myaesthenia gravis, the way the facial paralysis makes her face look like it's always smiling. I say 'No. What facial paralysis?'

She lived in terror of judgement and conflict as if these are the same thing. The destructive power of words, the permanent tearing that comes of the hard ire of a sister judged. That's not to say she didn't have a temper, not to say she didn't open her mouth with words that cut to the bone. She had a talent for sizing up people. 'He *loves* you but he's got too many problems to help *you*'.

And there were her eyes. These auratic watering eyes, now, in their blindness, one-hundred-percent open surface contact. Floating live surfaces. Concentrated yet diffuse points of contact with the world. She was afraid, but not in her eyes. It was the legs that shook, refused to hold her weight, curled up beneath her so that she had to be lifted – that terrifying blind lift from the wheelchair to the bed and back. Back and forth, back and forth, in a wild, abandoned confinement. A free fall for a woman who bore the weight of the world and found herself dealing, alone, with an unspecified unworlding that she could not grasp. She always had good legs. Her teacher friends, all much younger, said so when she was in her sixties. Claire always had the good legs, even at the end.

She hated overhead lighting; so do I, we all do, generations of people spread out across the country hating the cold illumination of an overhead light. The lamps she made are the centrepieces in our houses and when our cats finally tear apart the crumbling shades we make new ones. We scavenge for the right lamps. They can't cost much of anything if they are to have value. We walk across dark rooms to turn on the lamps even if it takes ten to light a room. Ten lamps, ten switches, the time, the careful, stumbling time-taking moving around the room turning on the lamps. We stockpile light bulbs against the demise of incandescent lighting.

People in this line don't use dryers, either. Especially not for underwear and socks, which dryers will rip and burn and shrink and destroy. Grammy Bea, of course, didn't have a dryer. She had a wringer she rolled over to the kitchen sink on washing day and she hung the laundry out on a line in the yard. In the winter she brought it in frozen stiff and hung it all over the house to finish drying. My mother and all her sisters had clotheslines in the back yard and wooden racks in the basement. Now it's mostly the wooden racks in basements in Massachusetts and Connecticut and just the underwear and socks. There are other truncated traces of a line in practices like writing Christmas cards or using grocery store bags to line trashcans instead of buying actual trash bags that fit.

My mother had five kids, one born each year, like a linked chain of Irish twins. The fourth was dead in the womb at four months and in those days they made the women wait to deliver them dead. My father wasn't even there for the birth of her first baby in Rhode Island. He was out playing cards and drinking with the boys, didn't even show up at the hospital until the middle of the next day. That's what men did then. There was no washing machine for the diapers, no money. They would save up to get a six-pack on Fridays. A rat in a crib prompted the move out of Navy housing to Vermont where my mother had gone to college on a basketball scholarship. A small Catholic women's school. My sister went there too, one of my brothers went to the brother college down the road. And every year the, finally, old ladies made the more and more heroic trek back to Vermont to see the classmates who called my mother 'Dric'. When the trips became boldly, stubbornly impossible, the kids propped up the efforts at reunion with their own increasingly heroic efforts. That trip, and their homes, were the last things they let go of, long after the driver's licences and the partners were gone.

Claire had the weight of the world. The kids, the job teaching English as a second language to violently poor immigrants. The suspicion that there was something wrong with my father, that one day it would be revealed to the world that he was crazy; he would do something to lose his job. He loved her. With the kids, he had favourites. He had beautiful hands. He loved Bea, cooked her dinner on Sundays, hated his own mother, still wanted to cut up my meat for me when I visited as an adult.

She always had projects. She furnished the house with antiques bought for two dollars a piece at barn sales in Vermont and New Hampshire and refinished in the driveway. She visited the families of her school kids. Once she brought a turkey for Thanksgiving to one of a student's family and discovered that there was no furniture in the apartment. She went out and found some. She could draw; she'd doodle gorgeous, bombshell women on scraps of paper when she was talking on the phone. She painted scenes on boxes and baskets, stools and dressers. She knitted comforters for the kids and then the grandchildren. She made the lamps and lampshades. She raised us Catholic, led the girl scout troop, modelled for charities, observed Lent, prayed on her knees every night, deposited her whole pay cheque into a college fund for us all those years, lined us all up and marched us off to the supermarket or set us onto our Saturday chores or took us on camping trips, setting up tents in the rain. A therapist I once had would have said to her, as she did to me, 'Who do you think you are, God?'

When we were four surly teenagers, she got season ski passes and got us up at 6 AM every blustery winter Saturday and Sunday to drive to Pat's Peak in New Hampshire. There were vacations at the beach or at little lakes, rowboats, clam digging, a moment with her head resting on my lap in a cabin, stroking her beautiful hair grown long for once, the pictures of her with friends on *chaise-longues* on beaches, the intimacy of those bathing suits.

There was all the trouble at dinner when my father got home. The rage. The humiliation. We, the witnesses. I would fall off my seat or drop the pitcher of milk or the bowl of squash on the floor to create a diversion. The youngest one, who lived in horror of vegetables, would be sitting at the table alone with the carrots and green beans on his plate while the rest of us got ready for bed.

There was a big group of friends who grew up together. All couples with piles of kids. They had dinner parties at which there were terrible fights between brothers. They travelled all over together, sending us postcards from Venezuela and Italy. They skied in Utah and visited Palm Springs. They smoked and drank and laughed hard together.

One day she killed all the kittens when she turned on the car. They had crawled up into the engine. She picked us up from school to tell us; we usually walked. She cried, her body shook. What she was going through was way more intense, we knew, than our loss of the kittens and so we kept still.

Sometimes we would catch her in a strange posture when she was coming down the stairs, or standing in a corner in an upstairs bedroom facing the wall. Her whole upper body would be bent a little forward and shaking, her shoulders sloped down. Her hands were up at her mouth and she seemed to be biting them while she shook. We never talked about it. We all watched her. Then, watching her dying, we'd mention things to each other – things telegraphed like a notification from life: her strange shaking, biting gesture, the rages at our father at the dinner table; she spanked us with a hairbrush; we had the fear of God. That was another world.

When the kids were gone she found the house in New Hampshire to buy and then traded it in for another one with a view of the mountains after carefully eyeing the new house for a couple of years, sizing it up with binoculars from the first house. In the new house she grew miraculous geraniums and a jade plant so big and healthy people were always saying it must be 500 years old. Those plants lived through the freezing winters and a month at a time without water. They flourished clinging to their windows with southern exposure.

For decades she choked on her dinner. She would get up and go into the bathroom while we sat there waiting to see if she would come out again. There were operations in Boston, bi-weekly blood transfusions. Once, when we were all grown, things looked bad. She sent us all a letter. My youngest brother says he never got one. I don't remember the letter either but I remember my father calling to tell me to come home. I remember not understanding how much care she needed right after the operation. I remember blithely going to bed and sleeping all night while she lay awake on her back all night in pain, weakly calling out to me that she had to get up to go to the bathroom.

I still have one green ceramic plate left from the set she bought me in Clearwater, Michigan, thirty years ago. She wanted to make a gesture to establish my household because I wasn't getting married.

Her house had the same phone number hard-wired into the wall in the kitchen for fifty years: 978-688-5444. For a long time I couldn't take the number off my cell phone because I wanted it to still be somewhere.

After my father died, we travelled together. Once we were outside Albuquerque visiting a dusty hill covered with ancient stones. I had to pee. There were public restrooms at the bottom of the hill and people were coming up the paths but still out of sight so I pulled down my pants and peed on the path. Much to my amazement my mother just followed suit. The direct contact of that quick imitation was more touching than sentiment and says something about the nature of her attachments and mine.

After my father died, her labours slowly cooked down to a sheer and potent will to fall into step with whatever was happening, even though it wasn't good, a surge to go on belonging to a something. Slowly, step by step, her enduring itself turned into a feeble performance of the effort to find a form and hold to it. The achievement of a life.

My father died one night without warning. After all those years of him failing to hold up his end of the world she was always in the middle of propping up and setting in motion, a fissure opened up and swallowed the whole thing, rage and all. She couldn't even remember what it was she had been so angry about. They had had a wonderful life.

She was small and frail from that day forward. That winter was horrible. No one visited her. She was in the dark, alone, she couldn't even push the snow back to open the door. She couldn't get out. Help dropped by sporadically and she would try to remember her list of things she needed help with. She thought about his body in the frozen ground; he must be so cold.

She became one of those doing what the living do. You make a cup of tea and an English muffin for dinner. You drive the SUV to the drugstore and back; you manage to get it into the garage without hitting the sides but the hatch is too heavy for you to pull down; you can't even reach it, so you spend hours in the freezing garage trying to rig up something to stand on, finding a rope, trying to attach it to the latch and tie it around your waist, your fingers frozen, fumbling, you don't see well, it gets dark, you have to give up, you turn off the lights in the back seat so they won't run down the battery, you don't tell anyone. You will have to wait until someone comes to visit. Every day is now a useless expenditure of effort. Your work doesn't work anymore.

You want the spring to come; you want the beautiful winter light to stay with you a little longer today, you settle deep into the chair by the wood stove, now converted for gas, you catch a glimpse of the scene of your life and you long for it.

You have to gather all the papers, the death certificate, the insurance, all the financial accounts, investments you and he made without professional help; some were disasters and some made money but they're here and there, scattered over a frighteningly obtuse unknown zone of financial reports you think you have to learn how to read. What number do you call? What do you do? What are these things? You do this for three years, all alone, in a torture and meanwhile you are having trans-ischemic attacks that leave you blank, aphasic, not yourself. You live through them alone, you don't tell anyone because you are clinging to your life.

Numbers get hard, then impossible. You are leaving little slips of paper and little notebooks all over the house with phone numbers written on them – your kids, your sisters, your friends, your doctor's numbers. Different versions of the numbers, you're trying to record them, to find a new system that will work for you; your writing is shaky, it goes off the page and you don't even realise it. Your son finally takes your chequebook away when he finds cheques half written all over the house.

You lose your licence because of the eyesight; a doctor turns you in; you try to enlist help to get it back; you call your daughters with hesitant opening lines for schemes that might work, baiting them to come up with something as they used to do, increasingly desperate at their evasion, the blank where the line of a plan once happened. Now you have to rely on walking downtown for a loaf of bread or your medicine. You realise, through episodes, through experiments, through great efforts, that that's all you can carry. It's not enough.

One day you take a bad fall on Main Street in front of the post office as you are trying to make it to the drugstore. The cobblestones are uneven; there is a deadly, large granite curb. You fall on your face. You are humiliated by this fall. A fool. A mistake to think you could go on, still belonging, still in place. You have been found out. You are taken in an ambulance to the hospital. Your glasses are broken, there are many stitches on your face, you are really shaken up, the whole town knows. Then you fall off the stool in your kitchen where you eat so you can look out the window at the shapes of people walking by, the neighbourhood kids playing basketball in the driveway. Your hip breaks. Now you go on secretly; you flop around the house, taking secret falls into corners until, weeks later, your situation is finally discovered. Then an operation, rehab, and home in a wheelchair. Your daughter arrives. That night, in a hurricane, the water logged hundred-foot oak tree in the front yard falls and splits the house in half. By 5 AM the Channel 5 weatherman is standing on the tree shouting through the wind into a microphone and looking into your bedroom where you have him on TV. For days the cameramen bang on the door trying to get in to get a picture of you in your wheelchair, the shut in.

Then for months you live in the detritus, through another winter. It's horrible. You love the physical therapists who come right to your house – they're so nice. They move you from the wheelchair to the shower or the bed, the bathroom is made accessible, a ramp is built into the house, finally the house is pieced back together again and you get back to your chair by the stove. There's a beautiful new master bedroom upstairs where they've added space. You make the trip up to see it only once. But it's not yours, you will never inhabit it. It's a house sliding onto the market.

You have to give up your home. There is a quick slide. You find yourself in an apartment in assisted living. You sit there for months like it's a box, only half furnished because your house hasn't sold yet, none of your paintings and photographs are up on the wall. Then your daughter and granddaughter come to stay for Christmas, put up everything, decorate, cook, make your life good again, give you a jump start. You learn the ropes. You walk down to get your mail everyday with your walker. You eat dinner in the dining hall and try to make friends. You take exercise classes. You try to go grocery shopping in the van but you can't manage it and have to give up. You set up a bank account in the place so you can get some cash when you need it. You deposit a hundred dollars. You find someone you like; she's blind; you go to her apartment a few times to hear someone read a book. This is the highpoint. You say you don't love it here, not like you loved your house, but you're content. That lasts for a few short months, and then it's the hospital and the nursing home upstairs and back to the apartment and a series of horrible moments, and through it all the dream of getting the licence back, of being able to drive yourself, morphs into a sharp, recurrent pang of a thought that breaks the surface over and over as the need to gather your things and get out of here. You want to go home.

Fast forward. Now living in the nursing home upstairs is permanent. A pile of steps got us here. Each one, we thought, was as bad as it could get, but now we know better. She can no longer push the call button. We push to get her a different kind of button that might work for her. We bring her eye pillows to soothe the blind eyes that weep, ache. We try to enforce a schedule of bedpans every two hours. We try to shore her up. She hates the dullness of the residents, only talks to the aides and the hospice people. Her old friends visit. Any real conversation will pull her out of the fantasy terrors that gather in her isolation. She was able to tell her friend Ellen which golf clubs to use in different situations – a three wood, a nine iron.

The nursing home is this weird bling thing. Bright colours, loud cheer, quick summations – 'Getting old isn't for sissies!' 'Doesn't she look pretty in her hat!' 'Are you going to a party?' At first she can muster a recognition of the gesture; she smirks. When it gets harder to stay in the game, the game itself becomes a hard necessity. The gesture at the lived world, the theatre of submission. They will leave you alone in the dark or abandon you again in front of the fish tank or at the nurse's station. As far as she knows, she has been put to bed without dinner. She calls out, 'Help me, please', so quietly but unrelenting. The aides have beautiful faces and big round bodies. They bounce in and out quickly. They care about the residents.

You're darkly floating. Things come up out of nowhere. Possibilities of meaning you can't formulate torment you. You are agitated without intention or direction, abandoned to a condition of living through the evacuation of projects and rhythms of living. You wish the things of the world could be close to your skin. Small tasks completed are a relief – your face is wiped with a warm wet cloth. A small gesture of care brings to life some 'you' who can now check something off a list or get a star next to your name. But they no longer brush your teeth; they are rotting, brown, and you know it. You miss the feel of clean teeth, the ritual of getting ready for the day, getting ready for bed.

I'm the visitor. I'm sitting by the bed or slowly dragging a cumbersome bed-like pink padded wheelchair around the halls, out the doors to flower beds or leaves rustling, the feel of a breeze, live smells. I take her to have a beer on the patio of the bistro downstairs. She remembers it as beautiful, up on a hill, a new restaurant opened by the Dougherties or someone; she's amazed; she never knew it was there.

Sister Mary Stuart died peacefully in her sleep. Her friend June says 'Well, I guess all's well that ends well'. My mother doesn't want to be left out. She thinks she'll go to Vermont for the funeral. Confronted with all the 'no' saying – no, you can't travel; no, they can't get you into a car, how would you go to the bathroom, etc. – she struggles to get herself back on the track of the bitter pill. She is ashamed.

I tell her the story of the cat on the roof. It was a stormy night – hard wind, hard rain, thunder and lightning. I could hear him crying up on the roof all night but he wouldn't come down the tree. Finally in the morning I got a tall ladder and went up and pulled him off. She says, full of concentrated purpose, 'Now you know how I feel'.

I just sit. I become a paralysed surface of despair that sometimes calms into a nap, a Sudoku puzzle or the reading aloud out of a novel. Philip Roth's *American Pastoral* works pretty well for the first fifty-eight pages, spread out over a couple of weeks. She would fall asleep within a minute or two but then we'd pick up again. The characters roused her – she enjoyed remembering what had happened to them the last time we read. Again, always, the falling asleep right away but the repetition produced a shot of life even though we knew it was only a pathetic little something being fabricated. Sometimes we could find her voice. The news of people she knew would pull her up into a well-worn groove of attending to the kinds of things that happen to people and the way they respond. But by the time we got to Stewart O'Nan's *Last Night at the Lobster* she could no longer pull her senses together with the characters or the plot.

You sit and watch. Leaning into her body, you see folds of an unstable and charged sensorium. Knowledges sometimes accidentally unearthed. Surprise. 'You won't believe what happened to me! I wasn't in my room, I was in the yellow chair, they said I wasn't, and we were in a big place full of blue'. The hard bearing of life as a scar of life as potential and loss. The cooking down to sheer tracks of effort, anxiety, love.

You stage rebellions in the name of humanity – 'We're going down to the café to eat real food'. You get caught, you get lectures from institutional voices you need but understand cynically – they're just covering their own asses. At least there's hospice. Hospice is better. This is the best place she could be. Are you kidding?

Conclusion

Here I have approached the social life of achievement through a cartography of a life. A biography distributed across a field of subjects, objects, circumstances, social aesthetics, dispositions, the charge of forces hitting bodies, the way that a tendency takes on consistency, some lines of contact and rupture, the durations of the living out of things, some things that get said, some possibilities. These are the lines of a life attuned to a series of worldings – a life unfolding, pausing and setting off again following the imperial promise of a form in whatever is happening.

The events of a life are the events of its worldings. Registers, spaces and temporalities are thrown together into something to be in, or to be next to, or to be wary of. Concepts of what constitutes a life, or an achievement, are percepts of what's happening, what achieves rhythms. Orienting kernels are fashioned out of an aesthetic, a sensory habit or a style of response – 'She lived her life as a stalemate', 'We don't drink with meals'. Small things index generative lines. They also spread out horizontally into lists of incommensurate elements that lightly touch, snap into an assemblage, or simply differently comprise the texture, density, tempo of a worlding. The lines of a life can start with anything, pick up speed, switch direction or attach to another line, pulling the life off course. Particular elements might live on, becoming phantasmatic or habitually comforting, or curiously emblematic. Over time, the lines of a life become prismatic.

They are scored onto forms of attunement – the watching and waiting to see what will happen, the ducking for cover, the grab and go, the improvising, the shouldering, the tallying up, the forgetting.

A life is an intimacy with worlds' promises laid down like tracks. A node that quivers through the labours of living out what emerges on the horizon or drags, becomes encrusted or slips, wears thin or implodes under the weight of its own compositional excess. A life's lines of contact and wavering registers have lifespans of their own. Its elements have a radical materiality that literally matters in the compilation of sensory alignments and losses, opportunities and the unspeakable sadness of being abandoned, in the end, by the world you have made matter in a life achieved.

References

Heidegger, M. 1975. *Poetry, Language, Thought* (trans. A. Hofstadter). New York: Harper Colophon.

Latour, B. 2007. *Reassembling the Social.* Oxford: Oxford University Press.

Lefebvre, H. 2004. *Rhythmanalysis.* London: Continuum Press.

Muecke, S. 2008. *Joe in the Andamans.* Sydney: Local Consumption Publications.

Sedgwick, E. 1997. *Novel Gazing.* Durham, NC: Duke University Press.

Thrift, N. 2007. *Nonrepresentational Theory: Space, Politics, Affect.* New York: Routledge.

2

Against the Odds
A Professional Gambler's Narrative of Achievement

Rebecca Cassidy

In this chapter I argue that both gambling and achievement should be understood in relation to the embodied and materialised technologies that frame interior processes. Interviews with a professional horserace bettor, who I shall call Brian,[1] will be used to show how changes in taxation and regulation have transformed the experience of betting on horseracing in the United Kingdom. Brian's narrative illustrates how achievements are mediated by material contexts which are themselves the result of broader political and economic shifts. Modifying Appadurai's concept of 'regimes of value' (Appadurai 1986: 15), I refer to these contexts as 'regimes of achievement' and explore the ways in which they frame Brian's self making. Appadurai created the idea of 'regimes of value' to account for the contrasting ways in which objects were valued in various contexts. These regimes are frameworks that are sufficiently stable to generate judgements, but also responsive to and generative of changes in the relationships that they constitute and are themselves constituted by. If one extends this insight to gambling (and indeed other kinds of speculation) one might usefully compare various 'regimes of achievement' or 'achievement regimes'.

The interdisciplinary field of gambling studies emphasises the prevention or reduction of what is referred to as 'problem' or 'disordered' gambling (Abbott et al. 2004; Cosgrave 2006; Reith 2007). Psychologists, sociologists, economists, geneticists and cognitive scientists have used studies of individual behaviour, quantitative surveys, genetic mapping and brain imaging to investigate problem gambling (Smith et al. 2007; Meyer et al. 2009; Williams et al. 2012). In addition to this policy-led research, a number of social scientists including anthropologists have conducted participant observation in gambling environments around the world.[2] These two approaches to gambling prompt different methodological impulses. The first limits the 'noise' of actual environments: soundscapes, visually arresting displays, aspirational architecture and interior design and other people, an approach most closely associated with experiments conducted by psychologists under controlled conditions (Anderson and Brown 1984). This approach has also dominated most enquiries into 'achievement psychology'. The second approach to gambling makes sense of behaviour through these experiential properties (Parke and Griffiths 2008). By doing so, the study of gambling environments provides opportunities to focus on change and cultural or other variation. Interior states may vary, of course, but the object of study in problem gambling research conducted under laboratory conditions has been conceived of as a universal relationship between certain activities or 'triggers' and addictive behaviour (see, e.g., Clark et al. 2012). One alternative is to assert that the meaning and purpose of gambling is created through practice, not freely but in dialogue with other processes, people and machines (Cassidy 2010, 2012). Given that most ethnographic studies of achievement focus on differing definitions of achievement rather than the experience of achieving, it is possible that the methods and perspectives being developed in studies of gambling environments may provide insights into not only gambling but also achievement more generally.

A Micro-Ethnography of Gambling

I began working with British horserace bettors in 1996 in Newmarket, a town in the east of England known internationally as Headquarters, a reference to its claim to have been the site of the creation of thoroughbred flat racing in the seventeenth century (Cassidy 2002). More recently, I conducted participant observation in betting shops in London, interviewing staff and customers and working as a cashier (Cassidy 2012). This chapter focuses on a professional horserace bettor, Brian, whom I met at Huntingdon racecourse in the U.K. in 1998. The advantages and limitations of what has been described as 'micro-ethnography', a focus on a particular research participant, are discussed by Jouhki (2011) in relation to online poker players. Jouhki acknowledges that the case of his research participant 'Mark' 'cannot be generalised to present whole cultures', but he nevertheless still wants to suggest that the case is 'a rather typical story of a poker player' (ibid.: 3). My argument is different. I do not wish to suggest that there are 'whole cultures', or that Brian's experiences might be representative of them. I believe that Brian's narrative is valuable because it complements more readily available, but temporally shallow, data about gamblers. A single narrative, though not generalisable, can contribute to our understanding of gamblers and gambling because it provides consistency and longitudinal depth in a field that is characterised by fleeting encounters between researchers and their participants. Temporally deep, micro-ethnographic accounts support the value of a focus on the social life of achievement as they show how understandings of achievement, and its consequences, unfold over time.

Throughout our friendship, I recorded details of Brian's betting life, from playing cards with his father and uncle as a child, to his retirement, in 2011.[3] Our conversations reflect our changing relationship as well as Brian's relationship with betting (Rabinow 1977). I have also spent extended periods of time with twelve other professional gamblers – eleven men and one woman. Where Brian's observations may usefully be regarded as characteristic of their stories, or on the contrary as importantly distinctive, I indicate as much. Brian is a generous and articulate research participant. The numerous recordings we made together show that he is reflexive and enjoys talking about himself. Brian was particularly interested in the impact of technology, regulation and administration on his every day practices. My decision to focus on the 'apparatus' of betting is, therefore, determined by his priorities.[4] In the rest of the chapter, I focus on the contrast that Brian drew between his career as a racecourse bettor between 1990 and 2001, and as a user of the online betting exchange Betfair[5] between 2001 and 2011 – two material and regulatory contexts that evoked strikingly different experiences of what it was to gamble and to achieve.

Gambling and/as Achievement

Ethnographic studies of gambling show that achievement cannot be equated with winning in any straightforward way. Working in bars in Massachusetts in the 1950s and 1960s, for example, Zola (1963) described illegal betting as a mechanism that offered working-class men the opportunity to accrue status and responsibility when conventional routes (education, nepotism) to success (wealth, family) were closed to them. Success in bars where betting was taking place was short lived and relative, and related to the creation and maintenance of 'face' rather than a straightforward reflection of profit or loss. To lose 'well', in a way that reinforced shared values, was as important as winning. To win 'badly', could be highly offensive. Similarly, among betting shop 'regulars' in the U.K., the long-term possibility of gains in status also rests upon responses to the momentary wins and losses that punctuate long periods of time spent in the bookies (Neal 1998, 2005). In Las Vegas, Schüll (2005, 2012) has described gamblers who envisage achievement as prolonging contact with electronic gaming machines, a phenomenon also recorded in Australia by Woolley and Livingstone (2009). Loussouarn's (2011) work with Chinese casino gamblers in London shows that it is quite possible to win too quickly.

Hayano (1982) is one of the few anthropologists to have worked with professional gamblers – in his case in the card rooms of Los Angeles County. Perhaps because of his own attraction to the game (he eventually became a professional player), Hayano was interested in the existential properties of games in general and of poker in particular. He refers to poker as 'the existential game' (ibid.: 138), an encounter with uncertainty which denies the prospect of any 'finality of gain' or 'peak existence'. This lack of closure 'manifests itself in an existential, if not socio-psychological, kind of imbalance' (ibid.: 139). According to Hayano, poker playing is an evocation of life, or indeed life itself, rather than a means to an end. His work contrasts with that of Rosecrance (1985, 1986a, 1986b, 1986c, 1988a, 1988b), who worked with professional horserace bettors in North America in the 1970s and 1980s. Rosecrance accounted for the persistence of betting among professional 'handicappers' through 'binding social arrangements' (Rosecrance 1986d: 357), including the sharing of information and contingencies, reciprocal lending and the kind of empathic social interaction that is only possible between 'track buddies' with similar experiences. In each of these geographically and historically particular cases the connection between winning and achievement must be investigated rather than assumed.

Horserace Betting in the United Kingdom

During the eighteenth and nineteenth centuries, religious organisations associated gambling, including betting on horses and dogs, with crime, violence and poverty, as well as decrying its sinful, anti-social, unproductive nature. Lampard (2004) identifies the Methodists' 1936 'Declaration on Gambling' as typical of the theological and ethical condemnation that gambling provoked. For Methodists, and many other faith groups at the time, gambling was both wrong in principle (it violated religious doctrine in the sense that, 'belief in luck cannot be reconciled with faith in God') as well as having dire consequences (poverty which led to crime, alcoholism and the breakdown of the family unit). When Brian was born in 1946, betting in cash (the likely medium of the poorest punters) was illegal anywhere other than the sixty or so racecourses around the country. Nevertheless, in larger towns and cities illegal bookmakers stood on street corners and used runners to visit factories to collect stakes from workers (Chinn 1991). Faced with the impossibility of enforcing such an unpopular law, the police, select committees, and finally members of parliament agreed that off-course betting in cash should be permitted.[6] Ten thousand Licensed Betting Offices (LBOs) opened in the first year after their legalisation in the Betting and Gaming Act of 1960, governed by strict licensing laws that were intended to prevent them from 'stimulating' demand, a principle that had been established by the 1951 Royal Commission on Betting, Gaming and Lotteries (Miers 2004). In keeping with the ambiguous morality of betting at the time, customers were able to place a bet, but they should not be encouraged to linger in the shop engaging in what was seen as an unproductive and even potentially harmful use of their time. Despite the fact that live television broadcasts of racing had taken place since the 1950s, for example, LBOs were not allowed to have televisions or to show live racing until 1986. Instead, results were broadcast over a tannoy and written on a blackboard by a specially employed 'board man'. Window and door screens made it impossible to see into the shops; chairs, toilets and the sale of refreshments were forbidden until the 1980s. Betting duty was first imposed in

1966, at a rate of 2.5 per cent, and was raised to 5 per cent in 1968 and 6 per cent in 1970.

Betting shops remained relatively unchanged until 1994 when the National Lottery was created in response to the loss of revenue to foreign lotteries. The U.K. government became both a participant in, and indirectly responsible for the regulation of, the gambling industry (ibid.). The climate of deregulation in financial and other markets that dominated the policies of successive Conservative governments in the 1980s, and the development of offshore and online duty-free bookmaking, encouraged the betting and gaming industry to begin lobbying for change. In 2001, with horseracing and therefore betting badly affected by the foot-and-mouth crisis[7] and the creation of betting exchanges, betting duty was abolished and replaced by a Gross Profits Tax. In the same year the Budd Report synthesised two hundred written responses and twenty sessions of oral evidence into recommendations that formed the basis of the 2002 White Paper, 'A Safe Bet for Success'.

After various additions and periods of consultation, the Gambling Bill was introduced on 18 October 2004, and became law in April 2005. The Act removed the ad hoc legislation that governed gaming and betting and replaced it with three core principles. Under the new Act, gaming and betting had to strive to be transparent, crime-free and protect vulnerable people from possible harms associated with gambling. After forty years of stagnation, the betting industry had entered an unprecedented period of change. New technology, regulation, fiscal organisation and changes in attitudes towards gambling (and towards risk and speculation in general) produced a new apparatus of betting. Most importantly, gambling was recast as entertainment, an important part of the leisure industry and of 'U.K. plc' more generally.[8] Tessa Jowell, then Secretary of State for Culture, Media and Sport, reiterated this categorical adjustment when she unveiled the Gambling Bill in 2003 and said: 'Attitudes to gambling have changed ... It is now a diverse, vibrant and innovative industry and a popular leisure activity enjoyed in many forms by millions of people. The law needs to reflect that' (DCMS 2007).[9] Brian's career, his understanding of his activities and those of his competitors, has been contained by these various regulatory and political framings.

Being Brian

Brian considers himself to be a member of a golden generation. He was born after the Second World War, and his life and those of his grammar school mates growing up in the suburbs of London during the 1950s, was, he says, comfortable and secure. After school he abandoned a degree in mathematics at a northern university after a year because his friends were making more money than him without higher qualifications. Jobs were plentiful: if he found work boring, he explained, he would simply leave and walk into something else. His mathematical ability enabled him to work in a variety of accountancy roles including in LBOs. He benefited from oil wealth in the 1970s and 1980s when he was employed by companies in the Middle East as a computer programmer. High wages and low living costs overseas enabled him to become a professional horserace bettor when he was made redundant in his early forties. At this time, deductions of 10 per cent from either winnings or stakes in betting shops (which included off-course betting duty) made it virtually impossible to make a living without travelling to bet duty free on the racecourses. For a decade or so Brian travelled most days to different racecourses around the U.K., in order to assess the 'going' (the firmness or otherwise of the ground – particularly significant in the U.K. where the majority of racecourses are 'turf' and the weather is variable), the horses, and the on-course market. Between 2000 and 2001, the launch of deduction-free offshore telephone and online betting services by Victor Chandler, William Hill and other large bookmakers, changes in taxation, and the creation of betting exchanges first reduced the incentive to travel around the country, and then made it counterproductive. The key to success in betting changed. Brian had excelled as a professional racecourse bettor. By 2001 he realised that in order to continue to pursue his career within such a radically changed environment he would need to develop an entirely new set of skills.

In 1998 when we began to spend time together, Brian was still travelling around the country, making bets with racecourse bookmakers. At our first meeting at Huntingdon racecourse he explained that he was planning to place a large bet but first we needed to go and look at the horse in the paddock. The way in which horses conduct themselves in the parade ring and on the way to the start is thought by many bettors to provide useful indications of their mental and physical well-being: 'sweating up' in the paddock is considered a sign of nerves; a horse that bolts to the start may have run its race. (In all cases there are exceptions: some horses will be expected to sweat up and if they don't this could in itself be a cause for concern.) In this case, the horse was well behaved in the paddock and took the pre-race routine comfortably in his stride. Brian, satisfied, made his way to the stand to use binoculars to watch the horse canter down to the start. All went well. The bet was on.

We returned to the betting ring. Brian said '£500 on number six' to one of the bookmakers, who nodded, and we walked away. At this time, bets placed by professionals with bookies known to one another were conducted on trust. No ticket was written, no money changed hands. I was surprised. I hastily gave the same bookmaker fifty pounds and took the 'price' or odds of 12/1. He gave me a ticket and wrote my bet in his ledger. We sauntered off to the stands to watch the race. At this point Brian began to tell me a story:

> I had a television crew with me not so long ago at Goodwood [racecourse]. They wanted to see how I did things, much like you, and to film me winning a big bet. I told them then and there: You won't be able to tell from my reaction whether I've won or lost. You won't see me jumping about or punching the air like those idiots in the betting shop. The same in victory as defeat. That defines my approach. Because I'm a

professional. This is my office. You don't see accountants jumping up and down when a column adds up, do you?

He continued. 'I bet I'm nothing like you expected in the flesh am I? I drive a Renault, not a Bentley. I'm not flash. I'm not a high roller. There's nothing flash about me'. Brian was trying to disassociate himself from the image of the professional gambler that he believed I had held before meeting him. In particular, he was intent on categorising gambling as 'work', as opposed to frivolous and irrational risk taking (Downes et al. 1976).

Our horse won the race, and true to form Brian did not leap about, high five me, or tell anyone. But he did seem to be restraining himself. We collected our winnings. Mine in a wad that wouldn't fit in my pockets, his in a solid brick in his camera bag. This process was repeated many times in the next ten years and Brian's reactions to wins and losses remained consistently understated. I learned that he excluded excitement as a reaction to favourable outcomes because it implied uncertainty. A losing bet was accounted for by a mistake, and by post hoc knowledge that had been temporarily unavailable. A small amount of pleasure (small because in order to be correct it must also have been expected), or rather satisfaction, was derived from being proved correct according to accumulated knowledge, hard work and dispassionate, rational calculations. On one of our trips we placed two bets, winning one and losing the other. Brian was disappointed. The winner came in first when the favourite fell while travelling well at the last fence. The loser failed to make an impression in the race. Despite having a profitable day, he had been wrong about both races and he drove home puzzling about what he had missed. When we ran into a fellow professional the next day, Brian asked me not to tell him that he had been on the long shot the day before; 'I don't want him to know I got lucky', he explained. Under certain circumstances, Brian took a certain amount of satisfaction from losing races. After a freak fall which caused a pile up of riders and horses, Brian expressed relief when his horse did not quite rally to win, and told me: 'You can't predict that kind of thing. Under those conditions, you may as well be betting on two flies on a wall'. We left the racecourse poorer, but with Brian's 'reading' of the race intact.

Betting Markets as Achievement Regimes

Brian's understanding of achievement in 1999 was framed by a particular arrangement for fixed-price betting that exists in the U.K. and a few other racing jurisdictions, primarily former British colonies. The simplest bet is a 'match bet' between two individuals, at evens. For example, I bet you £5 that Manchester United will beat Chelsea this evening, and you agree. The necessary conditions for our bet are that we hold differing opinions as to the likely outcome of the football match and we trust each other to settle the bet once the outcome is determined. According to British convention, a shake of hands marks our acceptance, and is a signal that our agreement is binding (Shapiro et al. 1992). There is no exchange of stakes before the outcome is decided and no third party involvement is necessary. Once the match is over, if Chelsea have won, I pay you £5, and if Manchester United have won you pay me £5. In the case of a draw we retain our money. In the U.K., the majority of bets took this form until the invention of bookmaking in the seventeenth century. Today the majority of betting takes place through the medium of a third party: the bookmaker.[10] There are two ways of conceptualising bets made with bookmakers. One could argue that the bookmaker engages in a large number of dyadic transactions, one with every punter. This is how bookmaking began. However, innovations including taking cash bets up front, offering odds on all the horses in a race, thus 'making a book', and the starting-price mechanism suggest a different business model.[11] The bookmaking industry developed to make money from the dynamic properties of risk, while limiting exposure. Exposure is limited in several ways: through the inherent properties of the market, controlling access to information, and controlling access to betting opportunities.

All betting markets offered by bookmakers include a percentage of 'over round'. The over round is the price of providing the book, also known in the U.S.A. as the 'vig' (from vigorish) or 'juice'. As well as building profit into their books, bookmakers limit their exposure to risk through knowledge management. Punters have greater access to information than ever before due to television and the internet. However, there is a close relationship between the racing media and bookmakers. Bookmakers own 42 per cent of Satellite Information Services, the sole provider of pictures in betting shops until Turf TV was created in 2008.[12] The small racing press is dependent upon the goodwill of bookmakers for advertising revenue, and in 2009 respected journalist Paul Haigh resigned from the *Racing Post*, the only U.K. daily newspaper devoted to racing, saying that, 'Almost all the racing media is now under the effective editorial control of the bookmakers either because bookmaker advertising is essential to their survival, or because other racing correspondents have been made aware of, er, the side on which their bread is buttered' (Luft 2009).

As well as managing knowledge, bookmakers are able to control access to betting opportunities by 'monitoring' accounts. Once they have attracted attention, by, for example, winning consistently, every bet by a monitored customer is recorded so that an informed decision may be taken to decline their bets (or accept them at a reduced stake). Brian proudly showed me letters from Ladbrokes closing his (winning) accounts – indicating that his custom was no longer required. In betting shops, as well as monitoring individual customers, cashiers are obliged to ask for 'permission to lay' certain bets above a threshold stake at particular prices. Not all winning customers have their business declined. In keeping with the knowledge-management strategy of leading bookmakers, some 'unprofitable' customers are retained on the basis that their bets may be used by in-house odds compilers to inform 'tissues' (early prices for all runners or competitors in a race or event).

Economists are interested in fixed-price betting markets because they are importantly different from financial markets in the way that they generate prices (Sauer 1998). In most financial markets, at least in theory, prices fluctuate, generated by the intersection of demand and supply. In fixed-price betting markets, bookmakers announce a price at which they are willing to take bets. The 'weight' or volume of money bet on particular horses will affect the odds or 'price' at which it trades, but this is influenced by the early price set and by 'industry' money which is used to change prices on the racecourse so that starting prices reflect activities off course. A short price may attract customers if they believe that it is based on inside information. Punters will ask, 'what does the bookie know?' Occasionally one firm will offer a far shorter price than all the others for a horse. If the horse wins, well known racing pundit John McCririck will explain by shouting, 'They knew! They knew'. Although in every event there will be outcomes that are more or less profitable for bookmakers (the favourite winning is usually a bad result for bookies, for example), one of the central tenets of bookmaking is that the bookmaker should make a profit regardless of the outcome of the event. In a sense, therefore, the bookmaker does not bet.

Despite the many practices that limit exposure to risk, fixed-price betting encourages the personification of bookmakers, and betting systems in the U.K. are often conceived of and marketed as a way to 'Beat the bookie!'[13] Comparisons with other betting markets emphasise this point. In the U.S.A., Japan, Hong Kong and France (until 2010), the massive amount of betting that takes place does so through the pari-mutuel or pool betting system.[14] Unlike fixed price bookmaking, pari-mutuel provision is risk free in practice as well as in theory. Punters place bets on horses by adding their stake to a pool which is divided up according to the odds at the off, minus the 'takeout' – money that is paid to the state, the racetrack, and to owners and trainers as prize money – usually around 20 per cent, but up to 30 per cent for certain bets. The takeout is the equivalent of the 'vig' in the fixed-price system. Odds fluctuate until the start of the race, according to the 'weight' of money they attract. Payouts are determined by the cumulative decisions of punters. The pari-mutuel system has proved historically unpopular in the U.K. because of high takeouts, and the fact that it makes it impossible to 'take a price', a practice which reinforces the sense that betting is a dyadic transaction between punter and bookmaker.[15] The fixed-price system and the pari-mutuel system are two quite different achievement regimes.

Against the Crowd

The idea that betting was a battle with the bookies was one that Brian rejected. Brian regarded the bookmaker as his colleague while he saw the other bettors as his opponents, referred to as 'mugs' and, sometimes, 'gamblers'. Invoking a conventional relationship between work and reward, Brian described his achievements as 'a transfer of wealth from the ignorant to the knowledgeable, from the feckless to the hard working. My success is a triumph of reason'. The bigger the win, the greater the contrast between himself and the mugs, and Brian's system ensured that this gap was often wide, as it was based on the concept of 'value'. Unlike a casino game, where the law of large numbers determines that the house will make a profit over the long term, betting on horseracing in the U.K. enables some people to make a profit on the basis of their specialised knowledge. As a racecourse 'pro', Brian described his strategy as going 'against the crowd'. This strategy depended upon identifying 'value' bets: bets that offered odds longer than the real chances of the horse winning.

Identifying 'value' is an aspect of many betting systems and is dependent upon the facility to take a price. One racing journalist explains the idea in the following erotic terms: 'the only time any halfway-intelligent punter becomes truly aroused is when the odds for certain horses do not reflect the true chances of those horses' (Thomas 2002). According to Brian, 'It's easier to find a 12/1 shot winner regularly than it is to have a lot of bets at 2/1 and have the number of them come off that I need to make it pay'. His understanding of the fixed-price system is that the bookmakers have advantages in terms of information, liquidity, price setting and control of access to betting opportunities. Competing with them is hopeless. However, the same could not be said of the average punter who bets for kicks and on impulse.

Brian depended upon hard work to identify value bets. He watched every single race and has a photographic memory. He identified horses that had been unlucky fallers, horses that had finished strongly, horses that had been ridden poorly, horses that were running on ground to which they were unsuited, changes in the ground, changes in the positions of the stalls from one side of the racecourse to another and its effect on draw bias, and so on. These were deductive, investigative, 'evidence based' predictions that culminated in a large stake on a particular individual at a rate of four to six bets a week. The particular rhythm of betting is a product of what Brian imagines himself to be attempting, and can be contrasted with a typical 'mug' punter (as envisaged by Brian), who goes into a betting shop on his lunch break, sees a race in South Africa is about to start and takes a punt on number three, the favourite, because three is his lucky number. Brian thinks that this is a person from whom he should be able to take money by approaching betting on horses – his trade – in a completely different fashion.

The era of racecourse betting, which involved a number of professional bettors travelling around regional circuits within the country's sixty-nine racecourses, was ushered in by the imposition of off-course betting tax in 1966 (initially absorbed by the bookie, but passed onto the punter as rates rose during the 1970s) and ended with its abolition in 2001. This fiscal arrangement also enabled Brian's definition of himself in opposition to mugs, the majority of whom frequented betting shops, where they were taxed by the state, cutting into their margin, as well as disadvantaged by the control of information and access to betting opportunities by the bookmaker. Under these circumstances, Brian defined his achievements in relation to two groups of significant others: the great mob of unknown betting-shop punters whom he regarded as subnormal, and his colleagues on the racecourse, fellow professionals and bookmakers, for whom he had the utmost respect.

Betfair: 'When You're a Trader, Losing Is the Same as Winning'

By 2009 Brian had completely changed his betting behaviour, watching races at home on television and using the online betting exchange Betfair to place a large number of small bets rather than more substantial, less frequent bets. As he told me:

> Things are going nicely on the punting front this month – I've now given up completely on trying to find 10/1 winners in big handicaps and am sticking to the sort of Betfair trading you watched me doing ... I reckon the word I'd use is trading, as opposed to gambling or betting. A stockbroker trades in shares, a broker trades in commodities or currencies, a gambler trades in sport, in my case racing.

Launched in June 2000, Betfair transformed the betting market in the U.K., by enabling punters to bet with each other rather than through bookmakers, and charging a commission on all winning bets of between 2 and 5 per cent. This new business model enabled them to undercut the bookies' margins and generate better odds (O'Connor 2011). Under these vastly different conditions, the rhythm of Brian's betting changed from a small number of large bets at odds of around 10/1 in large handicap races to a larger number of small bets placed on horses to lose. The facility to 'lay' has caused controversy. Bookmakers and regulators expressed their concern that allowing people to bet on horses to lose increased the potential for corruption as it is always easier to stop a horse than it is to make it win. Brian took some time to adjust to this idea too. He told me that he found it hard to look for 'dross', or overrated runners, as well as likely winners, until he started to think of the market as a whole, 'At first I thought, I don't want to spend my time looking for slow horses, or horses that flatter to deceive, that aren't genuine. Then I thought, actually, what you're talking about is just market imperfections, like value bets. Now losing is the same as winning, to me'.

Most strikingly, Brian's new strategy involved following trends in the movements of prices in the mornings before racing. As he explained, 'Betfair has taken out the middle man, it's an opinion poll on the right price for a horse'. He described it as, 'Unerringly and worryingly accurate up to midday. They do get it wrong, but if you went onto Betfair for a year and backed horses that shortened ...', and then he raised his eyebrows and pointed upwards, implying a profit. I was shocked when Brian, well known among betting insiders for going 'against the crowd', recommended I read James Surowiecki's book *The Wisdom of Crowds* (2004), excitedly citing the ability of a mixed crowd of non-experts to accurately predict the location of the submarine *Scorpion* as 'proof' of his thesis.

Despite the apparent contrast, elements of his former strategy survive in the way that he disparages other users of Betfair, telling me that, 'No one has the discipline, most use it exactly the same as they use the bookmakers, not thinking about it at all.' Nonetheless, there is a change from Brian's previous system which saw bookmakers and professionals as colleagues and mugs as sources of profit to a new system in which the cumulative actions of the majority tend towards the truth, enabling Brian to make use of their unwitting insights in order to extract a profit from them. Brian no longer had relationships with bookmakers or any other third party. It might be argued that he had become a bookmaker himself, a characterisation that Betfair are keen to resist.[16]

Brian's betting strategy no longer relied upon the organic rhythms of the racing calendar and the physical properties of horses and racecourses but on trends in betting behaviour expressed as graphs on computer screens. There was no need to watch races. Photographic memory no longer conferred an advantage as he was not studying form and its relationship to performance. He was not making money by taking the opposite opinion to a mug. He was betting blind, observing trends in one set of data and applying them to another. Perhaps not surprisingly, his feelings about these changes were mixed. Shortly before his retirement he told me, 'There are none of the big days when you can celebrate winning several thousands, but equally the steady drip of a few hundred here and few hundred there all adds up to the same at the end of each month. Just not so exciting.' Unless their system requires them to see horses in the flesh before they place a bet, there is no longer any incentive for professionals to bet on-course. On the contrary, anyone wanting to see a horse before a race would look at the horse and then place a bet using Betfair, where the odds are likely to be better than on-course. Punters continue to frequent high-street shops in order to do battle with the bookies or to play the machines (Cassidy 2012), but the serious players have migrated to Betfair, where they can name their price to back or lay, and hope it gets matched, or arbitrage ('buy' a horse at one price and then 'sell' it at another, higher price) either manually or using software that instantly detects the smallest movements in prices.

As a Betfair customer, Brian experienced the lowest operational costs of his career. No travel, no entry fees, no expensive and terrible racecourse food. Less 'over round', more efficient markets and lower prices. He was no longer subject to monitoring and the threat of account closure because, unlike bookmakers, Betfair does not close profitable accounts as they are not betting but gathering commission on the bets of others. Despite and perhaps because of these advantages, which in effect level the playing field for everyone, Brian stopped betting professionally in 2011. He had, he said, 'had enough of computer helplines and sitting in the spare room looking at a screen.' 'I've come full circle', he told me. 'I left a job in computer programming to take redundancy and give this game a go. I did okay, I liked working on the racecourse. And now I'm back here, sitting, working on a computer all sodding day. It might be the most efficient market, but the game's changed and it's not for me any more.'

Brian's betting in 2009, though very different to how he worked in 1998, was a mix of the traditional and novel. Although he is computer literate, Brian is no Mark Zuckerberg and he continued to read form in the newspapers and online, and to watch races on television. The current generation of punters raised on Betfair arbitrage on markets for horseracing using techniques and software borrowed from financial theory, rather than their knowledge of racing, in order to gain an edge. The new regime of achievement made the role of trader that Brian had worked so hard to realise under the conditions that obtained until 2000 possible. At the same time, the relationships that framed that struggle, with bookmakers, fellow professionals, horses, jockeys and even mugs, became increasingly abstract and depersonalised. The transformation of betting from gambling to trading, which Brian might once have referred to as 'a triumph of reason', in fact revealed the stark difference between winning and achieving. Although Brian was making the same amount of money, he was no longer able to account for that profit in a way that brought him any pleasure.

Conclusion

In this chapter I have described how changes to the apparatus of betting on horseracing in the U.K. between 1960 and 2011 affected one professional horserace bettor. During the 1980s and 1990s, fiscal policy and regulation made the racecourse the only space in which professional bettors could prosper. On the racecourse Brian used his senses and experience to try to identify winners and overpriced contenders. He regarded bookmakers as colleagues and defined himself in opposition to mugs in betting shops who chose to bet despite the handicap of deductions of 10 per cent and limits on information and access to betting opportunities. When betting exchanges were created in 2000, bookmakers were no longer able to set the terms of their trade. Competition between established firms also became more intense as websites such as Oddschecker enabled online punters to choose the best odds.[17] Gradually, Brian stopped travelling to racecourses to watch horses, ground and jockeys. He stopped trying to identify opportunities to disagree with people to whom he considered himself superior. Instead, he stayed at home in order to discern other people's opinions in the movements of markets and to bet with them. The maverick who made money by going 'against the crowd' constructed a new regime of achievement. He became profitable once again, but he could not reach the heights he had scaled in the 1990s under these new conditions, and in the end they made him miserable. The new stars of professional betting are the absentee software wizards who produce automated 'bots' (robots) which detect changes in prices and automatically arbitrage their positions into guaranteed profit.

This case has wider implications for the study of achievement in several regards. Firstly, it illustrates the role of the state in legitimising particular kinds of achievement. Secondly, it shows how individuals reformulate their understanding of achievement in order to resist or support particular interpretations of their activities. Thirdly, it shows that changes to regimes of achievement can have unintended consequences. Gambling is variously and arbitrarily distinguished from investment, speculation, insurance, entrepreneurialism and numerous other ways of making risk pay (Downes et al. 1976; Fabian 1990; Lears 2003). In Euro-America, despite the increased presence of gambling on television and in the online and print media, professional gambling is counter-cultural to the extent that it transgresses the relationship between effort and reward that is enshrined in institutionalised education and in property and employment law. As such, it can shed light on dominant ideas as well as their counterparts. Talking to gamblers about their work involves continual explicit comparisons with more conventional routes to wealth and fulfilment, leading to a re-examination of achievement and other, related concepts including winning, reward, luck, fate, fortune, desert, work and leisure, risk and uncertainty. If we are to live with the consequences of new relationships with risky methods of making wealth, we need to understand how they enable us to perform and achieve.

Notes

1. I'm grateful to Brian for his friendship and wisdom and for granting me access to a way of life that has now disappeared. I have changed his name in accordance with his wishes. The fieldwork on which this paper is based was supported by Edinburgh University, the Economic and Social Research Council and the Responsibility in Gambling Trust, grant reference RES-164-25-0005 and the European Research Council, grant reference GAMSOC 263433.
2. Outstanding examples include studies carried out in North America (Zola 1963; Hayano 1982; Rosecrance 1985, 1986a, 1986b, 1986c, 1986d, 1988a, 1988b; Papineau 2005; Schüll 2005, 2012; Sallaz 2009), Jamaica (Stone 1976), Greece (Papataxiarchis 1999; Malaby 2003), Sweden (Binde 2011), the United Kingdom (Newman 1972; Saunders and Turner 1987; Neal 1998, 2005), the Pacific (Zimmer 1986, 1987a, 1987b; Rubenstein 1987; Sexton 1987), Africa (Woodburn 1982) and the Arctic (Riches 1975).
3. For a description of Brian's early gambling career, see Cassidy (2010: 141–42).
4. I use the term 'apparatus' as a translation of Foucault's *dispositif* (Agamben 2009; cf. Deleuze 1989; but see Bussolini 2010 for a note on translation). The concept refers to 'a resolutely heterogeneous grouping composing discourses, institutions, architectural arrangements, policy decisions, laws, administrative measures, scientific statements, philosophic, moral and philanthropic propositions; in sum, the said and the not-said, these are the elements of the apparatus. The apparatus itself is the network that can be established between these elements' (Foucault 1980: 194).
5. Betfair, 'the world's biggest betting community', was launched in 2000 and, by 2007, had a million clients and a turnover of £1 million a week. For the latest information about Betfair, see: http://corporate.betfair.com/ (accessed 8 March 2013).
6. Relevant select committees include that On Betting Duty (1923) and the Royal Commission on Betting, Gaming and Lotteries (1949). Licensed betting followed in the wake of the Betting and Gaming Bill (1960).
7. The spread of this highly infectious disease affected the movement of livestock, thus preventing racing from taking place and reducing betting-shop turnover.

8. 'U.K. plc' refers to the idea that businesses based in the U.K. could be thought of as sharing a single, national identity, as in the patriotic headline, 'UK plc should do its bit for broken Britain' (*Guardian*, 9 February 2009).
9. Changes in the regulation of gambling have been discussed by Kingma (2008) in relation to the Netherlands, Rosecrance (1988a) in relation to the U.S.A., Cattelino (2008) in relation to Florida Seminole gambling, and more widely by contributors to Kingma (2009) and Raento and Schwartz (2011).
10. In the 2010 British Gambling Prevalence Survey, private betting was the sixth most popular activity, with 11 per cent of respondents reporting that they had bet privately in the previous year. Betting on horses was the fourth most popular activity (16 per cent). The National Lottery was the most popular (59 per cent), followed by other lotteries (25 per cent) and scratch cards (24 per cent). For more statistics about betting in the United Kingdom, see: http://tinyurl.com/d3b5sfs (accessed 8 March 2013).
11. The mechanism generates starting prices or odds for all races in the UK by gathering a representative sample from the market on-course to apply in the (much larger) off-course market. According to Gambling Commission figures for 2011/12, fixed-price betting turnover on horses on-course was £213.80 million, compared to £5,152.24 million off-course in betting shops.
12. Ladbrokes owns 23.4 per cent and William Hill owns 19 per cent: http://tinyurl.com/cmbbocb (accessed 8 March 2013).
13. The discussion of betting systems on the Racing Forum, for example, is called 'Beat the Bookie' (see: http://tinyurl.com/bqw7bgx), as is football tipster Kevin Pullien's popular column in the *Guardian*.
14. In 2011, Japan was the largest market for betting as measured by turnover, followed by Australia, France, U.S.A., Hong Kong and Great Britain. See the International Federation of Horseracing Authorities at: http://www.horseracingintfed.com/ (accessed 8 March 2013).
15. According to Gambling Commission data, in 2011/12 turnover on pool betting on horses was £408.21 million, compared to £5,366.04 million at fixed prices (£5,152.24 million off-course, £213.80 million on-course).
16. The dispute between bookmakers, the British Horseracing Authority and Betfair regarding whether or not exchange clients could be identified as 'bookmakers' and therefore regulated as such has been described by O'Connor (2011).
17 Oddschecker is an odds comparison website – see: http://www.oddschecker.com/ (accessed 8 March 2013).

References

Abbott, M., R. Volberg, M. Bellringer and G. Reith. 2004. A Review of Research on Aspects of Problem Gambling: Final Report. Report prepared for Responsibility in Gambling Trust, U.K. Auckland: AUT University.

Agamben, G. 2009. *What is an Apparatus? and Other Essays* (trans. D. Kishik and S. Pedatella). Stanford: Stanford University Press.

Anderson, G., and R. Brown. 1984. Real and Laboratory Gambling, Sensation Seeking and Arousal. *British Journal of Psychology* 75, no. 3: 401–410.

Appadurai, A. (ed.). 1986. *The Social Life of Things: Commodities in Cultural Perspective.* Cambridge: Cambridge University Press.

Binde, P. 2011. Trotting Territory: The Cultural Realm of Swedish Horse Betting. In *Gambling, Space, and Time: Shifting Boundaries and Cultures* (eds) P. Raento and D. Schwartz, 107–128. Reno: University of Nevada Press.

Bussolini, J. 2010. What is a Dispositive? *Foucault Studies* 10: 85–107.

Cassidy, R. 2002. *Sport of Kings: Kinship, Class and Thoroughbred Breeding in Newmarket.* Cambridge: Cambridge University Press.

——— 2010. Gambling as Exchange: Horserace Betting in London. *International Gambling Studies* 10, no. 2: 139–149.

——— 2012 Horse versus Machine: Battles in the Betting Shop. *Journal of the Royal Anthropology Institute* 18, no. 2.

Cattelino, J. 2008. *High Stakes: Florida Seminole Gaming and Sovereignty.* Durham, NC: Duke University Press.

Chinn, C. 1991. *Better Betting with a Decent Fella: A Social History of Bookmaking.* London: Harvester Wheatsheaf.

Clark, L., B. Crooks, R. Clarke, M. Aitken and B. Dunn. 2012. Physiological Responses to Near-Miss Outcomes and Personal Control During Simulated Gambling. *Journal of Gambling Studies* 28, no. 1: 123–137.

Cosgrave, J. (ed.). 2006. *The Sociology of Risk and Gambling Reader.* New York: Routledge.

DCMS. 2007. New Rules Would Ensure Children and Gambling Don't Mix. Press release, Department for Culture Media and Sport, 19 November, 132/03. <http://www.culture.gov.uk/reference_library/media_releases/2703.aspx> (accessed 2 April 2012).

Deleuze, G. 1989. Qu'est-ce qu'un dispositif? In *Michel Foucault: philosophe* (ed.) F. Ewald, 185–195. Paris: Seuil.

Downes, D., B. Davies, M. David and P. Stone. 1976. *Gambling, Work and Leisure: A Study Across Three Areas.* London: Routledge and Kegan Paul.

Fabian, A. 1990. *Card Sharps, Dream Books, and Bucket Shops: Gambling in Nineteenth-Century America.* Ithaca, NY: Cornell University Press.

Forster, M. 2000. A Policy Maker's Guide to International Achievement Studies. <http://works.bepress.com/margaret_forster/7> (accessed 2 April 2012).

Foucault, M. 1980. The Confession of the Flesh. In *Power/Knowledge: Selected Interviews and Other Writings, 1972–1977* (eds) M. Foucault and C. Gordon, 194–228. New York: Pantheon.

Hayano, D. M. 1982. *Poker Faces: The Life and Work of Professional Card Players.* Berkeley: University of California Press.

Jouhki, J. 2011. Moderate Expectations: The Case of a Normal, Level-Headed Semi-Professional Online Poker Player and his Family. *Global Media Journal, Polish Edition* 2, no. 8: 1–15. Available at: http://tinyurl.com/b9whocu (accessed 8 March 2013).

Kingma, S. 2008. The Liberalization and Regulation of Dutch Gambling Markets: National Consequences of the Changing European Context. *Regulation and Governance* 2: 445–458.

Kingma, S. (ed.). 2009. *Global Gambling: Cultural Perspectives on Gambling Organizations.* London: Routledge.

Lampard, R. 2004. Church Responses to Gambling. *Political Theology* 5, no. 2: 219–230.

Lears, J. 2003. *Something for Nothing: Luck in America.* New York: Viking.

Loussouarn, C. 2011. 'Buying Moments of Happiness': Luck, Time and Agency Among Chinese Casino Players in London. Ph.D. diss., Goldsmiths, University of London.

Luft, O. 2009. Writer Paul Haigh Blasts Racing Post in Resignation Letter. *Guardian*, 20 March.

Malaby, T. 2003. *Gambling Life: Dealing in Contingency in a Greek City.* Urbana: University of Illinois Press.

Meyer G., T. Hayer and M. Griffiths (eds). 2009. *Problem Gambling in Europe: Challenges, Prevention, and Interventions.* New York: Springer Science.

Miers, D. 2004. *Regulating Commercial Gambling.* Oxford: Oxford University Press.
Neal, M. 1998. 'You Lucky Punters!' A Study of Gambling in Betting Shops. *Sociology* 32, no. 3: 581–600.
—— 2005. 'I Lose, But That's Not the Point': Situated Economic and Social Rationalities in Horserace Gambling. *Leisure Studies* 24, no. 3: 291–310.
Newman, O. 1972. *Gambling: Hazard and Reward.* London: Athlone Press.
O'Connor, N. 2011. Betfair: An Alternative Exchange. http://tinyurl.com/ara9gp6 (accessed 8 March 2013).
Papataxiarchis, E. 1999. A Contest with Money: Gambling and the Politics of Disinterested Sociality in Aegean Greece. In *Lilies of the Field: Marginal People Who Live for the Moment* (eds) S. Day, E. Papataxiarchis and M. Stewart, 158–175. Boulder: Westview Press.
Papineau, E. 2005. Pathological Gambling in Montreal's Chinese Community: An Anthropological Perspective. *Journal of Gambling Studies* 21: 157–178.
Parke, J., and M. Griffiths. 2008. Participant and Non-Participant Observation in Gambling Environments. *Enquire* 1, no. 1: 1–18.
Rabinow, P. 1977. *Reflections on Fieldwork in Morocco.* Berkeley: University of California Press.
Raento, P., and D.G. Schwartz (eds). 2011. *Gambling, Space, and Time: Shifting Boundaries and Cultures.* Reno: University of Nevada Press.
Reith, G. 2007. Situating Gambling Studies. In *Research and Measurement Issues in Gambling Studies* (eds) G. Smith, D. Hodgins and R. Williams, 1–24. Amsterdam: Elsevier.
Riches, D. 1975. Cash, Credit and Gambling in a Modern Eskimo Economy. *Man* 10, no. 1: 21–33.
Rosecrance, J. 1985. *The Degenerates of Lake Tahoe: A Study of Persistence in the Social World of Horse Race Gambling.* New York: Lang.
—— 1986a. Adapting to Failure: The Case of Horse Race Gamblers. *Journal of Gambling Studies* 2, no. 2: 81–94.
—— 1986b. Attributions and Origins of Problem Gambling. *Sociological Quarterly* 27, no. 4: 463–477.
—— 1986c. Learning to Live with Variable Ratio Scheduling: The Career of a Horse Player. *Sociological Inquiry* 56, no. 2: 229–244.
—— 1986d. Why Regular Gamblers Don't Quit: A Sociological Perspective. *Sociological Perspectives* 29, no. 3: 357–378.
—— 1988a. *Gambling Without Guilt: The Legitimation of an American Pastime.* Pacific Grove, CA: Brooks/Cole.
—— 1988b. Professional Horse Race Gambling: Working Without a Safety Net. *Work and Occupations* 15, no. 2: 220–236.
Rubenstein, R. 1987. The Changing Context of Card Playing on Malo, Vanuatu. *Oceania* 58, no. 1: 47–59.
Sallaz, J. 2009. *The Labor of Luck: Casino Capitalism in the United States and South Africa.* Berkeley: University of California Press.
Sauer, R. 1998. The Economics of Wagering Markets. *Journal of Economic Literature* 36, no. 4: 2021–2064.
Saunders, D., and D. Turner. 1987. Gambling and Leisure: The Case of Racing. *Leisure Studies* 6, no. 3: 281–299.
Schüll, N. 2005. Digital Gambling: The Coincidence of Desire and Design. *Annals of the American Academy of Political and Social Science* 597: 65–81.
—— 2012. *Addiction by Design: Machine Gambling in Las Vegas.* Princeton: Princeton University Press.

Sexton, L. 1987. The Social Construction of Card Playing Among the Dualo. *Oceania* 58, no. 1: 38–46.
Shapiro, D., B. Sheppard and L. Cheraskin. 1992. Business on a Handshake. *Negotiation Journal* 8, no. 4: 365–377.
Smith, G., D. Hodgins and R. Williams. 2007. *Research and Measurement Issues in Gambling Studies*. New York: Elsevier.
Stone, C. 1976. The Political Economy of Gambling in a Neo-Colonial Economy. *Review of Black Political Economy* 6, no. 2: 189–199.
Surowiecki, J. 2004. *The Wisdom of Crowds: Why the Many Are Smarter Than the Few and How Collective Wisdom Shapes Business, Economies, Societies and Nations.* Garden City, NY: Doubleday.
Thomas, P. 2002. How the Value of Value can be a Virtual Concept. *Racing Post*, 26 July.
Williams, R., R. Wood and J. Parke (eds). 2012. *Routledge Handbook of Internet Gambling*. London: Routledge.
Woodburn, J. 1982. Egalitarian Societies. *Man* 17, no 3: 431–451.
Woolley, R., and C. Livingstone. 2009. Into the Zone: Innovating in the Australian Poker Machine Industry. In *Global Gambling: Cultural Perspectives on Gambling* (ed.) S. Kingma, 38–63. London: Routledge.
Zimmer, L. 1986. Card Playing among the Gende: A System for Keeping Money and Social Relationships Alive. *Oceania* 56, no. 4: 245–263.
——— 1987a. Gambling with Cards in Melanesia and Australia: An Introduction. *Oceania* 58, no. 1: 1–5.
——— 1987b. Playing At Being Men. *Oceania* 58, no. 1: 22–37.
Zola, I. 1963. Observations of Gambling in a Lower-Class Setting. *Social Problems* 10, no. 30: 353–361.

3

Men of Sound Reputation
The Achievement of Passionate Aurality in Guyanese Birdsport

Laura H. Mentore

Amidst the many rare and colourful birds that put Guyana squarely on the ornithological map and lend their songs to its distinctive soundscape, there is a small and rather plain looking bird, the chestnut-bellied lesser seed-finch (*Oryzoborus angolensis*). Known locally by the onomatopoeic name *towa towa*, these seemingly unspectacular finches enjoy perhaps the most curious and complex social life of all, for they hold centre stage in the arena of birdsport – a traditional and much beloved pastime among Guyanese men. The typical bird race entails placing two finches adjacent to one another in their respective cages, whereupon they embark on an acoustic race to a set number of songs which is agreed upon in advance by their owners. Races are typically held in parks and on street corners in the early hours of Sunday mornings. As male *towa towa* are territorial, their close proximity to each other is usually sufficient to stimulate a litany of complex and long-winded demonstrations of finch-style bravado. A third person acting as referee and judge keeps count, and the first finch to complete the agreed upon number of songs is declared the winner. It is not uncommon for bets to be placed on races, with centre bets between the owners and side bets between other men who gather around to watch and commentate. The ritual time–space of bird-racing is affectionately known as 'bird church'. This is not only because of the near-sacred value of 'passionate' birdsong in the schema of Guyanese aural aesthetics, but moreover because bird-racing marks one of the only occasions in which men of different socio-economic and ethnic backgrounds come together on equitable terms in this otherwise highly stratified postcolonial society.

Bird-racing is most common in Georgetown (the capital), and the other towns and villages that span Guyana's coast. There it falls within the realm of ubiquitous social activity, so interwoven with other strands of everyday life that it can easily go unnoticed unless one trains the eye to notice its telltale signs: macho young men in 'muscle shirts' walking or bicycling down the street at daybreak with a most delicate grip on the wire handle of their balsawood bird cages, exposing their birds to the morning's acoustics so as to expand their repertoires of songs; grown men on their hands and knees along the canals of the National Botanical Gardens, risking the spotlessness of their work uniforms as they search for the finest grass seed to nourish their mellifluous champions. Indeed, bird-racers care for their finches with the same intensity and devotion one might expect from the trainer of a professional boxer or racehorse. I should note that while the *towa towa* is the most common species in birdsport and my focus here, one occasionally finds other songbirds on the circuit, namely fire red (red breasted grass finch) or *twa-twa* (Bullfinch).

Above all, what bird-racers stress in their narratives is the passion they encounter and experience in birdsport. That is, the emotive zeal with which the birds project their songs into the soundscape and against that of their opponents. As one enthusiast explained, women prefer ornate, brightly coloured birds such as macaws and parrots, 'because they are nice to look at', but men are interested in birds entirely for the passion of their song. 'Men pay for passion', he aptly concluded. Through my research, I have come to understand that paying for passion bears significance far beyond the means by which songbirds are obtained with cash or, in the case of trade, in exchange for valuables such as a motorcycle or even a car. Bird-racers do not merely possess songbirds and, through a form of control implied by such possession, lay claim to the passion the birds embody. Rather, the passion of *towa towa* song contributes to an overall environment of passionate aurality that men draw from, embody and also contribute to themselves in the form of public, passionate speech events.[1] The relation that often emerges between a bird-racer and his *towa towa* could be described along the lines of a shared 'habitus' or recursive 'affective transmission' of the dispositions and capacities that performatively presence a masculine passion.[2]

Drawing from my ongoing research in various regions of Guyana, including the urban coast and indigenous Waiwai, Wapishana, and Makushi communities in the interior, this chapter provides an ethnographic account of bird-racing as well as providing some background on the complex array of other social practices that encompass and give way to the bird-racing arena. This includes indigenous men trapping songbirds from around their communities, the trade in songbirds as middlemen transport them from the interior to the coast and into diasporic communities in cities such as New York and London (where the tradition has been retained), and the intricate arts of training songbirds for competition. I use the term 'birdsport' to refer to this broader ensemble of activities and exchanges all fuelled by the desire for race-worthy finches. Tracing the social life of birdsport, it becomes possible to examine the kinds of relations that emerge between men and songbirds in these various stages and socio-geographic terrains, and to examine how, through such relations, men and songbirds mutually transform each other into social actors with specific capacities, skills and identities. In the process, of course, social relations between human actors themselves also take shape, and these too will be considered.

My analysis focuses on the cultural meanings and dynamics of achievement in the masculine world of birdsport. Although different components of birdsport may appear to be motivated by desires for monetary gain or a basic desire to 'win', I argue that, on a certain level, these are all regimes through which men ultimately strive to achieve reputation (see Abrahams 1972, 1983; Wilson 1973), a cultural concept I discuss in more detail in the following section. More specifically, in light of the aural and conceptual links that Guyanese draw between the passion of birdsong and the passion of masculine discursive performativity, I consider how birdsport enables men to assert their own passion, and in so doing to achieve reputations. Passion in this context is defined as a capacity to aurally presence one's self or point of view with great emotive zeal and persuasive force, which is considered a central component of masculine social identity in coastal Guyana.[3] As such, I suggest thinking about the social life of birdsport as a series of regimes of achievement through which the affective capacities of birds and men are circulated or transmitted.

Flexible and Rigid Routes to Achievement

When situated in relation to hegemonic notions of achievement in Guyana – as found in ubiquitous discourses on progress and development, governance, and education for example – birdsport can be seen as a counter-hegemonic or alternative form of achievement, one grounded in a moral code of egalitarianism and inalienability. Birdsport, and the possibility it presents for any and all participants to achieve masculine reputation, runs counter to the rigidly stratified configurations of power so often presented as the necessary or even 'natural' means of individual and group success. The differences between these notions of achievement can be further understood by considering the Guyanese (and more broadly, West Indian) cultural concepts of respectability and reputation.

Reputation and respectability were first systematically analysed by anthropologist Peter Wilson (1973), whose research was based on the Anglophone island of Providencia, off the coast of Colombia. As Freeman summarises, Wilson argued that Providencia and the broader West Indies can be understood as:

> steeped within the structures and ideologies of two competing but dialectically related value systems or cultural models: respectability, the inescapable legacy of colonial dependence through which patterns of social hierarchy are upheld and reproduced, and reputation, a set of responses to colonial domination and the elusiveness of respectability, through which people enact creative individualism and at the same time achieve a social levelling, or 'communitas'. (Freeman 2007: 253)

Respectability has been linked to the importation of Christian notions of virtue and propriety coupled with the stiff rationalism of Western legal, economic and educational principles during the British colonial occupation of the region. The root values of respectability remain firmly planted in many sectors of Guyanese society today, particularly in prevailing attitudes towards education, governance, and 'literacy events' (Mentore 2003).

As one might argue for all modern nation-states, literacy in Guyana is inexorably linked to, and 'on the side of', the state. That is, the hierarchical order of state governance is based as much on a distinction between literacy and non-literacy – the rationality of the literate world governed by text and the chaos of the non-literate world overrun by unrestrained utterances – as it is based on class, race and socio-geographic distinctions (such as urban/rural and coastland/hinterland). A Guyanese citizen's first and most palpable experience of this distinction is most likely in school, where literacy is privileged as the portal to legitimate knowledge and the standard by which educational achievements are measured; conversely, non-literate speech events are most closely identified with 'non-educational' spaces such as parks, the seawall, the street corner, and the 'backdam'. It is within the classroom setting that the State first seeks to instil a respect for the power of the written word as the means to achievement, not only in school itself but throughout one's entire life in all economic, political and social arenas. The relative scarcity of written materials in Guyana and the difficulty of preserving them in a tropical climate with limited resources help to extend an almost mystical power to written text and 'literacy events' in general.

Beyond school, the written word commands obedience and respect to such an extent that it often seems to take on a life of its own as 'an autonomous manifestation in the world, having its own force outside of and independent to society' (Mentore 2003: 265). Some of the most explicit statements of Guyanese notions of respectability can be found in the prominently displayed signs in front of all government institutions specifying their dress codes. For example, recently a forum in a leading Guyanese newspaper focused on the fact that persons with critical health emergencies are sometimes turned away from public hospitals as a result of wearing a 'sleeveless dress' or 'three-quarter length pants'. Although some contributors were critical of the dress code, one woman summarised the prevailing attitude where she wrote:

> The hospital is an institution that requires respect like any other ministry or proper office. Having a dress code in effect is a good thing which should not be ignored but adhered to. This helps in setting standards. While there are some of us who understand the moral value of dressing modestly there are those who can do better but just refuse to do so ... let's maintain respect. (Richards 2010)

Again, it is as if such codes wrote themselves into being – effectively masking the face of power behind their production. The hegemonic fantasies of a 'modern' Guyana are replete with images of a middle-class public that disciplines itself along literary avenues of achievement. The reality is that the vast majority of Guyanese people are systematically alienated from the production of this literary world and thus, not surprisingly, seem to take little interest in consuming it. Although the main newspapers are widely read where available, one is hard-pressed to find people interestedly reading books and there are very few spaces designed to accommodate reading of any kind, even within the national library and public university.

To the same extent that literacy events embody the general hierarchical structures and attitudes of respectability, it can be said that speech events embody the counter-cultural dynamics of reputation. These dynamics are found in less formal, public and predominantly masculine spaces such as the street corner, rum shop, market and park, which are all heavily associated with oral discursive performativity. This takes a wide range of forms, from passionate speech to 'busin and tantalisin' [verbal abuse and tantalising/taunting] (Edwards 1978) sweet talk and sweet singing (Abrahams 1972), joke-telling, story-telling, 'cat-calling' and informal debate. The ensemble of discursive capacities linked to being a man of reputation and passion are informally tested over the course of a man's life through various competitive and solo 'performances', usually of a casual and impromptu nature, in the midst of his friends and peers. Like the territorial male *towa towa* when confronted with an opponent – rapidly batting its wings, sometimes throwing itself against the sides of its cage while whistling away, and ideally 'shaming' his opponent into silence – a man can spend a lifetime learning how to better control and direct his acoustic energies, whether in the company of friends in the rum shop, or indeed in the aural space of 'bird church'. Far from being merely analogous, however, I will suggest in the following passages that the passion of *towa towa* plays a direct role in forging the reputations of men.

In a paper on passionate and literate ways of speaking in Grenada, Mentore distinguishes between the emphasis on calm, rational speech and text among the elite Grenadian class and what he refers to as 'the voice of the Creolese ... the alternative "nation language" ... filled with the noise of resistance' (Mentore 2003: 262; cf. Braithwaite 1984: 17). For elite Grenadians or 'Townies', he argues: 'A soft modulation of voice is the ideal ... Soft tones attempt to connote a reduction of expressive emotion. The desired effect is for one's argument to be "rational" in order that it may be accepted ... A soft, calm voice forces argumentation to rely upon "objective" textual sources and not upon subjective validations signalled by loud, emotional utterances' (Mentore 2003: 269). Conversely, in the kinds of public spaces marked by passionate speech, everyone has the right to assert their voice and to be heard, giving rise to what Reisman (1974) termed the 'contrapuntal conversation', a multi-vocal counterpoint of assertions in spontaneous self-expression (Mentore 2003: 273). 'An aggressive egalitarianism stems from the personal source of the equalising voice: an emotional voice sustained by cultural process to engage and to proclaim inner feelings' (ibid.: 273). It is this same robust, impassioned way of speaking that pervades street life in coastal Guyana, lending its distinctive sound and texture to those spaces where reputations are forged. For our purposes, I should clarify that reputation is not only achieved through actual 'performances' of passionate speech, nor is reputation reducible to passionate speech. While passionate speech largely reflects the moral codes and attitudes of reputation, men who trade and transport songbirds build up their reputations largely through non-aural means such as demonstrating their competence and reliability as trade partners in extensive exchange networks, or demonstrating their masculine virility through the seduction of young women in communities they visit. The key point is that these ways of achieving reputation are grounded in the same moral order as passionate speech, and indeed can be thought of as non-aural expressions of a capacity for it.

When framed by the workings of reputation, social life and business take on the very different demeanour of friendly bantering and informal dealings based on trust and entrepreneurial flexibility (Wilson 1973; Freeman 2007). In general, achieving a reputation means that a loose network of others (beyond family, neighbours and co-workers) recognises you by name. It also means that others have sufficient knowledge of your disposition, tendencies and general way of doing things that they can enter into informal business dealings or other forms of engagement with a high level of confidence in their expectations of you. In this sense, birdsport often provides men with valuable opportunities – economic, social, political, cross-cultural – to which they otherwise may not have access. In his paper on birdsport, Cambridge describes it as a training ground for 'functional attitudes beliefs and practices' such as solidarity, honesty, caring, cooperation and reliability while at the same time being a training ground for 'dysfunctional attitudes' such as smuggling (Cambridge 2005: 14). One of his informants, an Afro-Guyanese bird-minder in Richmond Hill, New York, described his membership in the birding social network as a means by which he gained exposure to the cultural practices of other ethnic groups in Guyana such as the Portuguese, and as a continuing source of connections with members of the Guyanese diaspora. He explained to Cambridge that birdsport provided him with employment opportunities he would not have otherwise had because, in Cambridge's words, 'the pastime helped to reveal personality attributes [given that] bird racing is a rules-based event that depends on adherence to rules, discipline, honesty, commitment and keen observations' (ibid.: 8). While bird racing is certainly rules-based, I would argue that other, more flexible aspects of birdsport beyond the racing arena, such as smuggling songbirds overseas, are equally 'functional' in that they too operate as indirect means of achieving reputation and reputation-based means of enacting relations that transcend class and ethnic barriers. Indeed, it is often these more flexible exchanges and dealings that provide men of low socio-economic status with otherwise unlikely connections to fellow birdsport enthusiasts, including employment, small loans and valuable overseas contacts.

To relate this back to the idea of birdsport as a counter-hegemonic framework of achievement, we can consider the many ethnic, class and regional borders and barriers that are cut across in the songbird trade, and which are also alluded to through terms such as 'bird church'. Hegemonic discourses on national progress and development stress unity, integration and collaboration across cultural and racial groups and regional/geographic sectors as necessary means of achievement – the suggestion being that positive change requires overcoming pre-existing forms of segmentation, fragmentation and isolation. Such themes are readily understandable given the historic deployment of discourses on essentialised differences as means of order and control throughout the British occupation of Guyana. Yet these very discourses stressing the need to overcome such differences and divisions also help to further reify them as concrete realities. Indeed birdsport offers sanctuary of an almost religious degree from the common trappings and reverse effects of these official discourses. Within its flexible and open corridors, men find creative ways to circumnavigate these hegemonic frameworks, and often manage to achieve – in quite informal and inconspicuous ways – the very thing such frameworks present as their lofty objective. Having laid out some of the basic features of reputation, we can now turn to a description of two of the preliminary regimes of achievement in birdsport: trapping and trading.

Of Nets and Cages: The Social Life of Birdsport in Southern Guyana

From time to time, tradesmen make their way across the southernmost reaches of Guyana, from the border town of Lethem to Erefoimo, a small Waiwai community on the Kuyuwini River – their trucks loaded with flour, sugar, rice, salt, batteries, clothing, radios, torches and other manufactured goods. These are exchanged for locally-made goods, farm produce, cash and/or monetary debt. A few others make the journey for the explicit purpose of obtaining *towa towa*, in which case they travel much lighter and deal more strictly in terms of cash and monetary credit and debt in exchange for birds and bird-trapping supplies. From Lethem, traders must first pass through surrounding Wapishana communities and Dadanawa Ranch (one of the most expansive cattle ranches in the world), then another 150 miles or so through alternating savannah and forest. The journey can take several days, for in the best of conditions the road is extremely rough and unpredictable, and in the rainy season it becomes a virtually impassable trail of mud, flooded creeks and enormous fallen trees.

It happens that the long rainy season (approximately June to September) is both the most difficult time of year to travel in southern Guyana and the optimal time for trapping *towa towa*. During this time, trappers in communities such as Erefoimo will hang fine nets at dawn and dusk in areas where the birds are known to feed, such as overgrown sections of their manioc gardens and the grassy outskirts of their household compounds. Sometimes a previously trapped *towa towa* with a strong whistle, referred to as a 'calling bird', is placed in its cage directly behind the net as a way of luring others towards it. Only the male *towa towa* are kept, and it is crucial that they are removed quickly before they injure themselves.

Once captured, the birds are kept in the same kind of cages found throughout Guyana – roughly twelve by nine inches, made out of balsa wood or thin bamboo slats and metal wire. Because the males are aggressively territorial, they have to be kept in separate cages or a single cage internally divided by pieces of cardboard.

To my knowledge, the Waiwai do not practice bird-racing themselves. Although I recorded a few instances in which families grew fond of a particular *towa towa* and kept it as a pet, they are trapped almost exclusively for the purpose of selling to traders. As a result of increased transportation in the region and demand among coastal bird-racers for birds from 'the bush', trapping has become more widespread in southern Guyana and is currently one of the only means by which Erefoimo residents can earn cash without having to leave the community. Yet due to the high mortality rates among captured *towa towa* and the infrequency of visits from traders, keeping the birds alive and healthy long enough to sell them is an arduous and time-consuming task that can detract from farm work, hunting and other subsistence activities.

When traders do make their way to Erefoimo, they typically spend the night (or several) before heading back to Lethem. During their time in the village, they are treated as guests according to traditional protocol – hosted by the village leader and fed most of their meals by his wife and other women. One of the main songbird traders who deals with trappers in Erefoimo is a man in his thirties from Lethem, whom I will refer to as Jerry. Like many people in Lethem, Jerry would describe himself as 'mixed', with Afro-Guyanese, Portuguese and Amerindian heritage. Depending on whether he is dealing with indigenous trappers, a shop vendor in Lethem, a transporter or other actor involved in the songbird trade, he may subtly evoke his identification with their respective ethnic group as a strategic way of establishing common ground. Erefoimo residents were aware of Jerry's indigenous maternal grandmother, but nonetheless referred to him as a *mekuru* (Afro-Guyanese, black) in the early stages of their relationship with him. This was less because of his appearance and more because of his way of life, centred around commercial activity and lacking any personal familiarity with indigenous practices.

Upon Jerry's arrival, everyone with *towa towa* brings them to the village centre for him to inspect. Some birds are refused on the basis of his determination that they are not healthy enough, and this can be the cause of some dispute. In one instance, Jerry agreed to purchase a large number of birds from one trapper only to discover the following morning that over fifty of them had died during the night. The trapper attributed this to the fact that Jerry put too many of them together in large cages, while Jerry argued that they must have already been sick and dying before he arrived. In contrast to the subtle circulation of food and other goods between household families in Erefoimo, dealings with Jerry usually take place in the open space of the village centre where everyone can observe and commentate. Transactions consist of either birds in exchange for cash, or birds in exchange for a reduction in the trapper's monetary debt.

In Erefoimo in June 2010, the price paid by Jerry for a healthy male *towa towa* was 800 Guyanese dollars (GY$), roughly US$4. At the time, there were a couple of other traders who paid GY$1,000 to GY$1,500, but they made the journey to Erefoimo less often. The few villagers who were able to transport their birds all the way to Lethem themselves, and thereby cut out middlemen such as Jerry, typically got GY$2,000 to GY$5,000 per bird. This price range is based largely on the bird's maturity (how many seasons it has moulted), and the buyer's informal evaluation of its potential as a racer.

Jerry not only buys birds from his suppliers in Erefoimo but also equips them with the necessary nets and cages. As I discovered, this is his main strategy for placing trappers in debt to him from the outset. While stores in Lethem sell the nets for GY$8000 to GY$9,000, when Jerry travels to Erefoimo he prices them at GY$25,000 (roughly US$125) – a sum far exceeding what most Waiwai would be able to accumulate in a given month or even year. After accepting a net from Jerry, the first twenty-five healthy birds a person traps are supposed to go towards paying off what they owe for the net (I was told he accepts these initial birds at a higher rate of GY$1,000 each). Cages are also supplied on credit, further indebting trappers and compelling them to deal exclusively with him. Some people lose the motivation to trap for Jerry as they discover how difficult and time consuming it is to catch twenty-five birds and care for them until he returns. Depending on the season and the person's level of commitment, it can take weeks or even months to accumulate the birds needed to pay off a single net. Thus it is hardly surprising that some opt to sell their birds to other traders in smaller quantities whenever the opportunity arises. If Jerry suspects that a trapper is using one of his nets to sell birds on a 'first come, first serve' basis to any interested buyer they encounter, he may demand back his net and cages. That is a risky venture, however, because it invariably triggers disputes and can compromise his dealings with others in the community.

While credit and debt are clearly driving forces in the initial stages of the songbird trade, it is worth taking into consideration some other dynamics of Jerry's relations with Erefoimo residents. Over the years, Jerry has shifted from being a distrusted stranger and *mekuru* to a full-fledged *parawan*, or trade partner, valued for the social and material wealth he brings from afar – including money, birding supplies and less-tangible forms of connections to other people and opportunities in Lethem. Like indigenous *parawan* who travel from other villages with handmade cooking and hunting implements, or the increasingly common shotguns and aluminium pots from Brazil, Jerry is invited to tie his hammock in the village leader's home. Women send their children to him with bowls of bananas and cooked meat; men make social visits late into the evening to tell stories and discuss the latest news.

Waiwai codes of sociability and generosity can bring about intensely awkward feelings, sometimes even anger, on the part of traders such as Jerry, as they are faced with incessant requests, questions and a general lack of privacy. But eventually they tend to develop a tolerance, if not a fondness, for this intensive form of engagement, so distinct from the increasingly impersonal hustle and bustle of Lethem. Some traders would explain their recurring visits to me less in terms of profit and more in terms of a desire to relax and visit, almost as if they were on holiday. This is not to suggest that profit ceases to be a principal motive, but that in cases such as Jerry's attempts to do business strictly according to capitalist codes of buying and selling are suppressed to an extent by local codes of interpersonal trust, delayed reciprocity and generosity. As a result of being hosted, fed and cared for according to the protocol of the *parawan* relation, men such as Jerry often find themselves entrapped in the sentiments of social debt. They become too 'shamed' to aggressively collect on monetary debts. They find it necessary to adopt slower, more roundabout ways of pursuing what they want. These pressures are compounded when they find themselves immersed in local household families who refer to them in kinship terms, and urge them to do the same.

In Jerry's case, the appeal to kinship took on a whole other dimension when the village leader discovered him lying in a hammock with a young woman of the community, whom I will refer to as Lynn, late one night at the guesthouse. Jerry is now the father of Lynn's only child, and although the couple is not considered 'married' in any sense of the term (indigenous, common-law or otherwise), her parents nonetheless make a point of referring to Jerry as their *wošin*, or son-in-law. While such scenarios are increasingly common given the increase in travel and communication across the region, this case was especially poignant. As Lynn gracefully passed from adolescence to womanhood, she was considered exceptionally bright and attractive, and there was greater than usual interest in the question of whom she would marry. Due to the Waiwai preference for village endogamous cross-cousin marriage, it was hoped that she would marry someone from within Erefoimo or at most, a neighbouring community. The sudden turn of events between her and Jerry clearly took the community by surprise.

Lynn and the baby have continued to live in her parents' household and receive occasional support from Jerry, who stays with them whenever he travels to Erefoimo. Throughout southern Guyana, Jerry has a wide reputation both for his successful songbird enterprise, and for fathering children in several indigenous communities in addition to Erefoimo in the process. From the perspective of non-indigenous, urban Guyanese in Lethem and the coast, having children with multiple women is not uncommon, and in fact gives testament to a man's virility and passion. From the perspective of Erefoimo residents, the situation is frowned upon but tolerated, with hopes that it might improve over time. Despite their much stronger emphasis on sustained co-residence between a child's parents, the situation has not brought an end to their dealings with Jerry. Songbird trappers continue to work with him more than other traders, and Lynn's family continues to demonstrate confidence in the affective force of kinship ties to further develop a mutually beneficial, familial relationship with him, and indeed to gradually transform him into what they would consider a more moral, trustworthy person. Through their firm cultural belief in the processual nature of personhood and social relations, Jerry continues to be seen as a rare contact point with the dangerous but desirable outside world – a kind of relation that can only be achieved through sustained, affective transformations.[4] As a result of their commitment to this process, coupled with their lack of other sources of monetary income, Jerry has been able to establish a veritable monopoly over the songbird trade in Erefoimo. In the process, he has significantly bolstered his reputation, while Erefoimo residents have gained a long-term relationship with someone dangerous but desirable because of the valuable ties he provides to other places and persons beyond their community.

While dealing with traders has its benefits, indigenous trappers in southern Guyana nonetheless aspire to transport songbirds directly to Georgetown with fewer middlemen cutting into the profit. They are well aware of the enormous disparity between the price in their villages and in Georgetown, where untrained juvenile birds directly from the interior can sell for GY$50,000 (US$250) or more. Yet for most of these trappers, simply getting to Lethem, much less purchasing an expensive bus ticket from Lethem to Georgetown, is not a realistic possibility. Then there is the risk of having birds stolen or confiscated by police at checkpoints along the way. One man who plays a role in trappers' attempts to transport their birds themselves is a driver for the lone coach service that runs between Lethem and Georgetown, whom I discovered to be somewhat of a gatekeeper for the entire trade.

Recently when I was travelling on the bus to Lethem, I noticed a covered bird cage on the front dashboard next to the driver. At daybreak, after hours of rattling along through the night, the driver removed the cover to reveal a young *towa towa*, who now enjoyed a privileged view of the towering forest that enveloped us as we approached the Iwokrama Rainforest Preserve. The driver, an Afro-Guyanese man from the coast, informed me that his bird was 'recovering' from a recent loss in a race. He always brings at least one of his birds with him on the bus, he explained, as a way of exposing them to the different bird songs found in 'de bush'. In light of the ban on exporting *towa towa* from Iwokrama, and the fact that surrounding Makushi communities had also recently adopted similar bans, I was intrigued that he made no effort to conceal the bird when we stopped at the police checkpoint at the entrance to Iwokrama. I had cause to reassess my impression of things when I saw half a dozen caged birds on the front porch of the police station itself.

A subsequent conversation with an indigenous trapper revealed further dimensions to this driver's apparently well-known involvement in the songbird trade. I was told the driver is the best person to work with if you have several *towa towa* that you want to carry to Georgetown yourself. Despite the apparently casual attitude towards songbirds at Iwokrama, ordinary travellers (and especially indigenous persons) are at high risk of having their songbirds confiscated by police at the various checkpoints along the road. If you are smart, I was told, you arrange ahead of time to give the driver one of your birds upon arrival in Georgetown, thereby ensuring that he will 'speak up for you' if the police should ask any questions about your birds. Apparently the driver has the necessary permits to trap *towa towa* in areas where it is not banned and will simply tell the police (with whom he appears to be on quite friendly terms) that all the birds belong to him. Through this informal system of bird 'trafficking', the driver has achieved a reputation for having the kinds of connections, guile and experience necessary to help others successfully navigate the songbird trade all the way to Georgetown with minimal losses.

Again, it is through his relationship with *towa towa* and his capacity to move through the many barriers and obstacles along the songbird trade route, more so than his official wage labour as a coach driver, that this man has achieved a reputation spanning the length of the single, treacherous dirt road from Lethem to Georgetown. In sum, the songbird trade is about far more than moving songbirds, for through the birds move the reputations of men.

With these insights into the social life of *towa towa* – that is, how they produce the social categories of trapper, trader and middleman through distinct regimes of achievement and imbue individuals who occupy these categories with distinct reputations – we can shift now to a description of what is often their final destination: Georgetown and its bird-racing arenas.

Sunday Mornings in a Coastal Soundscape

> Every Sunday just after daybreak flocks of men carrying small, covered bird cages start to gather at the Ramp Road just off Mandela Avenue. They come on bicycles, on foot, in four by fours, and from all walks of life. (Walker 2001)

Bird-racers customarily congregate on Sunday mornings between 5 and 7 AM, when *towa towa* are in their most mellifluous state. This is not a strict rule, however, and races can be held on any given day as an excuse for social visits and as part of the birds' training regimens. Races tend to be organised in advance through face-to-face communication or mobile phone. They are often planned several days in advance, providing sufficient time for the birds to be prepared and for the news to reach others who may want to attend. Even with more impromptu races on Sunday mornings, a man will make casual inquiries about potential opponents (or observe them in other races) before entering his bird into a race. Friends on the racing circuit share information about different birds at every opportunity, recounting the minute details of races they witnessed and how the two competitors performed, often referring to the birds by name.

The names of individual racing birds are often based on a specific performative trait: Drizzle, for example, 'because he's so fast, like the rain', or Baby, who demonstrated rare talent at an unusually young age (Sell 2009). Bird-racers have an impressive knowledge of the names of the birds owned by other men in their area. Many of my informants also knew the names of racing birds in more distant areas, or even abroad. Information sharing is instrumental in organising the races, and provides an opportunity for men to demonstrate the extent of their socio-spatial mobility and connections in a more general sense. Throughout the planning stages, the observations and discussions tend to focus on the central issue of which birds are likely to make a good (as in fair and equal) match – a key point to which I return below.

Upon arriving at the designated race site, the men remove the covers from their birds' cages and position them on either side of a vertical wooden post, usually by latching the wire siding of the cages onto nails that protrude from either side of the post. The first bird to complete the agreed upon number of songs (which typically ranges from twenty-five to fifty) is declared the winner by a third person who keeps count and acts as judge. The criteria for what constitutes a distinct song can vary somewhat from race to race (and this can be a source of dispute), but as a general rule of thumb a song begins when the bird opens its beak and stops as soon as it closes. *Towa towa* are said to have two main varieties of whistle, 'pee peh yow' and 'zeer', with some racers favouring one over the other. The ideal performance entails a rapid succession of strong, clear notes.

The most extreme outcome of a bird race is when one of the racers sings so passionately and continuously that it dies from exhaustion immediately after defeating its opponent – what is referred to as 'committing suicide'. Such self-sacrificial victories can cause considerable grief for the bird's caretaker but at the same time greatly contribute to his reputation as talk of the event quickly spreads. A bird that commits suicide is revered for its fearless passion, joining the ranks of others whose deadly feats will be vividly recounted in rum shops for years to come.

Depending on the pace of the birds' singing and the number of songs to which they are racing, a race can take anywhere from a few minutes to several hours. I was interested to find that the atmosphere among men attending a race tends to be quite subdued. Not only are they quiet, but it is as though the owners strive to appear indifferent to their birds, making 'small talk' with each other and looking off into the distance while the birds 'rackle' away. Yet subtle, furtive glances toward the cages and nervous, fidgeting hands suggest such indifference is an intentional form of posturing, perhaps in an attempt to appear humble in the event that their bird wins and equally unperturbed in the event that it loses. At the end of a race, the bird cages are taken down from the post and the covers are replaced, sending the birds immediately back into recovery mode.

Importantly, the outcome of a race is never reduced to good training or a bird's 'natural talent'. While some are reputed to be 'bad, bad birds', the question of whether or not they will win a competition against a well-matched opponent is considered first and foremost a matter of luck. This goes far in explaining men's apparent attitude of disinterest or nonchalance towards their birds during the races: to act otherwise would be to risk claiming to have a direct hand in their bird's victory should it win. The wide appeal of birdsport seems to have much to do with its level 'playing field' as a sport of luck between equally matched opponents. Because actively competitive birds are well known by broad networks of men, arranging races between birds of relatively equal talent is the principal way in which the element of unpredictability (and thus the gambling incentive) is retained. The egalitarian ethos of bird racing, which stipulates that all men can participate and have a fair chance at winning, seems to gain much of its appeal from the way it runs counter to the dominant forms of organisation and exchange surrounding it, which are very much premised on inequality, exclusion and one-way flows of wealth and resources. In the sanctuary of 'bird church', bricklayers and doctors compete on equal terms and find common ground in their mutual appreciation for the passion of birdsong. Immediately outside its corridors awaits the harsh reality that most Guyanese have to struggle everyday either to keep or lift themselves out of abject poverty, while only a small percentage have the fortune of a well-paid job, a luxury car and an 'upstairs house'.

The Art of Training a Bad, Bad Bird

Although the element of luck looms large in bird-racers' narratives of winning and losing, *towa towa* are nonetheless rigorously trained by men who aspire for reputations as trainers of notoriously 'bad birds' – birds full of passion and complex whistles who compete at the highest possible level and would rather die than be out-sung. The key component to training is the development of a distinct 'whistle' or ensemble of whistles through auditory exposure to the other mature *towa towa* and other songbirds. Compared to how *towa towa* sing in the wild, captive birds are trained to produce distinct songs in a more uniform or consistent manner. Other components to training include a good diet (including vitamins and supplements), special healthcare treatments at different times of year and at different stages of maturation, a low stress environment outside the competitive arena, and a sufficient amount of recovery time between races. *Towa towa* are especially vulnerable and require extra attention during moulting periods, when they shed their brown feathers and begin to acquire first their spotted feathers, then the glossy, black feathers of a fully mature adult.

Trainers utilise several techniques for exposing their birds to the whistles of mature and talented *towa towa* and other songbirds. The most common is by walking with the bird through the neighbourhood or parks in the early morning and late evening hours, thereby exposing it to the rich cacophony of other birds' songs. Another technique is to position a novice within close hearing distance of a 'trainer bird', a more mature *towa towa* with a well-developed whistle. Due to the risk of over-stressing the birds, this is typically done for limited periods of time and in such a way that the birds cannot see each other. Avid bird trainers, particularly of the older generations, will sometimes play tape-recordings of birdsongs for their caged birds. Only the closest of friends and relatives lend out their coveted tape cassettes to each other. There is an especially high demand for these among bird trainers in New York and London, where colder climates make it impossible to walk the birds for much of the year and the more industrial soundscape makes it largely ineffective, even in the warmer months.

As far as diet goes, local hand-picked grass seed is generally preferred over store-bought varieties, which are usually imported and available only in expensive pet shops. Thus, a familiarity with the plant life in gardens and along canals is another specialised form of knowledge that bird trainers develop through information sharing with friends, relatives and racing opponents. The three main types of grass seed I encountered are referred to as 'striker seed', 'black seed' and 'power seed'. Power seed, according to one informant, should only be used in moderation at strategic times before a race to 'power up de bird'. Many informants mentioned that they give their birds various tonics and supplements, which are sometimes store-bought brands of liquid vitamins intended for human use. One man, widely renowned for his talented birds, mentioned that twice a week he gives his birds two drops of a special mixture prepared for him by his uncle, which includes brandy, honey and one other ingredient he was unwilling to disclose. Its purpose is 'speed', he explained, meaning it enhances the bird's ability to complete distinct songs in rapid succession. In addition to seed and supplements, I was told there is an extensive range of treatments that can be used to 'clean 'e out' and 'build 'e up' in times of sickness and during the stressful processes of moulting and beak shedding.

In the constantly circulating knowledge and advice concerning training and care for songbirds, there is a common emphasis on wild as opposed to store-bought bird foods, birds caught from the 'bush' as opposed to bred in captivity, and the importance of exposing caged birds to the avian acoustics of un-caged, non-domesticated birds. Interestingly, these values appear to be largely retained, if not exaggerated, as some *towa towa* are transported overseas to Caribbean diasporic neighbourhoods such as Richmond Hill in Queens, New York. In the next and final section, we can trace this movement and get a glimpse of how the moral codes and social dynamics of reputation travel with *towa towa* across international borders and into the lives of Guyanese abroad. In this context, I suggest that birdsport not only continues to enable the achievement of reputation through the performance of passionate aurality but also helps to mark the masculine identities forged through such performance as distinctively Guyanese. The great demand for *towa towa* from Guyana (as opposed to bred in captivity abroad) speaks to the central importance of continued attachments to Guyanese aural and physical spaces in achieving masculinity and reputation among Guyanese men living abroad.

Hair Curlers in Flight

Early one morning in August 2006, a 35-year-old man named Terrence McLean boarded a flight at the Cheddi Jagan International Airport in Guyana. Seven hours later, he disembarked at John F. Kennedy Airport in New York and, along with the other groggy and bleary-eyed passengers, proceeded to the customs gate. Guyanese by birth but a U.S. citizen for many years, McLean had taken leave from his job as a maintenance worker in a Brooklyn nursing home to settle his grandmother's estate back in Guyana. Customs officials grew suspicious of McLean when they discovered 50 pounds of grass seed in his suitcase. Upon searching his carry-on baggage, they found a brown paper bag with thirteen plastic hair curlers, each stuffed with a live finch. McLean was charged with illegally smuggling the birds and failing to properly declare them on his customs form. Later he would explain to the court that he chose plastic instead of metal curlers so as to avoid setting off the metal detectors.

In a classic courtroom turn of events, the U.S. government's own witness, an ornithologist by the name of Dr Pepper Trail, testified that the finches in McLean's curlers belong to the Emberizidae family, which is not actually listed in the Wild Birds Protection Act of Guyana. As Trail explained, 'When the Guyanese law was written in 1919, all finches were lumped into one family [the Fringillidae], but understanding of the birds' evolutionary relationships led to separating the finches into three families' (Marzulli 2009). Notably, the Emberizidae finches carried by McLean are known for their song, whereas the Fringillidae finches listed in the Act are not. Because the scientific classification of finches has been revised since the law was enacted, and no law existed at the time pertaining to Emberizidae finches, the magistrate concluded that the case was defective and the smuggling charges were dropped. McLean only had to pay a small fine for failing to properly fill out his customs forms.

As readers have no doubt surmised, McLean's finches were male *towa towa* destined for sale as prize fighters. For the decades that Guyanese have been migrating to New York, they have carried their passion for birdsport, and their birds, with them. There too it seems that the races have gone virtually unnoticed on Sunday mornings in small parks tucked away in predominantly Guyanese neighbourhoods such as Richmond Hill. That is, until McLean's case drew the attention of reporters and, more recently, New York law enforcement, who suspect that illegal bets are placed on the races. In response to reporters who began to seek them out at local parks, Guyanese men would chuckle and dismiss the betting as false rumour. One man explained, 'We train our birds to be competitive, to sing the best ... but the most that happens is the loser will buy the winner a cup of coffee' (Sell 2009). Yet based on what I have been told (in less risky conversational settings), in New York, the wagers on races between notoriously bad birds can reach well into the thousands of dollars.

McLean told the court he was transporting nine of the birds for a particular man in New York who had purchased them in advance from a contact in Georgetown. McLean said he purchased the other birds for himself in an open-air market in Georgetown. Having come from overseas, he explained, he was charged a higher price of US$200 (GY$40,000) for each of the birds, because everyone knows they can sell for US$300 to US$1,500 in New York.

As a final note, we can consider the manner in which McLean was able to get the birds onto the plane in Guyana in the first place – where security was significantly bolstered in preparation for hosting the 2007 Cricket World Cup. According to McLean's testimony, he went through airport security without the birds. 'Meanwhile, [his contact] turned them over to an airport employee, who had been told what Mr. McLean would be wearing. "Are you Terry?" the airport employee asked, and told Mr. McLean to follow him to the cantina. There he handed over the bag of hair curlers and finches without a word' (Dwyer 2009). From a security standpoint, this transaction might be attributed to inadequate surveillance techniques or simply the indifference of a lackadaisical airport employee. Yet these explanations fail to help us understand why the transactions were performed in the particular way they were, or what ultimately motivated all of the men involved to take such great risks in getting a little bag of birds out of Guyana and across one of the most stringent national borders in the world. This is precisely where the dynamic forces of reputation come into play, as these risks enable men to partake in forms of connectivity and exchange that are simply not possible within the parameters of national and international regulations.

Conclusions

Here I have suggested an alternative understanding of why men such as McLean are willing to go to such great lengths for *towa towa* by considering the relationship between the passion of *towa towa* and men's reputations, as well as the overall importance of achieving reputation in establishing one's masculine social identity. Whether we focus on a Guyanese immigrant acting as a go-between for bird-vendors in Georgetown and bird-racers in New York, a songbird trader from Lethem successfully leveraging a credit and debt system while expanding his reputation and the kinship network of an indigenous community, a bus driver acting as middleman between police and indigenous persons travelling to the capital city, or a doctor and a bricklayer coming together in 'bird church', birdsport reveals a world of complex and unlikely exchanges and connections. It is these exchanges and connections that provide participants in birdsport with opportunities to acquire the affective, discursive, economic, interpersonal, sexual and performative capacities that ultimately mould them into men of reputation.

The arena of bird-racing itself consistently emphasises social levelling and conjures the image of an aggressive egalitarianism reinforced by the overarching role of luck in determining winners and losers. The tight embrace of these dynamics in the midst of Guyana's highly stratified political economy warrants closer examination as a source of an alternative social model. At the same time, however, we should not ignore those less 'sociable' elements of birdsport marked by exploitation, seduction, suicide, deception and secrecy. The fact that birdsport is such a mixed bag of forms of relationality only further begs the question of whether we should treat is as a singular system from which to draw some general analytic conclusions.

As a tentative step in that direction, it could be argued that the various regimes of achievement that comprise birdsport, whether seemingly symmetrical or asymmetrical in their power configurations, consistently place ordinary men within reach of the very thing that hegemonic discourses on progress and development present as their objective yet negate through their means: the ability to transcend the spatial, social and economic forms of division and fragmentation upon which the Guyanese nation-state and political economy were historically founded. In this paper I have argued that birdsport is able to provide this unlikely kind of transcendence because of the way it facilitates the transmission and circulation of reputation – an ensemble of affective capacities which is greatly valued and pursued by Guyanese men of all socio-economic, racial and ethnic backgrounds. Perhaps most significantly, while reputation is considered something that must be gained, forged or achieved, it is not spoken of, conversely, as something that can be lost or denied. Like the capacity for passion that remains inalienable from its speaker, men cannot be stripped of their reputations. To be certain, a man's reputation can morph and shift throughout his lifetime and take on more positive or negative values, but access to the overall arena of reputation-building remains open.

And again, if we take seriously the idea that affective capacities such as passion are 'transmitted' between social beings in ways that breach the presumed boundaries between their bodies (as well as the presumed boundaries between persons and environments), birdsport can be said to resist the hard logic of self-containment that pervades Guyana's hegemonic notions of the autonomous individual, the discretely bounded group, and the territorialised place or region. In so doing, birdsport essentially circumnavigates the hegemonic avenues along which individual and group achievements are typically measured and ranked, whether in school, the workplace, the official national economy or government institutions.

While some of my informants claim that captive breeding of *towa towa* is on the rise among Guyanese in New York, the illicit trade is not likely to dwindle anytime soon. Any enthusiast will readily tell you that *towa towa* from the grasses and forests of Guyana's interior have the sweetest whistle or 'rackle' and make for the most passionate racers. Whether or not this is true in an empirical sense is, of course, beside the point. The value of *towa towa* from Guyana is driven by their embodiment of acoustic, environmental, and affective connections to the homeland : the rich flora and fauna of its alluvial floodplains, savannas and forests; the relatives and friends who continue to live there; and above all, the vibrancy of a face-to-face Creolese culture that has yet to be stifled by centuries of literate speech. One might suggest that on another level the willingness of men to take great risk in smuggling the birds is driven by a desire to carry the masculine ethos of birdsport into their communities abroad, and in the process to continue to expand their reputations. As songbirds from Guyana enter into Guyanese households and congregations of Guyanese men in the parks of New York, London and Montreal, they carry with them all the egalitarian possibilities and prospects of the street corners, rum shops and parks of coastal Guyana. They sing the vital message of a masculine integrity of intrinsic worth that remains available to all participants.

We may conclude by returning to the fundamental question underlying all of this: Why the aural? What is the relationship between sound and counter-hegemonic forms of achievement in Guyana and among its diaspora? Why are songbirds such effective transmitters of the affective capacities and skills that constitute masculinity and provide alternative routes to achievement for Guyanese men? Here we might further consider the conceptual relations between the passion of birdsong and the passion of men. One could argue the bird race is like a 'contrapuntal conversation' (Reisman 1974). It is the auricular essence of the contrapuntal, only without the conversation. If passionate speech events are governed by fewer restrictions than literacy events, birdsong is passionate speech outside the cage of human language. From within the arena of birdsport emerges a simultaneous flow from multiple directions that never needs to be 'toned down'; where the overlapping and intersecting of songs never compromises the intelligibility of their message; where 'interruptions' create rather than negate meaning. While birdsongs have complex patterns and rhythms that elevate them far beyond mere noise, to the Guyanese bird-racer the crisp 'rackle' of a *towa towa* is the sound of passion unrestricted, unencumbered by the borders and boundaries of words and grammatical structures. On another level, it is a passion transmitted by the bodies of birds unencumbered by the weighty markers of race, ethnicity and class that are continually forced upon their human owners.

As I have sought to demonstrate here, the cultural understanding of a transcendent, masculine passion moves with songbirds across the various regimes of achievement in which they circulate. Indeed, in the world of birdsport, songbirds *are* passion, passion in a form that all participants can hear, transport, train or trade, as the case may be. In the process, they come to embody such passion as an aspect of their own social being, which in turn enables them to transcend the more restrictive categories of person to which they are bound in other facets of life. It is this capacity to provide such a common ground – not the winning and losing that take place within it – that marks the real achievement of birdsport.

Notes

1. For present purposes, 'passion' can be read as a Guyanese cultural term for highly charged affective energy in general, with passionate song and speech as its most common vocal projections. Depending on the context, passionate speech can convey a broad range of emotive states, from anger to love, hurt, injustice, grief, shame, pride, courage, infatuation or strong commitment with regard to an idea, cause, person and so on.
2. On the transmission of affect, see Brennan (2004). To be clear, when I suggest that the passion of the songbird's singing directly impacts men's capacities to express passion as an aspect of their own social identities in terms of an 'affective transmission', I am working with the Guyanese (and arguably, pan-Caribbean) understanding of passion as an essentialised, affective capacity (embodied by humans and songbirds alike) that nonetheless requires the performative arena in order to be enacted and circulated in society. This is

most explicit in the context of carnival and, in a sense, in the performance of spirit possession. Thus while all humans are understood to have the capacity for passion, it is the strong association of the particular arenas of birdsport with masculinity that causes its participants and their aural performativity to be identified with this specific gender.

3. Given the focus here on masculinity, I should qualify that women can and often do deploy passionate speech. Due to a common Caribbean distinction between masculine street life and feminine domestic life (Abrahams 1983), however, the kinds of public spaces in which passionate speech occurs are generally masculine regardless of the gender of the individual speaker, hence the 'man of reputation' as the iconic image of the passionate speaker.
4. On the widespread indigenous Amazonian notion of alterity and the transformation of 'dangerous' strangers into 'safe' kin through prolonged exchange relations, see Gow (1991), Howard (2003), McCallum (2003) and Mentore (2009).

References

Abrahams, R. 1972. The Training of the Man of Words in Talking Sweet. *Language and Society* 1, no. 1: 15–29.

——— 1983. *The Man-of-Words in the West Indies: Performance and the Emergence of Creole Culture*. Baltimore: Johns Hopkins University Press.

Braithwaite, E.K. 1984. *History of the Voice: The Development of a Nation Language in Anglophone Caribbean Poetry*. London: New Beacon Books.

Brennan, T. 2004. *The Transmission of Affect.* Ithaca, NY: Cornell University Press.

Cambridge, V. 2005. Birdsong and the Guyanese Diaspora in New York: A Preliminary and Orienting Study. Unpublished paper presented at the conference 'Soundscapes: Reflections on Caribbean Oral and Aural Traditions', University of West Indies, Cave Hill, Barbados.

Dwyer, J. 2009. Trafficking in Contraband that Sings. *New York Times*, 15 April 2009.

Edwards, W. 1978. Tantalisin and Busin in Guyana. *Anthropological Linguistics* 20, no. 5: 194–213.

Freeman, C. 2007. The Reputation of Neoliberalism. *American Ethnologist* 34, no. 2: 252–267.

Gow, P. 1991. *Of Mixed Blood: Kinship and History in Peruvian Amazonia*. Oxford: Clarendon Press.

Howard, C. 2003. Wrought Identities: The Waiwai Expeditions in Search of the 'Unseen Tribes' of Amazonia. Ph.D. diss., University of Chicago.

McCallum, C. 2003. *Gender and Sociality in Amazonia: How Real People are Made*. Oxford: Berg.

Marzulli, J. 2009. Bird-brained Guyana Man Terrence McLean Is Cleared in Finch Pinch. *New York Daily News*, 14 April 2009.

Mentore, G. 2003. Passionate Speech and Literate Talk in Grenada. In *Language and Social Identity* (ed.) R. Blot, 261–282. Westford, CT: Praeger.

Mentore, L. 2009. Trust and Alterity: Waiwai Analyses of Social and Environmental Relations in Southern Guyana. Ph.D. diss., University of Cambridge.

Reisman, K. 1974. Contrapuntal Conversations in an Antiguan Village. In *Explorations in the Ethnography of Speaking* (eds) R. Bauman and J. Sherzer, 110–124. Cambridge: Cambridge University Press.

Richards, C. 2010. The Dress Code at the Linden Hospital Complex. *Stabroek News*, 1 February 2010.

Sell, S. 2009. Guyanese in Queens Listen for a Different Kind of Tweet. *Columbia Journalist*, 20 October 2009.

Walker, W. 2001. The *Towa Towa*: The Prize-fighting Bird of Guyana. *Stabroek News*, 26 August 2001.

Wilson, P. 1973. *Crab Antics: A Caribbean Study of the Conflict between Reputation and Respectability*. New Haven: Yale University Press.

4

Political Dimensions of Achievement Psychology

Perspectives on Selfhood, Confidence and Policy from a New Indonesian Province

Nicholas J. Long

Achievement is a highly political issue. Under the conditions of contemporary globalisation, in which citizens of different nations are faced with the prospect of vying against each other for lucrative and prestigious jobs in the 'global knowledge economy', securing 'international competitiveness' is a priority for governments around the world. Indeed, the rise of achievement indicators that rank nation-states and regions according to how 'competitive' they are globally – something measured in terms of economic performance, poverty reduction and levels of 'human development' or 'well-being' – means that more than jobs and income are at stake. Success in these rankings is also a matter of national pride, and politicians wishing to prove themselves competent at governing will do all that they can to maintain or improve the standing of the area under their jurisdiction.

This means that citizens must be 'globally competitive' and attract high scores on indices of 'human development', leading to large numbers of schemes through which governments seek to boost levels of attainment amongst their populations. Some of these involve focusing attention on developing new sets of skills; others place an emphasis on the very motivation to achieve. Whether this is couched in the neoliberal rhetoric of encouraging individuals to 'fulfil their potential' or in the more starkly utilitarian celebration of a 'motivated workforce', states – and the companies, schools and families embedded within them – are actively striving to create what McMichael and Boyd (1994) have termed 'a climate of achievement'.

Acknowledging and analysing this political dimension of achievement discourse provides a crucial corrective to the ways in which achievement, and its effects, have been construed within both anthropology and developmental psychology. For example, within psychological anthropology, one of the most compelling models of how achievement should be studied has been Roy D'Andrade's (1992) suggestion that achievement be viewed as a 'goal schema'. Seeking to account for how ideas and motivations provide individuals with 'directive force', D'Andrade argues that 'achievement is not a brute fact; an achievement is a culturally constructed object which exists only because some group of humans have developed the notion of "achievement" and agreed that certain things will count as an achievement' (ibid.: 35). Such a formulation has merits but precludes the possibility that social and political relations between any given actor and that 'group of humans' who have devised the dominant notion of achievement might interfere with the way it proves 'directive' of action, let alone the consequences of its attainment or the ways in which dominant discourses of achievement might change over time. This issue goes equally unacknowledged in important recent psychological studies of how notions of the 'achieving self' are shaped by everyday practices of praise and criticism (see the introduction to this volume, and below, for further details). Perhaps as a consequence of their experimental, laboratory setting – or because of the researchers' latent assumptions about the relations between child research subjects and the authorities that assess them – these studies afford little scope for the possibility that praise and criticism might be seen as forms of political action, rather than as straightforward revelations of 'the self' and its attributes. Moreover, given achievement's increasing politicisation, this alternative dynamic seems not only possible but ever more likely.

If one of the most significant insights generated by these recent studies in developmental psychology has been that everyday instances of achievement and its narration can have powerful and long-lasting consequences for how 'achievers' understand themselves and engage with the world, the recognition that achievements and their celebration might be understood as thoroughly political opens up important new lines of enquiry. These centre on the ways in which achievement's prominence in policy rhetoric might have a bearing on the psychological and social consequences of achieving – as well as how dominant discourses and definitions of achievement transform over time. In this chapter, I want to illustrate quite how significant this political reframing of achievement psychology can be, drawing on over twenty-eight months of anthropological fieldwork in the Indonesian province of Kepulauan Riau (Riau Islands), known locally and hereafter as Kepri, between 2005 and 2012. Through participant observation of events and sites associated with achievement as well as semi-structured interviews with 'achievers', policy makers and members of the public, it became clear to me that many people's lives were being profoundly shaped by the ways in which achievement was politicised within the province. While my use of qualitative methodology means that the cases discussed below cannot be taken as statistically representative of achievement-thinking in Kepri, I follow Cole and Knowles (2001: 11) in their insistence that 'every in-depth exploration of an individual life-in-context brings us that much closer to understanding the complexities of lives' in any given setting. This chapter thus serves to illuminate both the range of ways in which, and the extents to which, the lives of people in Kepri mediate and have been mediated by the politicisation of achievement. Through such an analysis I argue that although recent advances in achievement psychology are of tremendous significance to anthropology, affording richer and more complex understandings of agency and the life course, they must in turn be combined with a close ethnographic attention to the political matrix in which achievement discourse is embedded, such that ideas of citizenship, political consciousness and engagements with the state are recognised as integral to any inquiry into what it means to have achieved.

Kepri's Achievement Programme

In 2004, Kepri became an autonomous province separate from the mainland Sumatran region of Riau Daratan to which it had previously been attached. While full details of the transition are beyond the scope of this chapter (see Long 2013), it was widely construed as throwing off the shackles of 'internal colonialism' by Riau Daratan. Riau Islanders had felt systematically neglected under the Daratan administration, which had provided only minimal investment in fields such as education, health and training. This, they felt, had rendered the population backward, unskilled and unable to meet the stringent demands of the contemporary economy.[1] The residents of the islands spoke of their province as suffering from a 'human resources crisis' – and indeed, one of the main arguments against provincial autonomy was that the poor quality of the human resources might render a new province unviable (Ardi 2002: 65). For the sake of their own legitimacy, as well as for the competitiveness of their newly decentralised province, the new government thus made it a priority to boost human resource quality, and to do so they turned to achievement psychology.

In the 1950s and 1960s, social psychologists in the United States instigated an ambitious research programme devoted to explaining the interior origins of the desire to achieve and the broader social consequences of that drive's expression. Much of this work is summarised in David McClelland's *The Achieving Society* (1961), which makes the bold argument that societies undergo economic development when their members exhibit a high degree of '*nAch*' – McClelland's shorthand for the psychological drive he termed, following Henry Murray ([1938] 2008), 'need for Achievement'. *nAch* was said to spur the values of entrepreneurship, competitiveness and a strong motivation to succeed, all qualities vital to being 'good human resources' but considered gravely lacking in Kepri.

McClelland had argued that *nAch* could be learned through exposing children to situations involving 'standards of excellence' that were 'impressed on the child by the culture' such that successful attempts to meet them produced positive affect, and unsuccessful attempts, negative affect (McClelland et al. 1953: 275).

As in other technocratic postcolonial states (see Nandy 1987: 51–52), these ideas had a significant impact on public policy in Indonesia as officials sought to improve the nation's economic growth, and were incorporated into the New Order government's project of fostering 'development mindedness' among the citizenry (Budiman 1979). By the 1980s, such ideas about achievement had become incorporated into an Indonesian term: *prestasi*, which began to pervade mainstream discourse. Informants told me that when they had been at school in the 1960s, *prestasi* was always used to refer to a discrete feat, such as coming top in an exam or winning a competition. It would thus have been translated as 'an achievement'. Now, by contrast, it not only meant this but also referred to a cultural value or an aspect of one's identity: 'achievement' in the abstract.

Simultaneously, Indonesia saw a surge of interest in the staging of state-sponsored competitions (Sutton 1991: 185). Whilst contests and competitive events have long been popular in Southeast Asia (Reid 1988), they now became explicitly anchored to – and in most contexts indissociable from – the discourse of *prestasi*: each contest generated achievement because it (necessarily) had a winner. Described by Karen Strassler (2006) as a 'culture of contests', this arrangement did not only invite popular participation in state programmes; it also aimed to provide opportunities to seize *prestasi*, generate a proliferation of motivating affects (as in McClelland's model) and through this foster the 'strong character' required for global competitiveness (Strassler 2006: 59–61).

These were and are national trends, but have been seized upon with particular fervour in newly created Kepri, where politicians, newspapers, advertising campaigns and commentators openly touted McClellandian psychology as the solution to the province's human resource problems.[2] In practice, this resulted in a plethora of contests associated with diverse age groups and activities. Many were directed at schoolchildren. Of these, the most prestigious were the annual Olympiads, in which students compete to prove that they are the best in their town, province or nation at a particular school subject, but the provincial and municipal government, NGOs and private tuition centres all sponsored 'one off' contests within particular municipalities or districts, which focused on fields as diverse as modelling, use of PowerPoint, public speaking, accountancy and sports. Within schools and private tuition centres, internal contests were regularly staged as an attempt to 'motivate students', whilst people who had left school still found they were able to participate in a whole host of contests, the most popular of which focused on various aspects of regional culture, such as dance, poetry and traditional songs – or Qur'anic recitation. Many also encountered opportunities to enter formal contests within their professional lives: during my time in Kepri I witnessed several contests designed to boost human resource quality and motivation within specific professions, such as teaching and minibus driving, whilst civil servants were regularly funded to enter contests organised by the Department of Tourism (including fishing contests and mountain trekking races) on the grounds that this will boost their awareness of the province in which they work, whilst also improving their human resource quality.

What such a diverse range of events have in common is the fact that they were all explicitly framed – at least in part – as governmental (or indeed societal) responses to a political problem: 'the human resources crisis' afflicting the province. That very fact, I argue, had a significant influence on the consequences of pursuing achievement for the individuals and groups who had been exhorted to do so. To illustrate this argument, I want to trace three ways in which the social life of achievement rolled forwards in the Riau Islands, exploring what their implications might be for the study of achievement more generally.

The Social Life of Achievement, 1: Prospects and Pleasures

The government-led attempt to create a more achievement-oriented population had its desired result, at least in so far as large numbers of Kepri youth (and also some adults) began to structure their lives around the pursuit of *prestasi*. When I asked contestants why they had got involved in competitions or tournaments their answers suggested the pleasures of achievement were far more compelling than those of the activity at hand:

> YUDITH: I love to compete in contests (*berlomba-lomba*). That's my hobby! I'm always looking for ways to increase my *prestasi*.

> HENDRA: This beauty contest is quite boring for me, and I don't think I'm very good at it. I would prefer to be doing a speech or debate competition ... But at the minute, the only competitions running are modelling and beauty contests ... so I've entered ... The more I enter, the more *prestasi* I get.

So what was the appeal that *prestasi* held? While its pursuit could be interpreted as simply the consequence of repeated injunctions to acquire it, there were also very tangible benefits that participants anticipated or experienced. In and of themselves, they might not seem remarkable, but – in showing just what was at stake in being identified as 'an achiever' – they shed important light on the dynamics discussed below.

Achievement has immediate practical benefits – and foremost amongst these is the prospect of a prize. Cash prizes would often be used to cover the cost of school and university fees, reducing the need to do part-time work, but whilst this was appreciated it was rarely talked of with enthusiasm. By contrast, material markers of achievement – whether this be a trophy or a 'luxury' commodity offered as a prize (such as a laptop computer) – elicited much greater interest. Prospective competitors fantasised out loud about how nice it would be to win a laptop or a luxury mobile phone. Others visualised the moment of holding a trophy aloft, and the thrill of pride they would feel whenever they walked into their house and saw the trophy on the mantelpiece.

Indeed, trophies often took pride of place in the rooms households used for receiving and entertaining guests. The presence of the trophy invites comment and reflection (indeed, many hosts told me that if guests did not pass comment on the trophy they probably did so out of jealousy and/or spite), and not just achievers but also their relatives relish the opportunities to narrate the circumstances in which the object was acquired. So important was this attachment to the 'material culture of success' (Rowlands 1994) that when my friend Cynthia hosted end-of-year competitions at her private tuition centre, which specialised in English language tutoring, parents wrote in to complain about the prizes that the children were receiving. While Cynthia was giving them dictionaries or textbooks that would assist them with their English, a group of parents approached her to request that in future the winners be given trophies:

> CYNTHIA: I said to them: 'But dictionaries are useful! Haven't you sent your children here so they can get better at English? They need a good dictionary! And trophies are expensive. I can't afford to give them both'.
>
> 'It's not that we don't like the dictionaries,' said one of the mothers, 'but children are disappointed if they don't get a trophy. If their friends win things, they get trophies. But if all they get is a dictionary, nobody knows they have won anything'.
>
> So what could I do? That was what they wanted!

The trophy's importance thus stems from its capacity to denote the recipient's 'achiever' identity over a period of time. It is a tool that helps create a 'social life of achievement' in which success is seen as enviable, and becomes a source of pride and esteem.

Achievement could also transform social relations in the future. Teddy, a vocational-school student who had achieved excellent results in modelling, speech and religious trivia contests, recounted that having been successful made his life 'a lot better' – now, whenever he passed by teachers who didn't know him, they would smile and say hello, something they had never done before. Likewise, Esther reported her pride that, amongst her friends, she alone was personally known to the mayor, 'because I am always representing my school, and always winning!' But the idea that one might be 'noticed' through achieving was particularly important in the field of employment. Kepri job application forms typically contain a specific section in which applicants are asked to list their previous *prestasi*, while candidates will often use trophies and rankings as evidence to argue for their employability in job interviews. Achievement could thus facilitate further success – or least the financial security of employment – a prime dimension of its appeal for young people (and their parents) on the brink of an uncertain future.

Affective dimensions of achieving were important too. Teddy explained a little of the thrill of *prestasi*. He recounted the day he had been announced as top of the school in his final year of SMP (junior high school). As he went up to the stage to collect the trophy he found that he was, 'dizzy and could hardly walk. I was crying, but because I was so happy. And then when I took the trophy and I heard the applause ... It was the most perfect moment of my life. After that I knew I had to enter a lot of competitions so I could experience that again'.

These remarks underscore how the emotional and sensory dimensions of *prestasi* make it appealing: the swimming legs, tears clouding his eyes, the sound of the applause – a sensation that he could not achieve elsewhere and that prompted him to search elsewhere for a repeat experience. What this material appears to demonstrate is a psychological positive feedback mechanism in which achievement engenders a further desire to achieve both in its terms and through its trappings. This, of course, is the key assumption underpinning the government's achievement programme – as is the belief that, in the words of one Tourism Department official, 'champions [will] become models for their classmates. Their classmates will see that they have won the prize, and that will give them motivation to be more disciplined so that they can win a prize in the competition next year. It is an excellent socialisation strategy'.

Of the people that I met who had not achieved very much success in competitions or tournaments, a large number did indeed say that watching their more victorious counterparts had motivated them to try harder. Some were spurred on to compete with their peers and try to win; but others – especially those who studied at schools with a poor reputation – told me that they just wanted to make sure they didn't look out of place at the competition; representing their school was already enough of an achievement for them. What was striking overall, however, was the general level of optimism that the proliferation of contests engendered. While some people (typically those from poorer districts of Tanjung Pinang) did express despair that they or their children would never stand a chance in academic competitions where they were expected to vie against wealthier, more cosmopolitan – and often ethnically Chinese – Riau Islanders, alternative arenas of contest, such as Qur'anic recitation, Islamic calligraphy and sport, afforded them opportunities for achievement that felt tangible and realistic.

Despite the general enthusiasm for such events, some Riau Islanders were cynical towards the government's interest in achievement psychology. One female student, a frequent competitor in contests herself, told me that she thought that many Riau Islanders had lost sight of what the events they entered were all about. 'They think they are getting achievement (*prestasi*)', she told me, 'but all they are getting is prestige (*prestise*). The difference between the two words is only two letters – but there's a very big difference in what they mean'. However, for many Riau Islanders, especially those confronted with the challenges of unemployment and poverty, the memory of seemingly trivial *prestasi* in their childhood – of coming third place in a sub-district swimming competition, or of representing their neighbourhood at Qur'anic recitation – was a treasured resource. As I became more closely acquainted with people living economically precarious lives, they would often confide to me of the moment in their past when they had received a ranking (*rangking*) or won a trophy. It reminded them, they told me, of a time that they felt their lives had value, and that they were full of potential, and it gave them the confidence that if they tried hard they might be able to make something of their lives once again.

The governmental and public endorsement of *prestasi* can thus be seen to have had a powerful effect on Riau Islanders' motivational structures, orienting the population towards a particular idea of being an 'achiever' in ways that gave many people direction and hope.[3] But those outcomes seemed to be most typical amongst those who rarely, if ever, experienced 'achievement' or had done so in the long-distant past. For in many regards, the 'social life of achievement' that I have sketched in this section was fantasmic; an illusory, aspired-for life that had little in common with the realities of experiencing achievement on a regular basis. For, rather than living a life in which they were motivated to strive for ever-greater success, Kepri's achievers often experienced rather more ambivalent engagements with notions of both self and citizenship.

The Social Life of Achievement, 2: Doubts and Disillusionment

Of all the people I met in Kepri, it was perhaps Teddy, with his insistence on entering as many competitions as possible so as to re-enact the buzz of success, who best exemplified the logic by which the province sought to engineer an achieving mindset amongst its population. It is thus, perhaps, particularly telling that it was Teddy, and four classmates of his, who lay at the heart of a rather curious ethnographic puzzle.

In February 2006, Teddy was selected to represent his home town of Tanjung Pinang in the provincial-level English debating championships. This had involved defeating over twenty other students from schools across the town. The selectors were so impressed with the quality of the trials – which they proudly announced were of 'national standard' – that they gave rise to ambitious aspirations that students from Tanjung Pinang might make it into the top five teams in Indonesia. Teddy added that he didn't mind if he was ranked lower, provided Kepri beat Riau Daratan, its former 'coloniser', and showed the rest of Indonesia that Kepri's independence had been successful and allowed its human resources to flourish.

On paper, the team looked strong enough to carry out these hopes. Both Teddy and Martina had been school champions, while Bella and Clarissa were top of their classes in English and ranked highly in other subjects. Nor was there a problem of motivation. When they were selected, the children were delighted – grinning broadly and, in Teddy's words, 'almost crying with excitement'. But different tears were shed in the first training session. Fadli, their coach, described how Martina had trailed off crying only twenty seconds into a five-minute speech, whilst Clarissa had arrived at the session with her father demanding she be withdrawn. Their anxiety was that their English was not of 'national standard' at all. Rather, it would not stand up against the students from the neighbouring island of Batam, and they would suffer a humiliating defeat. Far from instilling self-confidence, 'achievement' appeared to have inspired the very reverse: a lack of self-belief, and an aversion to risk. The puzzle that this case poses bears a striking similarity to several phenomena reported by social psychologists. Yet, as I will argue, the distinctive politics of the Riau Islands setting necessitates the development of new, supplementary theoretical concepts – which in turn might offer important insights for the cross-cultural study of achievement and its consequences more broadly.

In the 1970s, Pauline Clance and her colleagues identified the so-called 'impostor phenomenon' amongst high-achieving women (Clance and Imes 1978; Clance and O'Toole 1987). Subjects exhibiting this trait believed that their high achievements were not a result of 'genuine' ability but rather of 'hard work, luck, knowing the right people, being in the right place at the right time, or to their interpersonal assets such as charm' (Clance and O'Toole 1987: 51–52). Losing 'the sense of reward and joy that ordinarily accompanies success', sufferers turned down opportunities to advance due to a fear of discovery, thereby failing to realise their full potential (ibid.: 53). Clance and Imes's description of the affective trajectory 'impostors' undergo makes for a striking parallel with the Kepri example: 'The woman feels elated temporarily and such feelings of success make the cycle very hard to give up ... However, the success is an empty one, and the good feelings are short-lived because the underlying sense of phoniness remains untouched' (Clance and Imes 1978: 244).

However, the starting assumption behind this analysis is that the sufferer's success really is genuinely deserved and that their attitude betrays a 'lack of reality' (ibid.: 245). This assessment places tremendous faith in the authorities that devise and evaluate standards of achievement – a faith which 'impostors' may not share, for culturally and historically specific reasons. That is certainly the case in Kepri, where the category of 'achievement' is not only seen as politically motivated but – and here is the crucial irony – constructed and evaluated by those who are 'poor human resources' themselves.

In post-Suharto Indonesia, which has been construed in the press and popular understanding as a battleground between the forces of democratic reform and *KKN* (corruption, collusion and nepotism), achievement very often lies under a shadow. Frequent accusations against judges are that they are 'unprofessional', that they are too inexperienced to judge, that they might have accepted bribes, and, as an ultimate fall-back, that they are 'Indonesian'. As Teddy explained, 'Indonesia has very poor education and human resources, so obviously an Indonesian judge is going to be a lot less expert than a foreigner. Besides, Indonesia has a lot of corruption; I think Indonesian judges don't know how to be honest (*tidak tahu jujur*)'. *Prestasi* thus emerges as highly desirable in self-fashioning and yet widely considered to be an imperfect reflection of the self. It is therefore unsurprising that people who are deemed successful can be thrilled by this designation and all the benefits it brings, whilst being haunted by the grim prospect that, as 'achievers', they are expected to keep on 'achieving' well into the future.

This point has some important implications for the growing body of psychological evidence that people's experiences of achievement (and specifically the language through which they are praised) has a formative influence on the self-theory they acquire, and their consequent propensity for high-achieving or risk-avoidant behaviour in the future. A persuasive case to this effect this has been offered by Carol Dweck (1999), summarising decades of experimental and role-play research with young children in the U.S.A. Dweck identifies two kinds of self-theory, with particular regard to the conceptualisation of intelligence as a property of the self: 'entity theory', in which intelligence is understood as an entity that dwells within the person and which they are unable to change; and 'incremental theory', which considers intelligence to be cultivated through learning and positive effort. The distinction, she found, had significant consequences for how children coped with situations of difficulty or challenge. Those subscribing to an entity theory were more likely to display a 'helpless' response, feeling that the task was beyond the fixed limits of their intellect, which in many cases they explicitly condemned. Such reactions were associated with decreased performance and decreased self-esteem, and strong feelings of moral reprehensibility arise (ibid.: 17, 46, 100). By contrast, incremental theorists asserted that, by focusing on the task and trying harder, it would be possible for them to make a breakthrough. Entity theorists feel more validated by success than their incremental counterparts, but also risk depressive episodes if they encounter major setbacks and challenges. This means that entity theorists take pleasure in easy work and avoid (or self-handicap in) situations where they run the risk of failure – an important qualification to prevailing anthropological models of motivated agency.

It would also offer a perfect framework with which to make sense of the Kepri vocational schoolchildren's anxious and risk avoidant attitudes towards their own capacities to achieve, were it not for the causal analysis that is at the heart of Dweck's argument. She suggests that the implicit theory of self a person holds is a direct result of social discourses about achievement and the self that a child is exposed to whilst growing up. Foremost amongst these are practices of praise and criticism. Thus even innocuous remarks, such as saying 'who's a clever boy then?' as opposed to 'didn't you work hard?' subtly introduces an entity theory of self, encouraging the praised individual to relate their achievement to fixed attributes of intelligence, talent and ability. However, despite the force of this argument, and the compelling evidence with which it is supported, such a framework of explanation makes little sense in Kepri, where praise is not conventionally formulated in terms of implicit 'entity theory', as it is in the U.S.A. Indeed, the public discourse surrounding achievement in the Riau Islands plays up discipline, hard work, religious devotion, dedication and downplays the significance of 'innate talent'. Parents and educators regularly told me that the province's youth was capable of anything, given sufficient motivation (which they tried to provide by pointing to inspirational exemplars, including celebrities such as Daniel Radcliffe and David Beckham, as well as local competition winners).[4] Since this would seem to fit better with Dweck's notion of an 'incremental theory', the question is raised of whether additional ideal-type self-theories might need to be added to Dweck's model for the purposes of cross-cultural and cross-contextual research.

It is in this regard that I would propose the category of an 'environmental mindset', which reflects the ways in which Riau Islanders' thoughts on achievement are bound up with an awareness of the social and structural relations in which they are embedded. This, however, is not to argue for an essentialised distinction between the 'sociocentric' culture of Indonesia and the 'egocentric' culture of the West (cf. Shweder and Bourne 1984). Rather, I agree with Hollan's (1992) contention that, if one attends to narratives of subjective experience, then aspects of individuated and relational thinking can be found in both Western and Indonesian contexts. As such, examining how, and under what circumstances, relational thinking affects experiences of achievement might also prove to be of value in more familiar settings.

Although an incremental theory of talent is prevalent within Kepri, it is anchored to the belief that motivation, and with it the capacity to become achieving individuals, derives from social and structural conditions – in short, the environment in which one is emplaced. Relevant factors include the aesthetics of one's material surroundings, the efficacy of government policies, and perhaps above all the quality of the local human resources – from teachers to competition adjudicators, to doctors who can advise on the best diet to feed a child's growing brain, and the officials who design schemes aimed at improving human resource quality. The pernicious paradox – established during fifty years of 'internal colonialism' at the hands of mainland Sumatra – is that the only people in a position to improve human resource quality are themselves human resources of low quality. As such, their efforts are viewed as fundamentally flawed – flaws which are transferred to the citizens brought up in such a setting.

Framing the problem of achievement in this way constructs an important and deterministic relationship between the performance of the citizen and their home town or region which – through its administrative policies, facilities and human resources – delimits that citizen's capacity to achieve. I see a productive parallel here with recent Melanesian ethnography that has stressed the creative potential of land (Leach 2003). Creations, which may include pigs, crops, trees and people, are extensions of the land itself, and their mobility and detachability render them 'land that moves' – always associated with that originatory land until and unless they become attached elsewhere (Strathern 2009). Bearing in mind that Indonesian contests structurally enumerate administrative regions of sub-district, district and province, the competition context can activate exactly such an awareness. One is a creation of a region, and as such its extension. Indeed, one is there to represent it. But one can have been created badly, and it is precisely this fear that Kepri youngsters – who know the province that created them suffers from a human resources crisis – feel when entering translocal contests. It marks a fundamental alienation from, and disappointment in, the region that 'high achievers' (*anak berprestasi*) believe will hamper their performance. In this sense, those 'achievers' who celebrate their triumph can be said to be doing so in 'bad faith', enacting (and believing in) the dispositions and demeanours of 'an achiever' whilst simultaneously perceiving their authentic self to be something rather different (Long 2011; 2013). Moreover, the flaws in historic processes of regional creation are being brought ever more into the public eye by the increasing significance of district and provincial-level politics under the decentralisation policies of post-Suharto Indonesia (see Aspinall and Fealy 2003). In Kepri, this has been emphasised still further due to the widespread preoccupation with solving a 'human resources crisis' and the rolling out of policies that focus on cultivating – and demonstrating – the achievement hitherto considered lacking.

In some ways this model echoes Dweck's notion of an entity theory. A regional creation is, after all, an entity – with fixed limits on its ability to achieve, which can perhaps explain the 'helpless' reaction and the fear of being 'an impostor'. However, there are important differences. As a newly created province, Kepri shows considerable volatility in political consciousness, as citizens oscillate between the hopes that infused their secession from Riau Daratan and the sense of hopelessness and disillusionment that stems from feeling their prospects are over-determined by the colonial past. These assumptions are all put on the line every time that a contest –inherently unpredictable by nature – generates its own new hierarchy of ability in a specified domain. The contest affords the possibility that, if the results are in Kepri's favour, a participant's bad faith in their achiever identity might evanesce towards good faith, as that identity is ratified through the 'objective' and nationally endorsed measures of results and scores, which are considered to be much more trustworthy than the results delivered by assessors in the Riau Islands. Importantly, however, and unlike the notion of authentic fixity implicit in entity theory – where a good performance might reveal that one had been intelligent all along – this reflects an incremental change in an external variable, the province and its capacity to produce high quality human resources (or at least knowledge thereof), upon which a sense of the self and the limits of its capacity to achieve are fundamentally dependent.

This approach allows us to understand how Riau Islanders might come to live a social life of achievement that rolls forward in a much more contingent and underdetermined fashion than psychological models would seem to predict. The experience of achieving can follow a trajectory in which success is first met in bad faith and so engenders a helpless response when achievers realise that their attainment has also paved the way for future competitive encounters that will expose its own lie – only for this to give way to belief that one really is *berprestasi* and capable of achieving all that one might want. This happened for the Tanjung Pinang debaters when they defeated teams from Batam, and then such provinces as Southeast Sulawesi, Aceh and South Sumatra at the national finals, eventually being ranked sixth in the country. Heartened from such success, they transformed from being ashamed of being from Kepri to proud (if surprised) that their new province could be as good as those with a much more fearsome reputation.

The irony of this particular story, as discussed elsewhere (Long 2011; 2013) is that all funding was cut from English language debating activities later that year. The same Education Department officials, who had lauded the team as of 'national standard', told me that they ultimately felt that English language was not an arena in which the people of Kepri could achieve – showing their own bad faith in the politicised achievement discourse they were propagating. When the team and their friends heard this, they simply said that this proved how bad the province's human resources still were – and that they would be held back from developing any further if they continued to live in the Riau Islands. Some resigned themselves to this; others moved away. Both responses thwarted the provincial government's attempt to cultivate a high-achieving population within its borders.

The Social Life of Achievement, 3: Achieving in Record Time

If the first two social lives of achievement that I have outlined refer to the lives people lead after achieving, the third 'life' that I would like to sketch is that of the concept of *prestasi* itself – for the understandings of it that informed the proliferation of contests shortly after Kepri's was created as a province quickly proved unsustainable.

While every contest, examination or ranking generates achievers, it necessarily also breeds large swathes of people whose performance is identified as not quite up to scratch. In the eyes of officials (and here they once again echo David McClelland) the shame, dismay and envy that these people would feel was supposed to act as an incentive, inspiring them to work harder in the future so as to emulate the 'social life of achievement' of their more successful peers. As noted earlier, this did sometimes occur. Yet the fact that the achievement programme was embedded within a broader governmental matrix of policy promises to improve human resources frequently subverted the chastening effects of failure at any particular achievement event. Although an individual's failure to succeed might indeed be attributed to their lack of hard work, motivation, or practice, their friends and relatives proffered this in itself as evidence that the province was failing in its ambition to produce high quality human resources. The negative affects that failure to meet with standards of excellence evoked were often not those of personal shame but resentment towards the political forces that, my informants intimated, ought to have made the chances of success more likely.

The problem was compounded by a sense that allocations of *prestasi* were not strictly meritocratic but influenced by personal connections or sometimes even bribes. This fear led to a cynical attitude towards competition outcomes that rendered many participants unable to accept that their lack of success could be attributable to deficiencies in their own skill set or mentality. Secondly, in an effort to secure the legitimacy of their decisions, adjudicators and competition organisers displayed a tendency to favour candidates with 'a reputation' (see Long 2007). As a result, *prestasi* could come to acquire a relatively conservative dimension, replicating itself within particular individuals' biographies at the expense of others. By the end of my first period of fieldwork (February 2007) it was becoming clear to both citizens and officials that simply not enough people were achieving. It was against the backdrop of such frustrations and concerns that Riau Islanders embraced a new interest that was sweeping the nation: breaking records.

In August 2009, fifty-one students from School No. 1 in the central Javanese town of Boyolali built a giant model of a catfish, 12.3 metres by 3.7 metres, and filled it with 800 kilogrammes of fried catfish. This broke national record number 3846, for the greatest amount of catfish meat gathered in one place. Djoko Kirmanto, an alumnus of the school and national Minister of Public Works, was in attendance:

> According to [Djoko], this event proved that the human resource ethos at School No. 1 is extremely high. As well as promoting the name of their school, they have certainly also raised Boyolali's status in the public eye. Moreover, the catfish flesh was obtained from catfish farmers in Boyolali.
>
> 'It's clear that this is *prestasi* of which we should be very proud', said [Djoko]. (Suara Merdeka 2009)

The setting or breaking of national and world records is referred to by Riau Islanders as 'getting a MURI', after the acronym for the Museum Rekor-Dunia Indonesia (Indonesian World Record Museum) in which such a feat will be documented.[5] Jaya Suprama, the general chairman of the museum, explains in an introduction to the *2008/2009 Book of Records* his belief that the 'superlative intentions and acts in various fields of life' that each MURI represents will 'directly influence the enthusiasm of the Indonesian people to develop their nation and its population so that they can be of the very highest standard, status, and rank amidst the successive onslaughts of globalisation', and he ends his piece by stressing that MURI are 'superlative achievements' (Jaya Suprama 2012: ix–x). Such feats range from genuinely breaking records (whatever they may be) to 'one-off' accomplishments deemed impressive enough to be noted in the museum. Some recipients of the latter kind of award seem deserving of honours – such as Madiun Regency, which won an award for setting up a consistent house-to-house doctor service. Other accomplishments – such as designing a laminated furniture range in the style of Versace, or opening a promotional tourism and investment centre that was integrated with a café – seem more unlikely choices, and were the kinds of records that raised fears amongst some of my interlocutors that the MURI committee's attentions could be bought as well as earned. Although the Museum was set up in 1990, with many records set and broken ever since, the 2000s have exhibited an increased interest in MURI from public administrators, as well as an intensified association between MURI and ideas about 'human resources' and 'achievement'.

Boyolali was by no means unique in this regard; indeed, Kepri had taken up this project with enthusiasm. By 2008, MURI – not a major concern in the first half of the decade – were on everybody's lips as the provincial government hatched plans to break records for the most people ever to dance the Malay *zapin tempurung* dance (1,000 primary school children), the longest ever uninterrupted stretch of reciting *pantun* poetry (6 hours, 5 minutes and 5 seconds), the oldest human being in Indonesia (122 years old) and an effort to build the longest ever fish sausage (over 2 kilometres). The receipt of any such MURI was cast in the same idiom of achievement as a competitive victory: *prestasi*.

Most of Kepri's attempts at setting records were concerned with the scale of events or the number of participants. This allowed Kepri to be recorded in the MURI notebooks, setting its accomplishments on a national and global stage, but also for claims and material markers of *prestasi* to be distributed widely amongst the population. By expanding the definition of what counts as achievement – and what can be recognised through its hallmark symbols – the turn to MURI activities has allowed a lot more people to see themselves as potential achievers. This very fact can incite a motivational force that the fear of defeat in competitions might occlude. Unlike contests, then, the *prestasi* associated with MURI appears to support a more incremental mindset of achievement, whereby success emerges from participation and effort rather than any specific talent-entity. This accords with the explicit mission statement of the Museum (which officiates all MURI attempts) to 'inspire and stimulate enthusiasm amongst the people of Indonesia to always offer up their very best intentions and deeds in everything that they do'.[6] Similar ideas came through when I spoke to Nurul, a music teacher who worked at one of the schools participating in the attempt at breaking the record for *zapin tempurung* dancing.[7] She explained that one of the best things about the attempt was how many students could be involved:

> Each school gets to send some dancers. We are sending about twenty. The nineteenth and the twentieth would never win a dancing competition. But they are important! Without them, we don't have enough pupils to get the MURI ... It gives them motivation to make sure their dancing is good ... It will be nice for them to remember when they're older.

Not everybody had fond memories of their MURI-setting efforts. In June 2010, Edward Mushalli, the deputy mayor of Tanjung Pinang, announced to the newspapers and on his blog his plan that the town's annual marathon be nominated for a MURI as having the greatest number of participants of any marathon in Indonesia (Mushalli 2010). While this was an event that still counted as a competition, with prizes awarded to the winners of the race, the opportunity to win their town a MURI was supposed to have a galvanising effect on the town's population. (One resident posted in a blog comment: 'Ok! Let's all get together [for this] and celebrate our town ... Hopefully we will build up joy and it will always be like that. Tanjung Pinang!!!') The population did indeed turn out in force, and a MURI was secured. But while their participation in the marathon was precisely to obtain that MURI, Mushalli was quick to present the MURI as a testament to the community's enthusiasm for competing in the marathon. We can see in Mushalli's framing of the event an attempt to finesse different forms of *prestasi* that allows the population to feel that they are 'achieving' but also enables the government to put forward an interpretation of events in which this points to a motivated and competitive human resource base furnished with high levels of *nAch.*

However, what such an analysis downplays is the extent to which participation in the marathon was less motivated than coerced. All members of the civil service had been forced to participate so as to make up numbers. I asked one schoolteacher how he had found the experience:

> At the beginning I was not very happy – I felt a little bit under duress. It made me reluctant to do any training – I perhaps went for training about three times. But then as the day itself approached, I began to enjoy it more – because all my colleagues were forced to do it as well, so we could go along together, and there was a festive atmosphere (*suasana hiburan*) – and also the weather was good. It was drizzling a little bit, so it wasn't too hot and I could keep going. If it was hot and sunny, maybe I would have got tired, and would have stopped quite early. But since the weather was cool, I was able to complete the course. But I wouldn't enter again unless I had to. It's all politics.

There are several points here worth noting. Coercion breeds a resentful attitude at first, actually dampening motivation, but the sociality and 'festive atmosphere' it engenders actually leads to the MURI effort being fun and worthwhile. What shatters that impression, though, is the notion that 'it's all politics'. 'They just want to boost the name of Kepri,' he complained, 'not to raise educational standards. The trophy goes straight to the office of the organisers – a political office – and meanwhile our educational standards are falling behind worse than ever'.

A similar response of dismay was elicited when the fourteen-year-old daughter of my friend Widya – a vivacious entrepreneur in her forties – was forced to enter an attempt to break the record for the most scouts attending an anti-drugs education event (the record was broken, with 10,235 scouts in attendance). 'She really felt it, the coercion,' Widya told me. 'It meant she had no motivation, and she wasn't very happy to break the record'. She was equally critical of government officials' vested interests:

> You can see that Indonesian officials are at their happiest when they're organising something really silly. I look at that list of national records, and it makes me laugh. The *prestasi* that you get with a MURI is only ever as warm as chicken shit. They say it will increase human resource quality. Think about it. How can the longest ever chicken satay improve human resource quality?

'Maybe [it improved] the organisers?' chipped in her husband, a man often disposed to look on the brighter side of situations his wife found lamentable. 'No!' Widya replied, with a scornful laugh, 'They say those things to talk it up, to make it sound clever and intellectual. Actually it's just because they enjoy doing silly things. And they have no independent thought of their own. They see other provinces are breaking records and they just follow. Unthinkingly.' Once again, the configuration of political figures as 'poor quality human resources' had undermined the sense that one's province, family members, or even oneself, is achieving anything, limiting the extent to which *prestasi* associated with records was able to command genuine respect or induce a more motivated state of mind.

Finally, the interest in MURI was often met with hostility and cynicism by people who were concerned that it represented a dangerous slippage in the conceptualisation of 'achievement'. This perspective was articulated most eloquently by my friend Astrid, a Javanese woman in her early thirties who worked in a branch of the Department of Culture:

> It's certainly MURI madness (*gila MURI*) nowadays. They want to get certificates. If you're setting a MURI, it's actually a much easier way to get *prestasi* than a competition. If there's a competition, there are other competitors who can defeat you. But if you set a MURI, it's certain you'll get the *prestasi*. You see, Nick, we're seeing cultural change. I can see a change in the way people are thinking. Before, people would wait to be glorified (*dianugerahkan*). Now people are doing all they can to actively seek out glorification. They think it's their human right to have *prestasi*!

For Astrid, the passion for MURI was part of a broader trend in the way that people were thinking about achievement: as an entitlement, or as a 'right'. Citizens demanding achievement was a pernicious by-product of the government's desire to distribute achievement as widely as possible across the population, and a problematic consequence of committing themselves to the ideals of achievement as a means of testifying to the quality of their human resources.

Other critics of the MURI phenomenon focused on more practical concerns. Just two years after she had seemed so enthusiastic about the record-breaking *zapin tempurung* dance attempt, Nurul was amongst them. She admitted that the experience had been great for her pupils: they had trained really hard for the event, memorising all the moves perfectly, and had been rewarded for this by being placed right at the front of the stage, where spectators could see them – something that had made them very happy indeed. Nevertheless, she had concerns about the government's growing interest in MURI as a form of achievement, as she told me over snacks with her elder sister Lina.

'The trouble is that MURIs are always about food!' Nurul explained, 'Or rather, they are about making the biggest amount of food, or having the most participants doing something. That's what it's always like. They never involve any competition. They never involve trying to do better than something that someone else really talented has done.'

'No,' interrupted Lina, 'even though if they enter Olympiads, it turns out the kids from this province are capable of getting into the top three...!'

'Exactly!' Nurul agreed vigorously with her sister, pointing out that once they were adults, Kepri's youth would need to be able to hold their own against people from other provinces – and perhaps even other countries – in an increasingly global job market. 'But with MURI, it's just about having the most of them involved as possible.'

Following these accounts, one is led to the conclusion that the very understanding of what 'achievement' can comprise, and how one should relate to it – can one expect it, ask for it, or should it always be earned? – has a complicated 'social life' of its own. Moreover, this trajectory is strongly influenced by the standing of 'achievement' and 'achievement motivation' as policy objectives. The political origins of a valorised notion of competitive achievement thus laid the foundations for it to transmute into a broader notion of 'achievement' that inculcated novel – and contested – ideas about mindset, motivation, efficacy and deserts.

Conclusion: Policy, Regionality and Achievement

Achievement's prominence within the nascent province of Kepri's policy agenda both heightened its appeal and led to unexpected consequences. The starting assumption of the policy – that Kepri's human resource base is weak – undermined faith in the government's efforts to define and identify who was truly an 'achiever', meaning that many of those Riau Islanders who regularly experienced 'achievement' found their experiences of it to be either strikingly different from the life of improved employment prospects and social esteem that they imagined, or to combine those benefits with unanticipated and painful moments of self-doubt and existential angst. It also created incentives to democratise and widely distribute achievement, a process which involved a reconfiguration of its definition and scope that, as the discussion of MURI reveals, could be both enabling and disheartening.

These observations fit with the growing recognition that achievement can be a poisoned chalice, but do so in ways that reveal a set of dynamics that are strikingly different from those present in the existing literature. Most significantly, the very fact that 'achievement' and mindset were presented as policy issues heightened the sense that 'achieving' was bound up with relational and environmental aspects of selfhood. Whether it is the high-achieving debater who is afraid that his background will let them down, or the MURI hopefuls who are thrilled to achieve *prestasi* and national recognition for both themselves and their province, regional prospects are tightly bound up with personal aspirations.

Political consciousness and relationality thus emerge as crucial to understanding the consequences of achievement in this newly devolved region of Indonesia: achievement psychology in Kepri is resolutely political, not only in the way that political discourses might inspire people to understand certain things as achievement, but also in as far as the experience of existing within particular political relations shapes the interpretive beliefs through which actually achieving is experienced, understood and responded to: on how the social life of achievement rolls forward. This point – which is at once simple and yet opens a window into processes that are enormously complex – has largely been ignored by the huge numbers of researchers who have compared achievement psychology in different settings, who persistently interpret the difference they are exploring as one of 'cultural values' (often cast in rather a reified and immutable way) as opposed to existence within particular political matrices. Yet, as achievement levels become an increasingly explicit object of reflection amongst governments – and within schools and families – worldwide, the lessons that we can learn from Kepri stand to be of tremendous value in understanding – or at least opening up new ways of thinking about – social lives of achievement around the world.

Acknowledgements

Research for this chapter was supported by the Economic and Social Research Council (grant numbers PTA-031-2004-00183 and RES-000-22-4632), by a British Academy Postdoctoral Fellowship, and by a Junior Research Fellowship at St Catharine's College, Cambridge. Institutional sponsorship was provided by LIPI, Kementerian RISTEK, Universitas Riau, and STISIPOL Raja Haji.

Notes

1. The problem was compounded by the perpetuation of a (post)colonial stereotype that Malays – the ethnic group associated with the Riau Islands – were 'lazy' and unsuited to capitalist activity (Long 2009).
2. See, e.g., the arguments by M.S. Suwardi in Isjoni Ishaq (2002).
3. Contemporary human resource politics might thus offer an explanation for the seemingly high levels of 'social-oriented achievement motivation' – defined as self-realisation through conformity to the externally imposed values of an in-group (Yu and Yang 1994: 246) – that psychologists have recorded in Indonesia but hitherto attributed to a reifying model of 'collectivist values' stemming from an Islamic and agricultural tradition (e.g., Liem and Nie 2008).
4. Similar attitudes have been documented amongst Qur'anic recitation students in south Sulawesi, who told Gade that, 'one makes up for lack of talent by being motivated and inspired which is better than talent' (Gade 2002: 360).
5. The Museum was known as the Museum Rekor Indonesia (Indonesian Record Museum) until 2005.
6. See Museum Rekor-Dunia Indonesia: <http://www.muri.org/> (accessed 1 August 2011).
7. A video of this event is available online at: <http://www.youtube.com/watch?v=amnQbv4V6BM> (accessed 10 April 2012).

References

Ardi, S. 2002. *Amuk Melayu dalam Tuntutan Provinsi Kepulauan Riau*. Pekanbaru: Unri Press.

Aspinall, E., and G. Fealy (eds). 2003. *Local Power and Politics in Indonesia: Decentralisation and Democratisation*. Singapore: ISEAS.

Budiman, A. 1979. Modernization, Development and Dependence: A Critique of the Present Model of Indonesian Development. In *What Is Modern Indonesian Culture?* (ed.) G. Davis, 201–224. Athens: Ohio University Centre for International Studies.

Clance, P.R., and S.A. Imes. 1978. The Impostor Phenomenon in High Achieving Women: Dynamics and Therapeutic Intervention. *Psychotherapy : Theory, Research and Practice* 15, no. 3: 241–247.

Clance, P.R., and M.A. O'Toole. 1987. The Impostor Phenomenon: An Internal Barrier to Empowerment and Achievement. *Women and Therapy* 6, no. 3: 51–64.

Cole, A.L., and J.G. Knowles. 2001. *Lives in Context: The Art of Life History Research*. Lanham, MD: AltaMira Press.

D'Andrade, R.G. 1992. Schemas and Motivation. In *Human Motives and Cultural Models* (eds) R.G. D'Andrade and C. Strauss, 23–44. Cambridge: Cambridge University Press.

Dweck, C.S. 1999. *Self-Theories: Their Role in Motivation, Personality and Development*. Philadelphia: Psychology Press.

Gade, A.M. 2002. Taste, Talent, and the Problem of Internalization: A Qur'ānic Study in Religious Musicality from Southeast Asia. *History of Religions* 41, no. 4: 328–368.

Hollan, D.W. 1992. Cross-Cultural Differences in the Self. *Journal of Anthropological Research* 48, no. 4: 283–300.

Isjoni Ishaq (ed.). 2002. *Orang Melayu: Sejarah, Sistem, Norma dan Nilai Adat*. Pekanbaru: Unri Press.

Jaya Suprama. 2012. Sekapur Sirih dari Ketua Umum Muri. In *Rekor-Rekor Muri 2008-2009* (ed.) A. Sarwono, ix–x. Jakarta: Kompas Gramedia.

Leach, J. 2003. *Creative Land: Place and Procreation on the Rai Coast of Papua New Guinea*. Oxford: Berghahn.

Liem, A.D., and Y. Nie. 2008. Values, Achievement Goals, and Individual–Oriented and Social–Oriented Achievement Motivations among Chinese and Indonesian Secondary School Students. *International Journal of Psychology* 43, no. 5: 898–903.

Long, N. 2009. Fruits of the Orchard: Land, Space and State in Kepulauan Riau. *SOJOURN: Journal of Social Issues in Southeast Asia* 24, no. 1: 60–88.

Long, N.J. 2007. How to Win a Beauty Contest in Tanjung Pinang. *Review of Indonesian and Malaysian Affairs* 41, no. 1: 91–117.

——— 2011. On Having Achieved Appropriation: *Anak Berprestasi* in Kepri, Indonesia. In *Ownership and Appropriation* (eds) V. Strang and M. Busse, 43–64. Oxford: Berg.

——— 2013. *Being Malay in Indonesia: Histories, Hopes and Citizenship in the Riau Archipelago*. Singapore: NUS Press.

McClelland, D.C. 1961. *The Achieving Society*. Princeton: van Nostrand.

McClelland, D.C., J.W. Atkinson, R.A. Clark and E.L. Lowell. 1953. *The Achievement Motive*. New York: Appleton-Century-Crofts.

McMichael, P., and B. Boyd. 1994. *Towards a Climate of Achievement*. Glasgow: Quality in Education Centre, University of Strathclyde.

Murray, H.A. [1938] 2008. *Explorations in Personality*. Oxford: Oxford University Press.

Mushalli, E. 2010. Tri Lomba Juang Akan Masuk Rekor Muri. <http://edwardmushalli.wordpress.com/2010/06/29/tri-lomba-juang-akan-masuk-rekor-muri/> (accessed 9 August 2010).

Nandy, A. 1987. *Tradition, Tyranny and Utopias: Essays in the Politics of Awareness.* Delhi: Oxford University Press.

Reid, A. 1988. *Southeast Asia in the World of Commerce 1450–1680,* Vol. 1: *The Lands Below the Winds.* New Haven: Yale University Press.

Rowlands, M. 1994. The Material Culture of Success: Ideals and Life Cycles in Cameroon. In *Consumption and Identity* (ed.) J. Friedman, 106–119. Reading: Harwood Academic.

Shweder, R.A., and E.J. Bourne. 1984. Does the Concept of the Person Vary Cross-Culturally? In *Culture Theory: Essays on Mind, Self, and Emotion* (eds) R.A. Shweder and R.A. LeVine, 158–199. Cambridge: Cambridge University Press.

Strassler, K. 2006. *Reformasi* Though Our Eyes: Children as Witnesses of History in Post-Suharto Indonesia. *Visual Anthropology Review* 22, no. 2: 53–70.

Strathern, M. 2009. Land: Intangible or Tangible Property? In *Land Rights* (ed.) T. Chesters, 13–38. Oxford: Oxford University Press.

Suara Merdeka. 2009. Replika Lele Pecahkan Rekor Muri. *Suara Merdeka,* 9 August 2009. <http://suaramerdeka.com/v1/index.php/read/cetak/2009/08/09/76010/Replika.Lele.Pecahkan.Rekor.Muri> (accessed 9 September 2010).

Sutton, R.A. 1991. *Traditions of Gamelan Music in Java: Musical Pluralism and Regional Identity.* Cambridge: Cambridge University Press.

Yu, A.-B., and K.-S. Yang. 1994. The Nature of Achievement Motivation in Collectivist Societies. In *Individualism and Collectivism: Theory, Methods, and Applications* (eds) U. Kim, H.C. Triandis, C. Kagitcibasi, S.C. Choi and G. Yoon, 239–250. Newbury Park: Sage.

5

Directive and Definitive Knowledge
Experiencing Achievement in a Thai Meditation Monastery

Joanna Cook

The first time that I heard the famous life story of Khun Yai, one of the most senior *mae chee* (nuns) in the monastery where I do fieldwork, I was one of a large group of Thai and foreign meditation students sitting on the ground outside her room.[1] She spoke animatedly from her wheelchair and her words were translated by a junior *mae chee* for those who could not speak Thai. Her life story involves nine years as a peripatetic renouncer in the jungles of northern Thailand, meeting celestial beings, experiencing supra-mundane protection through the strict observance of her moral precepts, passing on these precepts to celestial beings and bandits, developing the power of 'divine eye', facing wild beasts with whom she communicated telepathically, and surviving as a result of the power of her meditation and morality. Each of these events is a recurrent trope in the hagiographies of Thai saints[2] and the life story was recounted in order to inspire each of us to be diligent in our meditation practice.

The story of this *mae chee*'s life was recounted in the exhortation for meditation students to be conscientious in their practice and disciplined in their observance of moral precepts in order that they might achieve meditative insight. The three tenets central to meditation as it is practiced and taught in this monastery are impermanence, suffering and 'non-self' (*anicca, dhukkha, anattā*). By bringing the three characteristics (as they are referred to) into their awareness on a moment-by-moment basis through mental discipline, the meditators with whom I work explicitly intend to change their world-view and cut attachment to a sense of self. Through meditation, practitioners intend to experience, not just to know, that there is no 'self' which exists. The Buddhist principle of 'non-self' (*anattā*) is intended to be realised as a psychological reality through the practice of *vipassanā*: it is intended that through this self-willed ascetic practice volition may be eradicated.[3] 'Non-self' presents an interesting counterpoint to analytical approaches to achievement that emphasise augmentation of the self, or directional striving motivated by desire to achieve a goal, both of which are understood in meditative instruction as premised on a delusional conception of 'self'.

It is the experiential insight into 'non-self' that is central to the hagiographic account of this *mae chee*'s life as it is recounted to meditators. In this chapter I consider how we might understand 'non-self' as an achievement in the context of meditation practice and hagiography (the biography of saints) in this monastery and what the implications of this might be for the anthropology of achievement more broadly. The proposition that a meditator achieves 'non-self' appears paradoxical because it problematically re-inscribes a category (meditator) which is negated through the act of achievement. Drawing on the work of Mair (forthcoming) and Elster (1993), I consider how a negation of the subject might be understood as an achievement. I suggest that an ethnographic exploration of different forms of negation offer alternative ways to explore what we mean by achievement.

Following the work of D'Andrade (1992), I consider 'non-self' as a cultural value that serves to motivate meditators in goal-oriented activity. The advantage of such an approach is to highlight the directive force of, and perceived moral responsibility to respond to, shared cultural understandings. However, I suggest that focusing on the relationship between culture and action in this way maintains a separation between subject and object (in this case between meditator and 'non-self') which does not account for the experience of 'non-self' through meditative discipline. As meditators commit themselves to meditative practice, if it is in any way successful the idea of 'non-self' as a goal or practice becomes incompatible with the end that they are trying to achieve. If this is the case we must conclude that the notion of 'non-self' is either aspired to insincerely or we must devise an alternative way of making sense of achievement and its telos that can take seriously the reported experience of the *mae chee* which whom we began. The analytic question here is how a telos of achievement might be sustained in a context in which notions of the person present in achievement theory cannot apply.

I then consider ways in which 'non-self' might be understood as definitive of the meditator. Rather than interpreting cultural knowledge as representation – as a value or model that can motivate action in pursuit of a specific goal – it is possible to understand the practice of meditation and the intended experience of 'non-self' as an ethical endeavour.[4] Through cultivating forms of mental discipline, meditators intend to attain experiential insight into 'non-self'. In such practice the value of 'non-self' is not external to the practitioner and internalised to a greater or lesser extent (and thereby motivational and directive). Rather, it defines what it is to be a meditator in this monastery. Such knowledge is both communicative and constitutive: the direction of achievement resides within the meditator and is thereby necessarily transformative.

This is illustrated in engagement with the hagiography of a senior *mae chee* recounted as expressive of the achievement of 'non-self'. The use of hagiographic tropes in the life story of a highly respected *mae chee* refers to classical constructs while actively shaping current understandings of 'non-self'. Narrative convention must be understood as constitutive as well as communicative. Such tropes become intrinsic to the way in which those who employ them perceive and organise their experience within the world. Hagiographic tropes include tales of virtues, dhammic teachings, practices and supra-mundane powers. They locate the subject of a particular narrative within a lineage of teachers that is understood to stretch back to the Buddha himself. It is this convention that connotes the authenticity of a saint's 'achievement' of the principles of renunciatory self-fashioning. But there remains a paradox between the loss of self, characteristic of the saint, on the one hand, and the communication of that loss on the other. What must remain central to our understanding of the narration is the impact that it has on the narrator, both as lived experience and as a means by which they organise their experience and self-awareness.

Negation as Achievement

In the meditation monastery, the Buddhist soteriological principle of 'non-self' is considered to be the way in which practitioners ought to understand themselves (but for the cognitive distortion of a perceived sense of self one would have a true understanding of the world in which the 'self' is rightly understood as nothing more than an impermanent compound); as such, the realisation of 'non-self' becomes a moral imperative.[5] Paradoxically, one's concern then becomes the ethical project of making oneself a certain kind of person – a project that is actualised through self-willed ascetic practice, the intention behind which is the eradication of the will and the direct realisation of 'non-self'. The achievement of insight into 'non-self' through meditation cannot be straightforwardly understood as 'meditator achieves 'non-self''. Framing the experiential insight into 'non-self' in terms of the language of the attainment of a goal implies an agentive self. As such, the proposition 'meditator achieves insight' – a formulation that would be very normal in most anthropologies of achievement – problematically re-inscribes a category of 'meditator' that is inconsistent with the nature of the insight achieved. The motivation behind and experience of meditation practice for these monastics demand that we consider possible forms of negation as achievement.

In a recent article, Mair (forthcoming) considers the ways in which we might understand claims to 'ignorance' in Buddhism.[6] Building on the work of the political psychologist Elster (1993), Mair examines the difference between forms of 'internal' and 'external' negation. He takes the affirmative proposition that 'A believes *p*' and considers Elster's three negations of this. He argues that while 'the passivity of external negation is uniform (everyone who is passively not a stamp collector is a non-stamp collector in the same way), there may be important distinctions between different forms of active, internal negation' (Mair forthcoming). The distinction between Elster's three forms of negation are important. If for example, the object is belief in God on the part of the subject ('Tom'), the distinctions in not believing become those between an active belief that God does not exist, reflective agnosticism, and the external negation of passive agnosticism:

> Tom believes God exists
> Tom doesn't have such a belief
> Tom believes God does not exist
> Tom disbelieves that God exists
> (Mair forthcoming)

Building on this, if the object of achievement is an ethical telos, such as experiential insight into 'non-self', say, on the part of a meditator, then we can identify a clear difference between internal and external negations:

> meditator achieves insight
> not (meditator achieves insight)
> meditator achieves not-(insight)
> meditator not-(achieves) insight

The external negation would refer to anyone who has not experienced such insight. Importantly, an external negation says nothing about the quality of the negative. Such a negation might refer to anyone who has not had this experience (as it would to anyone who does not collect stamps).

In the first of Elster and Mair's internal negations, the negation is of insight, the telos of meditation. The meditator has achieved the opposite of insight. Examples of such an achievement are common in the meditation monastery. It is thought that without proper guidance it is possible for meditators to have a few profound experiences during meditation and to take these to be evidence of substantial meditative attainment. Because of their delusional sense of their meditative achievement, the meditator would not be able to progress further in the practice and would remain stuck. This was referred to as *vipassanā kilesa* (or *vipassanā* defilement). This negation appears to be one of failure. The meditator has achieved something but it is not the experiential insight into 'non-self'. Claims to meditative attainment are problematic because they may be taken as evidence of a delusional sense of self rather than the attainment of 'non-self' through meditative discipline. Working out who offers an example of meditative mastery is of great concern to monastics and laity alike.[7]

The second internal negation would refer here to actively not-achieving. The negation rests on achievement itself. An obvious interpretation of this might be the active avoiding of spiritual attainment. One might have very good reasons for wanting to remain in a delusional world of sensory desire and gratification. This possibility formed the basis of a discussion I had with a group of *mae chee* about equanimity. One of the primary characteristics associated with the Buddha is his equanimity, to which monastics aspire. The ability to work tirelessly without emotion, to remain composed in the face of large demands, are experiences and concerns treated as an important index of meditative achievement. A senior *mae chee* reflected that, with experiential insight into 'non-self', our emotional state would be one of continuous equanimity:

> We'd still sweep the monastery, still have hunger, thirst, get tummy ache. We'd still have to be hot or cold in the same way as we do now but we wouldn't have emotion attached to any of this. If we have happiness then we also have anger, but a great teacher is still able to teach, it's not that they just stay doing nothing at all but that they have equanimity and so will not have happiness or sadness developing. They have loving-kindness to give and so have to smile, but they don't laugh like we do when we joke about. There is no like and dislike, no preference.

A junior *mae chee* in our party reflected on this possibility, wryly commenting that it sounded quite boring and that she liked laughing loudly, at which we all laughed and conversation bubbled along.

In the first internal negation (meditator achieves not-insight), it is the value of achievement itself that is negated. In the second (meditator not-achieves insight) the negative sign applies specifically to the act of achieving – it is an actively negative relation to the act of achievement. I would like to propose a fourth negation of the proposition 'meditator achieves insight', in addition to those explored by Elster and Mair, which might help us to account for the valorisation and recognition of forms of achievement in which the subject is negated:

not-(meditator) achieves insight

In this, a third internal negation, the meditator is negated but achievement of telos occurs. In the monastery where I work such an achievement is recognised as evidenced in the potential perfectibility to which monastics aspire. This highlights a problematic relationship between motivation and achievement: if the will is to be eradicated through the realisation of 'non-self', does this paradoxically eliminate the intention that motivates meditation?

Directive and Definitive Knowledge: Achieving 'Non-Self'

The relationship between motivational striving and goal-oriented activity is of central interest to the interdisciplinary study of achievement (see, e.g., Casson 1983; D'Andrade 1984, 1990, 1992; Strauss 1992; Elliot 2005). Within anthropology, theorists have been concerned with the relationship between culture and action, moving away from a fixed catalogue of human motivations and focusing instead on culturally specific interpretations of given situations. D'Andrade states: 'something counts as an achievement when certain actions, evaluated by some kind of standard excellence, are judged to be exceptional or outstanding. Standards of excellence are things which people construct, they are not things in the world. Achievement is a culturally constructed object *par excellence*' (D'Andrade 1992: 35). In his analysis of achievement, D'Andrade argues that goal-directed behaviour involves striving for something and emotional reactions to success or failure in pursuit of that goal. He identifies goals as motivational; motivation is experienced subjectively as a desire or wish, followed by a feeling of satisfaction once that wish has been fulfilled or frustration if it has been thwarted.

Human goals, in all their complexity, are interpreted as underpinned by forms of 'cultural schemas' – conceptual structures which make possible the identification of objects and events.[8] Schemas organise perceptions of action and form the basis for interpreting others' discourse about experience. They have a 'directive force' – the goals of a given schema are 'embedded' within the schema itself. Thus, a schema is a cultural model with a directive force (Casson 1983: 430), and the cognitive representation of cultural knowledge shapes motivation (Strauss 1992). Schemas, for D'Andrade, are processes related to specific interpretations:

> such a schema is more than just a recognition process by which an achievement can be identified when it occurs; it has the potential of instigating action; that is, for some people it is a goal. Of course, the strength of instigation depends at any one point on the important particulars involved in each interpretive instance – what can be achieved, the difficulties and rewards involved, how that kind of achievement is related to one's own situation and abilities, etc. (D'Andrade 1992: 29)

Particular cultural schemas for achievement may function as goals and have the potential to instigate action in pursuit of such achievements. Generic concepts are stored in memory as packaged units (schemata) (see also Abelson 1968), which are composed of both knowledge and information about how that knowledge is to be used (Rumelhart 1980). This knowledge is held in an isolated or bounded way. Rumelhart (ibid.) argues further that 'bounded knowledge' of this sort may also be joined to forms of knowledge that are less bounded, and that different forms of knowledge can be joined in diverse configurations.

If we interpret meditative aspirations and experiences in this way, 'non-self' emerges as a cultural value that motivates action. 'Non-self' is understood as a shared value in which the 'goal' of its experience is embedded. Indeed, the founder of the monastery states that it is the duty (*na ti*) of all human beings to free themselves from suffering and that the practice of *vipassanā* meditation is the only means of doing so. He argues that until this is realised, 'our lives will be aimless, like one who walks in darkness, unaware of dangers ahead; like a bird circling over the ocean, unable to find land'. In *dhamma* talks and meditation training, he teaches that the central focus of Buddhism is the purification of the mind, and for this reason (that Buddhism is true and its central teachings are there to be actualised by everyone) all humans are born to effect spiritual improvement on themselves. Just as D'Andrade (1984) interpreted American beliefs about success as a cultural model that has a strong directive force, we can understand 'non-self' as one of the fundamental principles motivating *vipassanā* practice in this monastery to provide a directional model for action. Monastics intend to experience 'non-self' through the practice of meditation and interpret monastic duty and their responses to interpersonal encounters through their awareness of this.

In a consideration of cultural schemas, Strauss suggests that we question what is meant by 'culture' in such an approach: 'If we conceive of culture monistically – everything is symbols or discourses, which differ only in meaning and position in the ordering of experience – then it is difficult to talk about different *kinds* of cultural values and motivational force' (Strauss 1992: 220–21). Strauss (ibid.) unpacks alternative ways in which cognitive representations of cultural knowledge relate to motivational effect. Focusing on five Rhode Island male blue-collar workers' discussions about what it means to 'get ahead', she considers three different types of knowledge that differ in content: cognitive representation, form of expression and motivational effect. Firstly, those values which are seen as cultural values (such as some success values) did not determine behaviour but had a directive force to the extent that they were internalised and affected each man's self-esteem. Secondly, 'experience-near' (Geertz 1984: 125) internalised social judgements, which were understood not as values but as inescapable facts of life, were much more influential in shaping behaviour. Directive force developed through adhering to what were seen as the constraints of reality rather than abstract social values such as 'the American dream' of the 'self-made man' (see also Schweder 1992). Thirdly, she identifies personal semantic networks, which also orient people towards goals but through self-defining efforts. These networks are partly understood as values but are not apprehended in their entirety: 'Personal semantic networks are the idiosyncratic webs of meaning carried by each person, linking individually salient verbal symbols to memories of significant life experiences and conscious self-understandings' (Strauss 1992: 211).

Thus, Strauss is able to demonstrate that while some cultural constructs are used in an 'un-self-conscious' way (because they 'go without saying') others are shared values and are consciously apprehended: 'Each of these models represents different forms of knowledge and awareness – different *ways of believing*. These ways of believing are not reducible to differences in content, but involve different forms of cognitive representation and conscious apprehension' (ibid.: 219). Bounded or unbounded forms of knowledge direct action to the extent that the practitioner engages with them in pursuit of goals for which they provide the motivating force. In this formulation, a separation between culture and action is fundamental to their relationship in order for culture to be the motivating force behind action. This is challenged by the experience of 'non-self' through meditative discipline to which meditators aspire. In order to understand 'non-self' as achievement, there must be a point at which cultural knowledge becomes definitive of the practitioner. Cultural 'schemas' are no longer 'out there' as motivation (predictive knowledge) but are defining of the practitioner (definitive). While exploring the content and directive force of cultural knowledge – cultural schema in D'Andrade's work – is useful for thinking about 'non-self' as a 'goal' of meditation, it remains antithetical to its practice and experience. The implication I identify in Strauss's work is that culture is not only motivational but has a constitutive or definitional relation to action.

It is not the case that 'non-self' is an experience either sought or achieved by all Buddhists, or even all meditators, but for monastics in this monastery it is a central concern. As Collins writes:

> Not-self is a secondary theory. In Buddhism human beings are 'directly given' as embodied persons and social agents, both monastic and lay; the ultimate truth of the changing, transmigrating flux of consciousness and karmic causality is hidden, and must be discovered through meditation ... [T]he occasions when secondary theory actually replaces primary theory are necessarily those of specialised practices conducted by trained experts: exorcisms and spirit lore, laboratories and academic publications, and in the Buddhist case the monastic practices of meditation and scholarly textual activity. (Collins 1994: 73)

The religious professionals with whom I work are striving to actualise such secondary theory as an embodied, ongoing reality. They engage in specific practices in order to change their experiences in relation to religious concepts; that is, they learn and practice with intent and in so doing religious tenets become real. By observing the conditions of the body and the mind, practitioners detach themselves from their involvement with these conditions sufficiently to be able to look *at* them rather than look *through* them. The individual is no longer exclusively identified with these conditions and this creates a psychological 'space' or perspective from which change is effected in the conditions of the body and the mind.

It is believed that through the practice of meditation it is possible to realise and experience ultimate truth: that there is no self that exists, that all things are imperfect and impermanent. The body is broken down into its constituent parts, the feelings are isolated and examined apart from their causes, bodily desire is subdued and the mind is quietened. During retreat this mental discipline slowly extends to a conscious awareness in minute detail of what one is doing both bodily and mentally in each moment. The practitioner uses the process of mental noting to observe and detach from the normal processes of the body and mind, such as grief, sleep, pain, doubt, restlessness or desire. In order to do this it is necessary to see all mental and physical phenomena as neutral, responding to them with neither desire nor aversion but rather developing a position of equanimity and balance. Through cultivated discipline, each mental and physical movement becomes evidence of religious principles at the same time as people actively learn to interpret their subjectivity through such principles.

Through disciplined meditation the practitioner learns to experience thoughts and emotions not as the uninteresting slough of the daily grind but rather as evidence of the fundamental truths of Buddhism: that all phenomena are conditioned by 'non-self', impermanence and suffering. Through dedicated work it is intended that the three characteristics are to be experienced.

Paradoxically, the subjectivity of the ascetic self contains an ambiguity between the intention to eradicate the will, the expression of will through ascetic practice and the experience of the dissolution of the will as a result of that practice. Practically, this involves the experience of 'non-self' by the individual as a result of the assertion of the self in willed ascetic practice.

In a consideration of the transformational capacities of religious language, Latour argues that some language 'does not speak *of* things, but *from* things': 'there exist forms of speech – and again it is not just language – that are able to transfer persons not information, either because they produce in part personhood, or because new states, "new beginnings" – as William James would say – are generated in the persons thus addressed' (Latour 2005: 30). Rather than the content of the speech act having a directive force on something or someone separate from it, it is itself transformative. The transformation is not external to the person participating in the act (either speaking or being spoken to) – it is not the transformation of the person in response to the cultural value; rather, it is internal to the person: the act itself becomes definitive of the person. In such speech acts, cultural value is not principally about the transfer of information in relation to which one might orient oneself. Similarly, I understand the experience of 'non-self' through the practice of meditation and (as I will argue below) hagiography may be understood as constitutive of the monastic. 'Non-self' as a secondary theory is no longer a cultural value which may be internalised to a lesser or greater extent and thereby act as a directive force for the disciplined meditator. Rather, achievement and 'non-self' are understood as definitive of experience. In so far as achievement of 'non-self' is understood as internally definitive of the person, it cannot be understood exclusively as an external category or type of cultural value (cf. Ryle 1949). It is not 'out there' having directive force on action but rather creatively recast in the relationships in which it is iterated; it does not represent but transforms. As Holbraad sums up Latour, 'each of these "speech-acts" conspires to efface its own propositional force so as to render present, in the act, the intimacy of the relation itself' (Holbraad 2004).

This is to draw a distinction between predictive and definitive relations. 'Meditator achieves 'non-self'' is predictive when 'meditator' is a substance and 'non-self' is one of its qualities; 'meditator achieves 'non-self'' is definitive when 'non-self' serves to define the meaning of 'meditator'. Definitional relations (such as that between meditator and 'non-self') are 'internal' while predictive ones are 'external'. The ascetic paradox – of the dissolution of the will through self-willed discipline (see Flood 2004) – rests on the relation 'meditator achieves 'non-self'' being predictive (external). However, if 'meditator achieves 'non-self'' is construed as definitive then the paradox is dissolved. The meditator is now 'defined as' the achievement of 'non-self'. In other words, to be a meditator in this monastery is to have the capacity to experience 'non-self' (see also Viveiros de Castro 2007). Meditation, then, is a matter of directing capacities in particular ways. This is not necessarily a resurfacing of the paradox – if it were, who would be doing the directing? Direction is an immanent property (definitive) of any motion, and as such resides 'within' it. Directive force is no longer dependent on the extent to which the meditator internalises an external cultural value (the relationship between culture and action so clearly illustrated in theories of cognitive schema). 'Non-self', in others words, resides within the meditator as an immanent possibility (cf. Holbraad 2004). The representation of 'non-self' as cultural schema identified in the duty to actualise such a potentiality through meditation is itself transformative because it is constitutive of the meditator. 'Non-self' is external as a motivating cultural value and internal to the meditator as potentiality.

For monastics in this monastery, the cultivation of mental and moral discipline becomes a central concern. Senior meditation masters offer examples of mastery and transfer protective power to meditators through blessings, the sharing of merit and guidance. Reynolds (2005), writing of widespread interest in protective media in Thailand, highlights lay concerns about potency and perfectibility. He argues: 'to be a human in Buddhism is to have the potential for enlightenment as well as for divinity. The Buddha is both the perfected human being and a manifestation of the transcendent potential of becoming perfected' (ibid.: 217). For Reynolds, then, Buddhist practice is largely a self-directed pursuit: 'one relies on one's own reasoning rather than on the authority of someone else, although teachers are of inestimable assistance' (ibid.: 213). The potential for perfectibility through mental and moral discipline is recognised in the aspirations of monastics – a recognition of the forms of potentiality and perfectibility all humans might achieve, as well as a recognition that for some (such as meditation masters) this is already an experiential state. The meaning of achievement in this instance is generated through inter-relational networks, but this cannot be separated from individual responsibility for self-development and the cultivation of moral virtues on the part of the religious practitioner: reflection on the qualities of achievement is of inestimable value in the ongoing and intentional subjective development of the practitioner.

Communicative and Constitutive Narrative Achievement

The story of Khun Yai's life was recounted in the exhortation for meditation students to be diligent in their practice and disciplined in their observance of moral precepts. At key points in Khun Yai's narration she paused to emphasise the need for meditation and moral observance:

> Start from morality, concentration and then wisdom. If you set half an hour for meditation before you go to sleep, you see who will come to visit, what will happen. And on the next day it is as you saw it in meditation, even the colour of the clothes they wear. The light of the mind has power more than any light; it is the light of wisdom.

The account is beautiful – it tells of hardships, heroic discipline and the steadfast faith of the protagonist. It vividly demonstrates some of the things that are of value in the community and that are respected by renouncers and laity alike. It connects the spiritual heroism of the Buddha, the lives of Thai saints, and is embodied in the personage of the narrator at whose feet the listeners sit. Khun Yai is widely believed to possess the supra-mundane powers of 'divine eye' and 'divine ear', and she is a renowned fortune-teller. Devotees throughout the country make pilgrimages to the monastery to receive her blessing. Sitting at the feet of a senior *mae chee* listening to the account of her life, it was impossible to distinguish between hagiographic trope and personal detail, and this is precisely why the account was of such value.

Hagiography may be interpreted as curricular of achievement; it connotes an exemplary life. Others recognise the authenticity of a saint's perfection through their total occupation of the hagiographic narrative.[9] In the Buddhist textual traditions, hagiographies establish a connection with a pristine past, and establish lineages of teachers and lives. The subjects of hagiographies may have their past lives revealed to them in meditation, or may be taught divinely by the Buddha or arahants,[10] thereby establishing a teaching lineage connecting them directly with the Buddha. Importantly, traditions are transmitted and subsequently traced through accounts of teaching lineages and genealogies. The form that the narrative takes implicitly associates the subject with other hagiographical subjects (the content sometimes does so explicitly), so that each story is associated with those that preceded it. It is expected that the life of a saint, recounted in biography, will encompass miracles, healing and other expressions of holiness. Through the transfer of stories from the Buddha and arahants to the stories of twentieth-century saints, that which indicates holiness remains constrained. However, de Certeau suggests that hagiography should not be limited to its 'authenticity' or 'historical value' (de Certeau 1988: 270), whether or not the story is true, and that the hagiographic conformity of these tales and their location in relation to different lineages connotes for the reader precisely the authenticity of a saint's compassion and renunciation of worldly attachment. In hagiographic writing, the acts, places and themes documented in the life of the saint refer not only to 'what took place' but also, importantly, to 'what is exemplary' (see Schober 1997: 2). The stories of the Buddha and arahants offer exemplary models for Buddhist practice, discipline and moral precepts. Subsequent biographies have repeated aspects of, or sequences from, these lives. While maintaining formulaic episodes, hagiographies provide important details about their subjects, located in a specific time and place and in relation to other teachers and students. This contextualisation of the saint (and, by extension, the biographer) within a lineage provides an important verification of the purity of their teaching.

So, what we might take from the 'cavalier plagiarism' (Tambiah 1984: 127) of hagiographic narrative is that which is significant in Buddhist culture. The life of the Buddha is, after all, an exemplification of Buddhist values (Carrithers 1996): his witnessing of sickness, old age and death, his subsequent turning away from worldly pleasures and renunciation of family life; his forays into austere self-mortification before discovery of the 'middle way'; temptation and enlightenment beneath the bodhi tree; and subsequent teaching, meditation and peripateticism – these moments in a life, his or those of subsequent saints, may be used to teach the value of abstract moral principles, such as renunciation, compassion, 'non-self', mindfulness. Thus, it is possible to remove the narrative from the context in which it was told in order to say something abstract but nonetheless significant about Thai Buddhist values.

For all its conformity to convention it would be wrong to suppose that hagiography has one true meaning; it may maintain a permanent meaningfulness but it does not only do this.[11] Carrithers (1992: 105–6) argues that the meaning of narrative is negotiated through relationships (see also Gergen and Gergen 1984). It cannot be understood exclusively in terms of an abstract schedule of motives, which are themselves explicable in terms of culture. Rather, common meaning is created interactively and it is this which is primary for understanding which interpretation of narrative is taken seriously. As he puts it, 'The sense of all stories, indeed all utterances, is dependent on the character of the human relationships that bear them' (Carrithers 1992: 106). Narrative at once preserves 'cultural values' and at the same time is 'subject to the vicissitudes of the actual historical relationships within which it is recounted' (ibid.: 107).

Hagiographic accounts bespeak spiritual attainment. If followers are to have the same experience, it is unlikely that they will be capable of having it yet. In the exhortation to practise meditation through the example of this *mae chee*'s own experience, the narrative takes the form of 'how I came to be who I am' (Lejeune 1989). The apparent risk of performative contradiction (I assert I am not a self) is avoided through hagiographic convention. Thus, the portrayal of 'non-self' through the narrative of the life-story locates the speaker within the tradition of 'non-self'. Listeners place themselves in the story and are marked by its impression (Stewart 1996: 31): 'stories not only allow but actively produce an excess of meaningfulness, a constant searching' (ibid.: 58; see also Sperber 1975; Chambers 1991; Strathern 1991). The boundary between the subject and tradition is obscured, and it is the total occupation of this discourse that identifies one as a saint. If hagiographic tropes are to be understood as cultural schema in this instance, they have been totally internalised by the subject. This suggests that they are fundamentally transformative and definitive of both narrative and narrator. Rather than understanding them in terms of their representation of cultural values, narrative tropes here cannot be removed from the 'flow of action' (Carrithers 1992: 93).

The evocation and interpretation of the life of the Buddha demanded by the meeting of the narrator and the listener suggests that the telling is itself a space of imagination produced and mediated through the form of the narrative itself. It is the experiential insight into 'non-self' – a secondary concern for the vast majority of Thai Buddhists – that is evidenced in this *mae chee*'s narrative of achievement and in the imminent potential of the meditator. Rather than reducing the hagiography to a plotted collection of abstract and conventional ideas grounded in 'tradition', its meaning is dialogic and emergent in practice (see Bakhtin 1981); importantly, what makes it so is its textual fidelity. While the hagiography may be abstracted as a fixed representation of achievement it is also a transformative space; as Stewart writes of 'culture', 'a space produced in the slippage, or gap, between sign and referent, event and meaning, and gathered into performed forms and tactile reminders' (Stewart 1996: 26–27).

Conclusion

Focusing on the exhortation to be diligent in meditation practice intended through the recounting of Khun Yai's life story, I have examined what meditative insight in a Buddhist monastery in northern Thailand might mean for the anthropology of achievement. It is possible to interpret 'non-self' as goal and motivation in the achievement of meditative insight. Through an examination of the work of D'Andrade and Strauss I suggested that we may interpret 'non-self' as a form of culturally valued knowledge which motivates action and which may be internalised to a greater or lesser extent. However, an implication of Strauss's work on the internalisation of cultural schema is that it must at some point move beyond the motivational – cultural value is not necessarily always motivating action from a position external to the subject. Using the work of Latour I suggested that an understanding of culture as speaking *from* achievement rather than speaking *of* the subject offers particularly useful insights for this case (and affords the possibility that those insights might apply to other fields) because it makes more sense of the monastic ethical endeavour in the ongoing process of self-cultivation.

The implication here is that the internalisation of certain notions of achievement is not just a cognitive process but also an ethical one. For monastics, the achievement of 'non-self' is definitive of how they understand themselves and of the 'selves' that they progressively produce through disciplined practice. Through dedicated work this religious value is to be experienced by the practitioner. Such an achievement appears to challenge the formulation 'meditator achieves 'non-self'' – which problematically re-inscribes the category of meditator with the achievement of its negation. I suggested that the internal negation – not (meditator) achieves insight – points towards the potential perfectibility to which monastics aspire. 'Non-self' is not reducible to an external cultural value which is either in a predictive relationship to the meditator or exerts a directive force on the meditator. While such external relationships are an important motivation for achievement because they provide models for behaviour, they are also transformative to the extent that they are the grounds from which the meditator apperceives all phenomena – they are implicit in the potentiality from which the meditator acts. Negation becomes definitive of the meditator as they experience themselves through ethical endeavour.

Hagiography here provides a clear illustration of the point at which 'cultural schemas' intersect with transformative processes of person-making. This demands that we reframe 'culture' not only as representation with directive force (as this implies a unitary notion of the self in an external relationship with culture) but also as constitutive of the relationships that bear it. I considered both the constancy of hagiographic tropes that are used to identify experiential insight, and the transformative nature of hagiography in context. While we might interpret hagiography as a narrative of achievement which reflects Buddhist values, to do so exclusively would occlude the dialogic character of narrative by which it is made meaningful in practice. Hagiographic convention may connote multiple values – in the context of the meditation monastery it is coupled with the injunction to practice diligently in order to achieve insight into the Buddhist tenet of 'non-self'. Hagiography may be understood as communicative and constitutive. For this reason, I suggest, achievement here is not reducible to the ability to occupy a 'cultural schema' to a greater or lesser extent. This approach emphasises the demands of the relationship with oneself and others in aspiring towards personal achievement. While recognising the significance of the constancy of hagiographic tropes in this context, I suggest that aspiration, recognition and achievement are dialogically constituted. Narratives, like culture, are transformative; it is through them that 'meaning' is mediated.

Acknowledgements

I am grateful to Nick Long, Martin Holbraad and the anonymous reviewer for insightful comments on earlier drafts of this chapter.

Notes

1. There are no formally recognised, fully ordained Theravada Buddhist nuns in Thailand. Women who wish to be ordained can do so either by seeking an ordination abroad or by becoming a *mae chee*. *Mae chee* receive either eight or ten Buddhist precepts, wear white-coloured robes and shave their heads. They commit themselves to a life of renunciation, usually living in monasteries or nunneries.
2. 'Saint' here is used to refer to an individual who is believed to have achieved transcendental states of mind by Thai Buddhists. I do not limit the term 'saint' to persons who are believed to have attained full awakening (arahant).
3. I interpret the intended shaping of the monastic self through disciplined meditative work in this monastery as a form of ascetic practice. Buddhist monasteries in Thailand vary wildly in focus and institutional organisation, and we must be careful not to assume a necessary correlation between monasticism and asceticism, or indeed between meditation and asceticism, in any given context. I do not use the term 'ascetic' to describe all people who 'renounce the world' or become monastics: to be a monastic one does not have to engage in ascetic practices and vice versa. I employ an analysis of 'asceticism' in the Greek sense of *askesis*, or way of life by which some forms of activity are inhibited, while others are developed, through specific strenuous forms of religious discipline (cf. Brown 1988;

Ishwaran 1999; Flood 2004). I argue that ascetic practice gains its force as the means by which individual monastics in this monastery develop subjective processes of interiority within the context of the monastic community, which ultimately lead to the removal of individuality. In Dumont's (1980) terms, it is through ascetic practice that people become 'individuals': they develop a 'self', which it is their duty to patrol and fashion. At the same time, however, it is through such practice that the person cultivates what Flood (2004) terms an 'ascetic interiority' through which self, desire and volition are eradicated.

4. I argue that the existence of an ascetic and ethical ideal provides a telos and a technology for cultivating such a reality, which individuals incorporate into their understandings of themselves and by which they constitute themselves as ethical subjects. The focus upon ethical self-formation as a means of understanding the psychosocial experience of monasticism resonates with a broader emerging field in the anthropology of ethics (cf. Laidlaw 2002; Robbins 2004; Lester 2005; Mahmood 2005; Hirschkind 2006).
5. On ethical practice and moral imperative in Jainism, see Laidlaw (2002: 321).
6. Mair's concern is to consider the relation of potential knowers to potential knowledge, and cultivated detachment from knowledge that might make forms of not-knowing a distinct ethical virtue: 'One might speculate that the number of things one is passively agnostic about is limitless, whereas the number of things one actively refrains from believing is strictly limited' (Mair forthcoming). Mair demonstrates that for the Inner Mongolian Buddhists with whom he works, a relation of 'not knowing' best exemplifies the most pious and appropriate relation to the Dharma. This is an active not-knowing which is cultivated as a disposition, evidenced in an understanding that the deeper knowledge of Buddhism cannot be accessed by the unenlightened. Through talk of ignorance, devotees develop faith in the 'limitless superiority of the Buddhas and lamas of the past who are the objects of their devotions' (ibid.). 'Awareness of this ignorance needs to be nurtured, deepened, and brought constantly to mind in order to guard against the careless arrogance that might allow a novice to act as if it were possible to draw conclusions about any aspect of the teachings, or even to act on those conclusions, or worse still to think that the consequence of acting on those conclusions could ever be calculated' (ibid.). Mair argues convincingly, in my opinion, that non-attainment or not-knowing may themselves become an ethical project.
7. It is forbidden to speak about the attainment of experiential insight, levels of enlightenment or supra-human states; it is considered as major offence (Somdet 1989: 27; Payutto 2010: 338) and the penalty for doing so is expulsion from the order.
8. For a useful review discussion of schemas in cognitive anthropology, see Casson (1983).
9. While the hagiographies of males who have attained the position of the accomplished and charismatic teacher is a long-standing academic and anthropological concern, there is relatively little scholarship on outstanding female Buddhist practitioners (see Cook 2009). See Seeger (2010) for a thorough account of the life of one of the most venerated female saints in contemporary Thai Buddhism.
10. An arahant is one who has attained the highest level of spiritual development, who is free, who will not be reborn again; an enlightened person who has eradicated defilements.
11. See McDaniel (2011) for alternative engagements with the hagiography of the widely revered Thai Buddhist monk Somdet To.

References

Abelson, R. 1968. Polls and Public Opinion: Some Puzzles and Paradoxes. *Transaction* 5, no. 9: 20–27.

Bakhtin, M. 1981. *The Dialogic Imagination* (trans. C. Emerson and M. Holquist). Austin: University of Texas Press.

Brown, P. 1988. *The Body and Society.* New York: Columbia University Press.

Carrithers, M. 1992. *Why Humans Have Cultures: Explaining Anthropology and Social Diversity*. Oxford: Oxford University Press.

——— 1996. *Buddha: A Very Short Introduction*. Oxford: Oxford University Press.

Casson, R. 1983. Schemata in Cognitive Anthropology. *Annual Reviews in Anthropology* 12: 429–462.

Chambers, R. 1991. *Room for Maneuver: Reading (the) Oppositional (in) Narrative*. Chicago: University of Chicago Press.

Collins, S. 1994. What Are Buddhists Doing When They Deny the Self? In *Religion and Practical Reason: New Essays in the Comparative Philosophy of Religions* (eds) F. Reynolds and D. Tracy, 59–86. New York: State University of New York Press.

Cook, J. 2009. Hagiographic Narrative and Monastic Practice: Buddhist Morality and Mastery amongst Thai Buddhist Nuns. *Journal of the Royal Anthropological Institute* 15, no. 2: 349–364.

D'Andrade, R. 1984. Cultural Meaning Systems. In *Cultural Theory: Essays on Mind, Self, and Emotion* (eds) R. Schweder and R. LeVine, 88–119. Cambridge: Cambridge University Press.

——— 1990. Some Propositions about the Relations between Culture and Human Cognition. In *Cultural Psychology: Essays on Comparative Human Development* (eds) J. Stigler, R. Schweder and G. Herdt, 65–129. Cambridge: Cambridge University Press.

——— 1992. Schemas and Motivation. In *Human Motives and Cultural Models* (eds) R. D'Andrade and C. Strauss, 23–44. Cambridge: Cambridge University Press.

De Certeau, M. [1975] 1988. *The Writing of History* (trans. T. Conley). New York: Columbia University Press.

Dumont, L. 1980. *Homo Hierarchicus: The Caste System and its Implications* (rev. edn). Chicago: University of Chicago Press.

Elliot, A.J. 2005. A Conceptual History of the Achievement Goal Construct. In *Handbook of Competence and Motivation* (eds) A.J. Elliot and C.S. Dweck, 52–72. New York: Guilford Press.

Elster, J. 1993. *Political Psychology*. Cambridge: Cambridge University Press.

Flood, G. 2004. *The Ascetic Self: Subjectivity, Memory and Tradition*. Cambridge: Cambridge University Press.

Geertz, C. 1984. 'From the Native's Point of View': On the Nature of Anthropological Understanding. In *Culture Theory: Essays on Mind, Self, and Emotion* (eds) R. Schweder and R. LeVine, 123–136. Cambridge: Cambridge University Press.

Gergen, M. & K. Gergen. 1984. The Social Construction of Narrative Accounts. In *Historical Social Psychology* (eds) K. Gergen and M. Gergen, 173–189. Hillsdale, NJ: Lawrence Erlbaum Associates.

Hirschkind, C. 2006. *The Ethical Soundscape: Cassette Sermons and Islamic Counterpublics*. New York: Columbia University Press.

Holbraad, M. 2004. Response to Bruno Latour's 'Thou Shall not Freeze-Frame'. Available online at <http://nansi.abaetenet.net/abaetextos/response-to-bruno-latours-thou-shall-not-freeze-frame-martin-holbraad> (accessed 30 April 2012).

Ishwaran, K. (ed.). 1999. *Ascetic Culture: Renunciation and Worldly Engagement*. Leiden: Brill.

Laidlaw, J. 2002. For an Anthropology of Ethics and Freedom. *Journal of the Royal Anthropological Institute* 8: 311–332.

Latour, B. 2005. 'Thou Shall Not Freeze-Frame', or, How Not to Misunderstand the Science and Religion Debate. In *Science, Religion, and the Human Experience* (ed.) J. Proctor, 27–49. Oxford: Oxford University Press.

Lejeune, P. [1971] 1989. *On Autobiography* (trans. K. Leary). Minneapolis: University of Minnesota Press.

Lester, R. 2005. *Jesus in Our Wombs: Embodying Modernity in a Mexican Convent.* Berkeley, CA and London: University of California Press.

McDaniel, J. 2011. *The Lovelorn Ghost and the Magical Monk.* New York: Columbia University Press.

Mahmood, S. 2005. *Politics of Piety: The Islamic Revival and the Feminist Subject.* Princeton: Princeton University Press.

Mair, J. forthcoming. The 'Buddhist Knowledge Gap': Ignorance and the Ethics of Detachment in Inner Mongolian Buddhism. In *The End(s) of Engagement: The Ethics and Analytics of Detachment* (eds) M. Candea, J. Cook, C. Trundle and T. Yarrow.

Payutto, P.A. 2010. *Dictionary of Buddhism.* Nonthaburi: Phoem Sap Publishing.

Reynolds, C.J. 2005. Power. In *Critical Terms for the Study of Buddhism* (ed.) D. Lopez, 211–228. Chicago: University of Chicago Press.

Robbins, J. 2004. *Becoming Sinners: Christianity and Moral Torment in a Papua New Guinea Society.* Berkeley: University of California Press.

Rumelhart, D. 1980. Schemata: The Building Blocks of Cognition. In *Theoretical Issues in Reading Comprehension: Perspectives from Cognitive Psychology, Linguistics, Artificial Intelligence, and Education* (eds) R. Spiro, B. Bruce and W. Brewer, 33–58. Hillsdale, NJ: Lawrence Erlbaum.

Ryle, G. 1949. *The Concept of Mind.* London: Hutchinson.

Schober, J. 1997. Trajectories in Buddhist Sacred Biography. In *Sacred Biography in the Buddhist Traditions of South and Southeast Asia* (ed.) J. Schober, 1–18. Honolulu: University of Hawaii Press.

Schweder, R. 1992. Ghost Busters in Anthropology. In *Human Motives and Cultural Models* (eds) R. D'Andrade and C. Strauss, 45–57. Cambridge: Cambridge University Press.

Seeger, M. 2010. 'Against the Stream': The Thai Female Buddhist Saint Mae Chi Kaew Sianglam (1901–1991). *South East Asia Research* 18, no. 3: 555–595.

Somdet Phra Maha Samana Chao Krom Phraya Vajirananavarorasa. 1989. *Ordination Procedure and the Preliminary Duties of a New Bhikkhu.* Bangkok: Mahamakut Rajavidyalaya Press.

Sperber, D. 1975. *Rethinking Symbolism* (trans. A. Morton). Cambridge: Cambridge University Press.

Stewart, K. 1996. *A Space on the Side of the Road: Cultural Poetics in an 'Other' America.* Princeton: Princeton University Press.

Strathern, M. 1991. *Partial Connections.* Savage, MD: Rowman and Littlefield.

Strauss, C. 1992. What Makes Tony Run? Schemas as Motives Reconsidered. In *Human Motives and Cultural Models* (eds) R. D'Andrade and C. Strauss, 197–224. Cambridge: Cambridge University Press.

Tambiah, S.J. 1984. *The Buddhist Saints of the Forest and the Cult of Amulets: A Study in Charisma, Hagiography, Sectarianism and Millennial Buddhism.* Cambridge: Cambridge University Press.

Viveiros de Castro, E. 2007. The Crystal Forest: On the Ontology of Amazonian Spirits. *Inner Asia* 9, no. 2: 153–172.

6

Autism and Affordances of Achievement
Narrative Genres and Parenting Practices

Olga Solomon

The concept of achievement demands a narrative lens: achievement is durative and agentive and thus by its very nature it denotes a narrative of becoming. To capture a phenomenology of achievement, I propose to direct this narrative lens at autism, a developmental disability that disrupts normative expressions of sociality but that, as Murray (2008: 5) suggests, 'contains its own logic and methods' that command analytic attention. The view can be traced to Hans Asperger, who, writing in 1944 in Vienna about what is now known as 'Asperger's syndrome', commented that in autism there is difficulty in learning in conventional ways; instead 'the autistic individual needs to create everything out of his own thought and experience' (Asperger 1991 [1944]: 56). This view, however important, suggests that the autistic individual's pursuit of achievement is a solitary process and is consistent with clinical descriptions of autism as a disorder of intersubjectivity (Hobson 1993; Trevarthen 1996). It also implies a contrast with non-autistic processes of pursuing and experiencing achievement. I seek to problematise these distinctions related to autism and achievement in two ways: firstly, I examine certain kinds of 'stories to be in' (Mattingly 1998) that are constructed by parents, especially mothers, from published life stories of successful adults with Autism Spectrum Disorders (ASD), and from memoirs of other parents. When mothers craft these stories, they create, for their children and for themselves, courses of action toward desired subject positions and ways of being in the world that stand in contrast to other possible but undesirable futures, futures that these mothers strive to escape. Secondly, I identify certain kinds of experiences and occupations afforded by engagement in such narrative co-construction that may have profound and tangible effects on the achievement of children, youth and adults diagnosed with ASD.

The interplay of autism and achievement merits a discussion located at the intersections of the discursive and the embodied, the developmental and the socio-interactional, the individual and the collective, the relational and the solitary, the routine and the improvisational, the cross-cultural and the sociopolitical, and the institutionally sanctioned and the institutionally prohibited. To move the discussion in such a multi-faceted analytic direction, I draw upon three kinds of narratives: firstly, interviews conducted with African American mothers who live in Los Angeles about their experiences of raising children diagnosed with autism; secondly, published first-person accounts of autism that are publicly recognised as stories of achievement; and thirdly, published parental memoirs of raising a child with autism who grows into a professionally successful adult. Within this chapter I am especially interested in the narrative framing of the experience of achievement in relation to the diagnosis of autism. Does achievement in these narratives happen in spite of autism or because of autism? Is achievement in these narratives always desirable and laudable?

My goal is to describe the 'expressive, storied dimensions' (Yanow 1999: 31) of autism and achievement and to identify narrative processes involved in making sense of autism as it relates to achievement, and achievement as it relates to autism, across the lifespan and from multiple perspectives. These narrative processes frame developmental differences and potentialities as visible, interpretable, ratifiable and contestable against the horizon of future-implicative social actions that permeate everyday life. To understand this narrative framing, I consider the three narrative sources with an eye for the everyday activities that afford individuals with autism experiences of achievement.

The concept of 'affordance' is complementary to this phenomenological, process-oriented view of achievement, and it denotes an engagement in an activity with others that enfolds over time. 'Affordances' are understood as opportunities for action provided by a particular object in the environment (Gibson 1977), and human perception of the self is directly linked with 'perceiving affordances for acting in the world' (Gibson 1993: 32). A critical part of the theory of affordances is the idea of 'fit' or 'scale', reflecting that the affordances have to be of the right scale to be perceived by the organism as relevant – that is, to fit the parameters of the organism, its anatomy and capacity for action. The concept of 'affordances of achievement' allows us to examine the processes by which parents and children make certain cultural and symbolic objects – such as a book or a movie based upon a life story of a successful person with autism – 'fit' their lives and make it relevant to their circumstances and challenges. These narrative texts of achievement are shared among parents of children with autism as a collective experience, engendering a sense of community, belonging and hope. Such uses of these narrative texts by parents illustrates, in a novel way, the Russian philosopher of language Mikhail Bakhtin's notion that 'the life of the text … always develops at the boundary between two consciousnesses, two subjects' (Bakhtin 1986: 106). Parents, as the audience of these texts, become their co-authors, interpreting and re-crafting these narratives of achievement as relevant to their children's and families' lives.

To consider these processes, I draw upon a data corpus collected for an ethnographic study conducted by an interdisciplinary team of researchers and clinicians at the University of Southern California.[1] The study examines African

American children's pathways to ASD diagnoses, interventions and services, and their parents' experiences and interactions with practitioners across multiple healthcare and educational systems. The study involves extensive clinical, home and community observations and video- and audio-recording of clinical encounters, ethnographic interviews with family members and practitioners, and narrative-based family group meetings. Twenty-three families living in Los Angeles, including twenty-two mothers and fourteen fathers and stepfathers, took part in the study. These participants represented a wide range of educational and income levels. The children's cohort consisted of twenty-two boys and three girls aged four to nine. In addition, medical practitioners and other professionals who served the children – paediatricians, neurologists, occupational therapists, physical therapists, speech therapists, nurses, teachers and service coordinators – also participated in the study.

Following Lawlor (2004), the chapter draws upon narrative, interpretive, phenomenological approaches to understand children's and families' experiences related to an autism diagnosis, and the implications of these experiences for children's achievement. The next section of the chapter addresses ways in which narrative genres construct certain subject positions for the children and their caregivers that can be transactionally pursued or resisted (Connolly 2000; McDermott 2006).

Autism and Achievement: The Narrative Genres

From a constructionist perspective, 'achievement' is a kind of narrative, one that provides an interpretive framework for categorising certain kinds of people who carry out certain kind of actions (D'Andrade 1992). Narratives of 'achievement' can be described, following Yanow (1999: 31), as '"an ensemble of texts" that display and enact cultural meanings and that the anthropologist seeks to read over the shoulders ... of those engaged in them'. An analysis of narrative genres illuminates the relation between narrative text and social action, or, as Hanks (1987: 670) writes, between 'the linguistic form of such texts and the broader social and cultural world in which they are produced'. The relation of the 'thematic, stylistic and compositional elements' of a text and the 'historically specific conventions and ideals according to which authors compose discourse and audiences receive it', makes visible the 'orienting frameworks, interpretive procedures, and sets of expectations' occasioned by these discourse genres (Hanks 1987: 670; see also Ochs and Capps 2001).

In the contemporary United States, children's 'achievement' has come to be associated with a certain kind of activity called 'learning'. The narratives of 'achievement' are constitutive of institutional constraints that organise learning, and even of institutions themselves. Arguing for a situated understanding of this process – that is, for a 'theory of situated genius' – Ray McDermott offers a powerful critique of theories of learning, knowledge and accomplishment that put

> learning and achievement in individual heads far from conditions of its use. This way, individuals and groups can be celebrated for learning more than enough, degraded for not learning enough, and, the key to the system, destroyed for learning too much ... A theory of situated genius ... demands that conditions of practice become the focus of any ascription of learning. (McDermott 2006: 299)

In McDermott's view, it follows that procedures for ascribing genius should be problematised, as the ascription can do 'more harm than good' (ibid.: 299).

Some adults diagnosed with ASD later in life may agree. Consider the recollections of Tim Page, a Pulitzer Prize-winning classical music critic and a university professor diagnosed with Asperger's syndrome in late adulthood, about his childhood experience with the ascription of 'genius':

> From early childhood, my memory was so acute and my wit so bleak that I was described a genius – by my parents, by my neighbors, and even, on occasion, by the same teachers who handed me failing marks. I wrapped myself in this mantle, of course, as a poetic justification for behavior that might otherwise have been judged unhinged, and I did my best to believe in it. But the explanation made no sense. A genius at *what?* Were other 'geniuses' so oblivious that they needed mnemonic devices to tell right from left, and idly wet their pants into adolescence? What accounted for my rages and frustrations, for the imperious contempt I showed to people who were in a position to do me harm? (Page 2009: 3)

Page's unique account is a peering back through memory, with the hindsight of post-diagnosis and the self-understanding and self-forgiveness that it brought, to the childhood and youth fraught with, as he writes, 'an excruciating awareness of my own strangeness', and a relentless pursuit of 'something around which to construct a life' (ibid.: 4, 6). Besides the challenges of self- and other-understanding that have become a familiar theme in personal accounts of the high-functioning autism experience, and the story of achievement 'perhaps not *despite* Asperger's but *because* of it' (as the anonymous writer of the text on the cover of Page's book put it), the other important part of Page's narrative of achievement is his family. His 'patrician mother' saved everything that originated from her son's penmanship beginning from the time he held a crayon in his hand, creating an archive that became the material for his book. She took the twelve-year-old Page to the original New York Metropolitan Opera House to hear *Madama Butterfly* before the building was demolished, an event that Page remembers as a transformative experience of his childhood. This trip, and his mother's keen attentiveness to Page's infatuation with classical music, made it possible for him to 'visit the place where so much musical history had been made' (ibid.: 44), and to recognise what that musical history meant for him. Page remembers his father being similarly involved. He served as a patient and understanding scribe who typed the 'doom-laden narratives' Page wrote as a child, as well as Page's advocate and defender who protested his school suspension in a four-thousand-word letter to the school principal. The prodigious classical music record collection the family had at home became

Page's personal, passionately experienced, life-world, something around which he did 'construct a life'.

Kamran Nazeer, a policy advisor to the British government who was diagnosed with autism as a child, also reflects on the ascription of 'genius' in his memoir *Send in the Idiots: Stories from the Other Side of Autism*, providing a counter-argument to Asperger's ([1944] 1991: 56) observation that 'the autistic individual needs to create everything out of his own thought and experience':

> Sometimes our use of the term 'genius' implies that we believe that there is a group of people with some fantastic natural capability to produce thoughts and objects out of thin air ... Genius has to work hard too. Our conception of the privileges of genius is a false one ... The term 'genius' may be one element of our broader view in which progress relies on the series of daring leaps made by great individual minds. However, this view neglects to consider how it is that great individual minds come to the point at which they can make a leap, and the extent to which other people and institutions are involved in that. (Nazeer 2006: 83–84)

Such writings of adults with ASD have altered the landscape of possibilities for children diagnosed with this condition and their families. Perhaps to a lesser degree, these writings have also altered the language of science used to describe ASD. Far from taxonomies of deficits or deficit-related savant abilities, these first-person accounts described a way of being, a world as perceived and experienced, the people and other important actors – some animate, some not – with whom the world was shared, and the opportunities for action that engagement with these existential companions offered. Most importantly, these narratives plotted 'stories to be in' (Mattingly 1998), pathways to achievement that, at least in imagination, others with ASD and their families could travel as well.

These narrative accounts also set precedents for autism and achievement co-existing, contradictorily and often unfathomably, in the lives of real people. Achievement may have uniquely personal, multifaceted and yet ordinary meanings for these authors with ASD, from marriage and parenthood to education and professional success (e.g., Prince-Hughes 2004, 2005; Prince 2010; Perner 2012). This is an important development because until recently autism and achievement have been a relatively rare and unlikely pairing in the social science and education research. Examining autism and achievement together may have appeared questionable: autism is a life-long pervasive developmental disorder that is highly heterogeneous, which makes developmental trajectories difficult to predict (e.g., Lord and Spence 2006). Nevertheless, autism often presents a barrier to the achievement of adult autonomy, let alone to the achievement of financial independence through participation in a market-based economy.[2] With the exception of hypothetical, after-the-fact diagnoses of famous, usually deceased, scientists, musicians and others (Fitzgerald 2004; James 2005), and the assignment of autistic cognitive profiles to the 'extreme male brain' (Baron-Cohen 2003, 2004) or other cognitive differences (Happé and Frith 2009; Happé and Vital 2009), autism and achievement are usually not discussed as relevant to each other. Public figures who have an autism diagnosis are often portrayed ambivalently in the media, as anomalies whose achievement exists in spite of, but possibly also because of, autism.

Such ambivalence has not always been the case. In his original article 'Autistic Psychopathy in Childhood', Hans Asperger, who first described what is now called 'Asperger's disorder' (APA 2000), writes:

> To our own amazement, we have seen that autistic individuals, as long as they are intellectually intact, can almost always achieve professional success, usually in highly specialized academic professions, often in very high positions, with a preference for abstract content ... The superficially surprising fact that such difficult and abnormal children can achieve a tolerable, or even excellent, degree of social integration can be explained if one considers it a little further. A good professional attitude involves single-mindedness as well as the decision to give up a large number of other interests ... With collected energy and obvious confidence, and yes, with a blinkered attitude towards life's rich rewards, they go their own way, the way to which their talents have directed them from childhood. Thus, the truth of the old adage is proved again: good and bad in every character are just two sides of the same coin. It is simply not possible to separate them, to opt for the positive and get rid of the negative. (Asperger [1944] 1991: 89)

This hopeful view has since been considered more as an oddity – there is an opinion that Asperger himself was 'on the spectrum' – than as a call to action. Notably, some individuals, such as artists Jessica Park and Stephen Wiltshire, who would not have been considered 'high-functioning' or 'intellectually intact' by Asperger, have nevertheless achieved a high level of professional success. Missing in Asperger's account is what Kamran Nazeer emphasises in the above quote: the transactional nature of achievement and the role of other people and institutions in autistic individuals' professional success. This is conveyed by Clara Claiborne Park who writes about her daughter Jessica in an interview-format chapter co-authored by them both and titled 'Living with Autism: A Collaboration', "It is something more than a joke when I say that Jessy is the lowest-functioning high-functioning person with autism I have ever seen" (Park and Park 2006: 83).

Temple Grandin's Story: A Meta-Narrative of Autism and Achievement

Temple Grandin's story is a particularly important narrative of becoming because it has turned into a meta-narrative of autism and achievement. After Grandin was already a well-known animal science researcher in the U.S., a public speaker and an author of several books, some of which were national bestsellers, her life story was recently made into an HBO film (Jackson 2010). The film, with much publicity, received seventeen Emmy awards, and many families of children with autism saw both the film and the Emmy award ceremony where Grandin's life was celebrated. Grandin's mother, Eustacia Cutler, was in the audience. During the ceremony, the film's executive producer, Emily Gerson Saines, whose son has autism, held high one of the Emmys and said, 'Temple Grandin, you are our hero, and Eustacia Cutler [Grandin gave Saines a long embrace] – and Eustacia Cutler, you are our inspiration.' Grandin then pointed to her mother in the audience, and demanded that she stand up. Cutler, author of the memoir *A Thorn in My Pocket* (2004), which documented Grandin's childhood, did just that. This was an emotional, and very public, moment: Cutler's role in her daughter's achievement was publicly recognised at a televised event viewed by millions. It was perhaps even more significant that Grandin herself initiated her mother's public recognition. This scene brought tears to the eyes of many people in the audience, as well as those watching it on their television screens, and was especially memorable for parents of children with autism.

Behind this moment was a life story that could have gone very differently. Temple Grandin was diagnosed with autism during the time when the psychogenic theory of this disorder was widely accepted; and her mother, like most mothers during that time, was blamed for her autism. A noteworthy detail of Grandin's narrative of becoming is that her parents were advised by the diagnosing physician to place Temple in a 'foster home', a euphemism for an institution. Grandin's mother firmly resisted this advice (Cutler 2004) and Grandin herself reflects on this choice: 'I owe my success to my mother, who defied the professionals who told her that I belonged in a school for the retarded' (Grandin 2005: 1276). This narrowly escaped possibility is very much on Grandin's mind when she writes:

> Many people ask me: 'What was the big breakthrough that enabled you to lead a successful life?' There was no such single breakthrough. My development was a gradual evolution that had many small but important steps. If I had fallen off any of these steps, I would have ended up in a school for the retarded or at a job that would have been below my abilities. (ibid.: 1276)

Grandin's life story, perhaps because of its traumatic beginnings and consequent success, and its wide coverage in the media, presents a powerful cultural resource of hope for families of children with ASD. Consider this excerpt from an interview with Stephanie whose eight-year-old daughter Tina was diagnosed with ASD.[3] Stephanie, Tina and several members of their extended family participated in the 'Autism in Urban Context' project. In this interview, Stephanie describes ways in which the film *Temple Grandin* had changed how she thought about Tina's abilities and interests, and how she organised Tina's everyday activities.

> STEPHANIE: I've been trying to work things out a little bit more, um, to find out what she likes. And last week, I want to say two weeks ago, there was a movie, um, I don't know if you've seen it, uh – *Temple Grandin*?
>
> INTERVIEWER: Oh yeah. I've seen it.

> STEPHANIE: I saw that movie. And, um, I wanted to watch it because, um, a friend of mine was saying that there was this movie on TV that you have to see. It's about an autistic girl – she grows up, she does so and so and such and such and I saw it and I been trying to tell people about the movie as it relates to real life, you know ... But it – it kind of gives you hope that – it's a movie, still. So you can tell that it's a movie. But, it kind of gives you the hope that something can really happen, and with little kids like this you see the foreshadowing, and Tina, that if Tina had these skills that she could, like, cultivate and, and when she becomes a certain age if she sticks to it and her mind is going to go towards being productive and that, then, you never know what she could do with that talent, and that was the reason why I wanted to watch the movie.

Stephanie describes a sense of collectivity and belonging that this movie created. She explains how she learned about it from a friend who insisted that she had to see it; she also describes what she has done with this experience: she has been telling other people about it. She struggles with her experience of having hope engendered by something that 'is a movie, still', that 'you can tell it's a movie'. Nevertheless, the movie affords a narrative foreshadowing of a desired future (Bernstein 1994; Morson 1994): that if Tina 'cultivates' her skills and 'sticks to it', then 'you never know what she could do with that talent'.

> STEPHANIE: Plus I really think it's what the child devotes themselves to. Whether it be art or music or agriculture, in Temple Grandin's case, whatever it is, I believe that, that's what kind of struck me to take this next two weeks as a project on myself to try to see what she's really interested, that way I'm able to, um, give her a focus. Because what hit me the – the most is that these kids need focus. They can really be productive members of society. Temple Grandin is now a doctor, you know what I mean? And she's teaching other people and whatever, and she's gotten her doctorate – from a person who didn't even learn to talk till they were four.

The story of Temple Grandin's life, with its difficult beginning and a long path to achievement – 'Temple Grandin is now a doctor ... she is teaching other people ... she's gotten her doctorate – from a person who didn't even learn to talk till they were four' – is perceived by Stephanie as an affordance that she can use to make a story she wants to be 'in' with her daughter. This story-making is carried out through practical engagement with Tina in activities that allow Stephanie to see what Tina is 'really interested in, that way I'm able to, um, give her a focus', because 'these kids need focus' to be 'productive members of society'.

> STEPHANIE: That was the other scene that got to me there was the mother who was sitting on the steps, and she says well the doctor says, 'your child will probably never speak'. And – and Temple is like gazing at this like chandelier and – as her mom tries to teach her to talk, and her hair is like tousled and she's like about to cry and Temple is just staring off into space at the chandelier and she keeps turning her head back and trying to get her to talk but the child is absolutely just like, enthralled in this like structure over here because in her mind she's seeing the shape of the chandelier, she's probably thinking how many crystals does it have,

> she's looking at the colour of the crystals, you never know, like they inte- – she intensely thinks about things, even Tina nowadays, when we were playing Wii last week, and I don't know if it's my turn, or her turn, she says to me, she says, 'Well, you could tell it's your turn because the background is white'. And which is something that, you know she didn't see the names, she didn't see the pictures. Her mind goes to different things that are way too detailed for us to pick up on some times. She's like – 'well the background is white. When it's white it's your turn, when it's blue it's my turn'.

As Stephanie recalls a scene from the movie, she engages in intersubjective imagining of her daughter's perceptual world, a world where Tina has an advantage over her mother because she can see 'different things that are way too detailed for us to pick up on sometimes'. Stephanie uses this understanding to newly interpret a specific recent event: Tina and Stephanie playing a video game on their Nintendo Wii.

> STEPHANIE: You know, because I guess people don't see these kids for what they are. To me, if you can get past having all the fits, and you can get past to what, whatever it is that their emotional lack is, what their emotional lack is, the kids are genius [...] Tina has said so many things, she has done so many things, created so many things, that makes us think that she is just way advanced in certain things, and may- – she's not, um – I don't know – who she is yet? She's only eight. There's so many possibilities.

Stephanie laments that 'these kids are not seen for what they are', with all their potentialities and unique challenges ('if you can get past all the fits and whatever it is their emotional lack is'). Implicit in this lament is the realisation that more should be done for them to develop their talents because 'these kids are genius'. Like any genius, as McDermott argues, Tina's is situated in an environment created at home by her mother and other family members, and at school by her teachers and other professionals, that not only enhances certain kinds of learning but also allows her to grow into a certain kind of person, one who has already achieved 'many things' and one that has many possibilities in the future. Stephanie also voices the ontological uncertainty, open-endedness and promise of Tina's life story: 'I don't know – who she is yet? She is only eight. There's so many possibilities'.

At a practical level, Stephanie uses Temple Grandin's story as a guide and an existential roadmap to choose and orchestrate activities for her eight-year-old daughter. Echoing Asperger's observations quoted above, Stephanie reflects on ways in which the film affected her understanding of her daughter and her daughter's autism. She describes how she deliberately structures Tina's everyday activities to support a certain kind of development. Temple Grandin's story of achievement, both in spite of autism and because of autism, affords a narrative landscape against which Stephanie and Tina can improvise their own life stories and their own narratives of becoming.

Such narrative processes, however, are often complicated by portrayals of autism and achievement characterised by ambivalence and contradictions. The narrative genres of 'achievement because of autism' and 'achievement in spite of autism' are not easily reconcilable, perhaps because they each could successfully generate a narrative of achievement but do not easily fit together in one narrative plot. An example of such ambivalence can be seen in an article posted on the U.S. TV station MSNBC's website – titled 'Can Animals You Eat Be Treated Humanely?' – where Temple Grandin's career in animal science is discussed:

> An Associate Professor of Animal Science at Colorado State University, Grandin can take more credit than almost anyone for trying to make modern slaughterhouses efficient and humane. Once considered curious, if eccentric, her audits and remodeling of processing plants have set new standards in the meat industry, which has come to embrace her message: Give the animals you eat a decent life and a humane death. 'They just walk up there in a quiet line, and they walk up the conveyor and they're shot, and it's over before they know what's happened', she says. 'It's almost hard for me to believe it works'.
>
> She says this while cutting into a thick steak following an afternoon spent among cows. For Grandin, eating meat requires accepting where it comes from and what's needed to put burger to bun. (MSNBC 2004)

The argument is often made that, because of her autism, Grandin has a unique ability to see the world from a cow's point of view (e.g., Dolgert 2009: 235).[4] This understanding enables Grandin to design slaughterhouses in a way that takes this view into account, a practical and unsentimental expression of empathy directed towards reducing animal suffering. Yet there is considerable ambivalence about this kind of empathy as reflected in the MSNBC journalist's musing that Grandin describes slaughterhouse operation while 'cutting into a thick steak following an afternoon spent among cows', or Dolgert's assessment that: 'Grandin designs humane slaughterhouses using, among other things, her insights into animal cognition based in her experiences as an autistic human. This is objectionable not only because of the insipid definition of humane which she operates, but also because of the implicit hierarchical way of viewing animals as cognitively-deficient humans' (ibid.: 235).

In the face of such ambivalence, the analytic vocabulary to describe the relationship between autism and achievement, its subjunctive, socially co-constructed nature, and the socio-cultural practices and processes that afford it, has not been well developed. Beyond the cognitive psychological accounts of savant abilities that are assumed to result in extraordinary, super-human skills (see Mottron and Burack 2001; Mottron et al. 2006, 2009; cf. Treffert 1989), such notions as 'motivation', 'desire', 'activity', 'practice', 'mastery', 'expertise' and 'imagination' are not often applied to understanding the achievement of individuals diagnosed with autism.[5] It does not mean, however, that because such a vocabulary does not exist to describe it, children, youths and adults with autism do not pursue or experience achievement, or that they are not members of communities of practice where what is called 'achievement' takes place. They do, often to the researchers' surprise, and in spite of numerous challenges imposed on them by ASD, as well as the prevailing assumptions about the degree and scope of their limitations.

Narratives of Autism and Achievement that Leads to Trouble

Sometimes the success of individuals with ASD comes in unexpected forms and goes against the norms of socio-culturally sanctioned, and even legal, conduct. A third narrative genre that captures such successes by linking autism and achievement is 'achievement that leads to trouble'. This narrative genre makes it possible to tell stories about a type of activity such as computer hacking, especially when national security-sensitive data are involved.

Three autistic hackers – Gary McKinnon, Viacheslav Berkovich and Adrian Lamo – have particularly attracted the attention of the media. Their stories are all of the genre 'narrative of achievement that leads to trouble', demonstrating the development of high-level expertise while simultaneously showing significant disregard of and resistance to structures of power. Unlike 'neurotypical' hackers who often pursue financial gains accessing credit-card data bases, autistic hackers so far have been unmotivated by the possibility of accessing information for these reasons. Their heightened proclivities in pattern recognition and hyper-focused attention to details have turned into idiosyncratic, determined pursuits of information. For example, between 2001 and 2002, Gary McKinnon, a 35-year-old man born in Glasgow and diagnosed with Asperger's syndrome, broke into the NASA and U.S. Department of Defense computer systems and tried to download a photograph of what he thought was a UFO. When the U.S. government demanded his extradition to the United States so that he could stand trial, the National Autism Society in the United Kingdom intervened on McKinnon's behalf, arguing that, because of his ASD diagnosis, he would psychologically deteriorate if he was moved away from home and jailed in a high-security prison. Although the extradition order was passed, it was eventually blocked in 2012 by Britain's Office of Home Affairs. This unprecedented move, which took place in spite of the U.S.-British extradition treaty, was based on McKinnon's mental health problems and his ASD diagnosis. British prosecutors, however, may still consider the possibility of trying McKinnon in Britain. The fact that McKinnon's achievement of high-level computer skills and his interest in UFOs led to 'trouble' is at once tragic for him and his family, and revelatory of how ideologically structured notions of 'legitimate achievement' are, even for those diagnosed with developmental disabilities.

Ideologies of autism and achievement come into focus even more vividly when narratives of 'achievement that leads to trouble' are contrasted with narratives of achievement of creative artists on the autism spectrum. A case in point is Clara Claiborne Park's memoir *The Siege* (1967), about raising her daughter, Jessica Park, now an artist with a gallery in New York. Jessica's life story can be characterised as achievement both in spite of autism and because of autism, but perhaps even more importantly – as the feminist scholar Jane Taylor McDonnell (1991) has highlighted – as the consequence of a distinctive form of mothering that Park's memoir not only describes but serves to promote amongst its readership. Like Nora in Ibsen's *A Doll's House*, mothers have to seize their own interpretations of their children, their potentialities and the horizons of their relationships, and 'record reality which perhaps has never been recorded before' (ibid.: 60).

The 'siege' that Park mounts takes the form of minute, momentary approaches that end up constituting interventions directed at such seemingly mundane activities as turning on a water tap, using a cup or turning on a light. The recording of these mothering practices in exhaustive detail is accompanied by Park's description of her own mental processes. McDonnell observes that Park is able to tolerate a high level of 'ontological insecurity': she does not know her daughter, is wise enough not to understand her, does not engage in the 'terrible arrogance' of forcing her daughter into the human social world, which allows Park to avoid inflicting the kind of violence of interpretation and intervention that the forcibly separated twins John and Michael, the numerical savants described by Oliver Sacks (1970), were obliged to endure (see Solomon 2010).

There is, however, a recognition that each of Jessica's 'special interests', an existential aspect of autism that is considered a 'symptom' and not a positive attribute of a person – numbers, radio dials, record players, railway crossings, electric blanket controls, quartz heaters – were intensely meaningful, compelling and a major organising principle of Jessica's reality, 'something around which to construct a life', as Page writes (2009: 6). Interestingly, Stephen Wiltshire, an artist with autism living in the U.K. known for his project *Floating Cities* (Wiltshire 1991), also had a progression of specific kinds of objects he liked to draw, moving from animals to London buses and finally to architectural landscapes.

These autistic artists' life stories combine both experiences of challenges and limitations, and of remarkable success and achievement, both because of and in spite of autism. Their distinct experience of the world as an aesthetic endeavour, and the works of art they created, highlight another important aspect of achievement in autism – that is, a lack of concern for ratified and familiar ways of engaging in the practice of art, exactly the same impulse that underpins the claim that autism leads to trouble. Stephen Wiltshire, for example, takes helicopter rides over cities he plans to draw so as to visually access his material in minute detail. Both Jessica Park and Stephen Wiltshire possess a highly focused and disciplined attention to detail and paint almost photographic images from memory. Their process of creation appears to be almost effortless and full of aesthetic pleasure derived from portraying quintessential qualities of buildings and other material objects (see Figure 6.1).

It seems fortunate that Jessica Park and Stephen Wiltshire escaped the fate of John and Michael, the twins described by Sacks (1970) who were evicted from

Figure 6.1 Jessica Park, *St. Paul's and St. Andrew's Methodist Church #2, with Migraine Lightning and the Elves* (1997). Acrylic on paper. Courtesy of Pure Vision Arts.

their numeral universe by well-meaning professionals: no one has told these artists that their way of practicing art was somehow deficient and unhealthy, and therefore should be abandoned. Thus they each developed successful, albeit unorthodox, careers as creative artists based upon what was a disability but also an asset. About the special interests of those with autism, McDonnell notes: 'none of us has ever seen before such narrowness of focus, such total concentration and dedication to task – or such oddity of interest in a child' (McDonnell 1991: 65). McDonnell quotes Ruddick (1980) in arguing that mothering is a very normative activity, the central challenge of which is raising the child to become an acceptable adult through shaping his or her interests into a culturally normative form. This is reminiscent of what Lareau (2003) calls 'concerted cultivation' with one important difference – 'concerted cultivation' is a familiar practice of 'intensive' parenting (Hayes 1996; Wall 2010); in parenting a child with autism, parents often have to engage in what Daniel (1998) has termed 'fugitive practices', improvised parenting practices in the face of crisis.

This is a success story, McDonnell writes, in many ways: Jessica Park now has a successful artistic career, a remarkable gift that her mother helped her develop. Her mother re-invented motherhood as a 'social activist position, turning her personal pain into the wisdom and courage to help others' (McDonnell 1991: 73). But Clara Claiborne Park may have given her daughter another gift: by writing two books about Jessica's childhood – *The Siege* (1967) and *Exiting Nirvana* (2001) – Park has attracted attention to Jessica's art, which may have contributed to her achievement as an artist. In this sense, Jessica has experienced multiple affordances of achievement, including the appreciative public attention possibly generated by her mother's memoirs.

Diane Savage's (2003) story about her son Matthew Savage, an accomplished young jazz musician and a founder of the Matt Savage Trio, is a more recent narrative of becoming, and illustrates how the narrative genres of achievement because of autism and achievement in spite of autism may collide in one story. Matthew was diagnosed with a Pervasive Developmental Disorder Not-Otherwise Specified (PDD-NOS) at age three and has been called a 'musical savant' by specialists who, as the term suggests, attributed his musical talent to savant skills. A young person with a similar extraordinary musical talent but without a clinical diagnosis would have been called a 'musical prodigy'. A leader of a jazz trio, an accomplished jazz pianist and a prolific composer with many music CDs to his credit, Matt Savage has performed with Dave Brubeck, Wynton Marsalis and other world-famous jazz musicians in well-known locations including the Lincoln Center in New York (Solomon 2009).

Diane's experience of Matthew's infancy and childhood is reminiscent of other parental stories of autism: a colicky, inconsolable baby, a sensory defensive child unable to ride in a car seat, to be near a vacuum cleaner or a popcorn maker. Highly perseverative and hyperlexic,[6] Matthew was also highly intelligent. He started playing a toy piano at age six and soon was taking classical piano lessons, improvising and playing music when the music sheet was turned upside down. His main challenge in music is 'making mistakes': he is terrified of not being able to play a piece perfectly. Diane Savage writes about Matthew's challenges and his achievement in spite of autism:

> Don't misunderstand me. There are many, many difficulties with which Matthew copes everyday. He still shows signs of his autism. People immediately notice him in a group! He still has inappropriate behaviors and regresses in new situations. But he is making progress. We focus on how many things he has been able to accomplish, not on the things with which he will always struggle. (Savage 2003: 290)

As with Jessica Park's and Stephen Wiltshire's stories, Matt Savage's narrative of achievement could be seen as portraying his success as both because of autism and in spite of autism. The ontological uncertainty of his musical talent is best left alone: it would be difficult, and perhaps unnecessary, to determine whether he is a talented jazz musician who happens to be autistic, or if there is something about his music, or the way that he engages in his creative process, that reflects his autism. As Asperger ([1944] 1991: 89) wrote, 'It is simply not possible to separate them, to opt for the positive and get rid of the negative'.

Conclusion

The three narrative genres – achievement because of autism, achievement in spite of autism, and achievement that leads to trouble – may occur simultaneously, occasionally producing contradictory accounts. These narrative genres may also guide parents in their work of structuring experiences and occupations for their children, thus creating opportunities for action and affordances of achievement. Such work of narrative imagination (Mattingly 2010) can be well understood from an occupational science perspective that places analytic focus on everyday activities, engagement and participation as related to human health and well-being.

Related to the discussion of autism and achievement, Christenson argues:

> occupations are key not just to being a person, but to being a *particular* person, and thus creating and maintaining an identity. Occupations come together within the contexts of our relationships with others to provide us with a sense of purpose and structure over time in our day-to-day activities. When we build our identities through occupations, we provide ourselves with the contexts necessary for creating meaningful lives, and life meaning helps us to be well. (Christenson 1999: 547)

There is nothing inevitable about the ways in which autism and achievement manifest themselves in children's and families' lives. As I have shown, narrative genres create certain subject positions for children and their families as desirable and possible, and as potentially leading to achievement. Achievement is transactional and is afforded by the children's and their mothers' engagement with one another in seemingly mundane but significant activities in their life-worlds. It is in the context of this engagement that the children are afforded the freedom to develop their relationships with the world they inhabit and to be 'at home' in this world (Reilly 1962: 2). Finally, I would suggest that granting children with ASD the freedom to be in the world in a certain way rests upon an acceptance of an ontological uncertainty of those children's development and achievement, a difficult and precarious parenting task.

I would like to end this chapter by stressing the role of collective, relational, interactional and imaginary work in the achievement of people with ASD. I see the work of families as the organising force that creates environments in which children, youths and adults with ASD engage with 'something around which to construct a life' (Page 2009: 6). Returning to McDermott's theory of situated genius, the case of autism and achievement suggests that achievement is better conceptualised as an attribute of learning environments rather than of individual cognition: 'The locus is people organizing collective problems well defined enough for a solution to be advanced and noticed ... Genius in a situational analysis is *ordinary* in the best sense of the term: people doing what has to be done with the materials at hand' (McDermott 2006: 294). For children with ASD and their families, 'the materials at hand' are stories about others who experienced autism before them: narratives of achievement with which they can craft their own stories of life with autism.

Acknowledgements

I am grateful to two anonymous reviewers for their insightful feedback and helpful criticism and to Nicholas Long and Henrietta Moore for their editorial guidance. I wish to acknowledge members of the 'Autism in Urban Context' project research team at the University of Southern California: Mary Lawlor, Sharon Cermak, Larry Yin, Marie Poulsen, Marian Williams and Thomas Valente. I am forever indebted to the children and families who shared their experiences and stories with me and other members of the research team. I also gratefully acknowledge funding from the National Institutes of Health/National Institute of Mental Health grant 'Autism in Urban Context: Linking Heterogeneity with Health and Service Disparities' (R01 MH089474, 2009–2012), that supported the collection of data analysed in this chapter. The content of this chapter is solely the responsibility of the author and does not necessarily represent the official views of the National Institute of Mental Health or the National Institutes of Health.

Notes

1. This study was entitled 'Autism in Urban Context: Linking Heterogeneity with Health and Service Disparities', and funded by the National Institute of Mental Health (R01 MH089474, 2009–2012) with myself as principal investigator.
2. The importance of being a 'productive' and market-value-producing member of society is not lost on McDermott who laments that, 'Genius ... became worth money, and conceptions of genius have delivered their object ... to be measured, quantified, bet on, and bought and sold as a unit of exchange and capital investment ... Its current packaging displays our own situation and illustrates the cultural demands we place on theories of intelligence, learning and achievement' (McDermott 2006: 287).
3. All names used are pseudonyms.
4. Grandin describes her experiences of understanding animals in Grandin and Johnson (2005, 2010).
5. But see Kasari et al. (1993).
6. Perseveration is engagement in repetitive behaviour: repeating others' utterances or stretches of talk from movies, or motor behaviour such as hand flapping. Hyperlexia is a spontaneous and precocious mastery of single-word reading emerging ahead of the development of comprehension.

References

APA. 2000. *Diagnostic and Statistical Manual of Mental Disorders.* Washington, DC: American Psychiatric Association.

Asperger, H. [1944] 1991. Autistic Psychopathy in Childhood (trans. U. Frith). In *Autism and Asperger Syndrome* (ed.) U. Frith, 37–92. Cambridge: Cambridge University Press.

Bakhtin, M. 1986. *Speech Genres and Other Late Essays* (trans. V.W. McGee). Austin: University of Texas Press.

Baron-Cohen, S. 2003. *The Essential Difference: The Truth About the Male and Female Brain.* New York: Basic Books.

——— 2004. *The Essential Difference: Male and Female Brains and the Truth about Autism.* New York: Basic Books.

Bernstein, M.A. 1994. *Foregone Conclusions: Against Apocalyptic History.* Berkeley: University of California Press.

Christenson, C.H. 1999. Defining Lives: Occupation as Identity: An Essay on Competence, Coherence, and the Creation of Meaning. *American Journal of Occupational Therapy* 53, no. 6: 547–558.

Conolly, P. 2000. Race, Gender and Critical Reflexivity in Research with Young Children. In *Research with Children: Perspectives and Practices* (eds) P. Christiansen and A. James, 173–188. New York: Routledge.

Cutler, E. 2004. *A Thorn in My Pocket: Temple Grandin's Mother Tells the Family Story.* Arlington: Future Horizons.

D'Andrade, R.G. 1992. Schemas and Motivation. In *Human Motives and Cultural Models* (eds) R.G. D'Andrade and C. Strauss, 23–44. Cambridge: Cambridge University Press.

Daniel, E.V. 1998. The Limits of Culture. In *In Near Ruins* (ed.) N.B. Dirks, 67–91. Minneapolis: University of Minnesota Press.

Dolgert, S.P. 2009. Citizen Canine: Humans and Animals in Athens and America. Ph.D. diss., Department of Political Science, Duke University.

Fitzgerald, M. 2004. *Autism and Creativity: Is There a Link between Autism in Men and Exceptional Ability?* New York: Routledge.

Gibson, E.J. 1993. Ontogenesis of the Perceived Self. In *The Perceived Self: Ecological and Interpersonal Sources of Self-Knowledge* (ed.) U. Neisser, 25–42. New York: Cambridge University Press.

Gibson, J.J. 1977. The Theory of Affordances. In *Perceiving, Acting, and Knowing: Toward an Ecological Psychology* (eds) R. Shaw and J. Bransford, 67–82. Hillsdale: Erlbaum.

Grandin, T. 2005. A Personal Perspective on Autism. In *Handbook of Autism and Pervasive Developmental Disorders* (eds) F.R. Volkman, R. Paul, A. Klin and D. Cohen, 1276–1286. Hoboken: Wiley.

Grandin, T., and C. Johnson. 2005. *Animals in Translation: Using the Mysteries of Autism to Decode Animal Behavior.* New York: Scribner.

——— 2010. *Animals Make Us Human: Creating the Best Life for Animals.* New York: Houghton-Mifflin Harcourt.

Hanks, W.F. 1987. Discourse Genres in a Theory of Practice. *American Ethnologist* 14, no 4: 668–692.

Happé, F., and U. Frith. 2009. The Beautiful Otherness of the Autistic Mind. *Philosophical Transactions of the Royal Society* 364, no. 1522: 1345–1350.

Happé, F., and P. Vital. 2009. What Aspects of Autism Predispose to Talent? *Philosophical Transactions of the Royal Society* 364, no. 1522: 1369–1375.

Hayes, S. 1996. *The Cultural Contradiction of Motherhood*. New Haven: Yale University Press.

Hobson, R.P. 1993. *Autism and the Development of the Mind*. Hove: Erlbaum.

Jackson, M. (dir.) 2010. *Temple Grandin*. HBO Films.

James, I. 2005. *Asperger's Syndrome and High Achievement: Some Very Remarkable People*. London: Jessica Kingsley.

Kasari, C., M.D. Sigman, P. Baumgartner and D.J. Stipek. 1993. Pride and Mastery in Children with Autism. *Journal of Child Psychology and Psychiatry* 34, no. 3: 353–362.

Lareau, A. 2003. *Unequal Childhoods: Class, Race, and Family Life*. Berkeley: University of California Press.

Lawlor, M. 2004. Mothering Work: Negotiating Health Care, Illness and Disability, and Development. In *Mothering Occupations* (eds) S. Esdaile and J. Olson, 306–323. Philadelphia: F.A. Davis.

Lord, C., and S. Spence. 2006. Autism Spectrum Disorders: Phenotype and Diagnosis. In *Understanding Autism: From Basic Neuroscience to Treatment* (eds) S.O. Moldin and J.L.R. Rubenstein, 1–23. Boca Raton: Taylor and Francis.

McDermott, R. 2006. Situating Genius. In *Learning in Places: The Informal Education Reader* (eds) Z. Bekerman, N. Burbules and D. Silverman-Keller, 285–302. New York: Peter Lang.

McDonnell, J.T. 1991. Mothering an Autistic Child: Reclaiming the Voice of the Mother. In *Narrating Mothers: Theorizing Maternal Subjectivities* (eds) B.O. Daly and M.T. Reddy, 58–77. Knoxville: University of Tennessee Press.

Mattingly, C. 1998. *Healing Dramas and Clinical Plots: The Narrative Structure of Experience*. Cambridge: Cambridge University Press.

Mattingly, C. 2010. *The Paradox of Hope: Journeys through a Clinical Borderland*. Berkeley: University of California Press.

Morson, G.S. 1994. *Narrative and Freedom: The Shadows of Time*. New Haven: Yale University Press.

Mottron, L. and J.A. Burack. 2001. Enhanced Perceptual Functioning in the Development of Autism. In *The Development of Autism: Perspectives from Theory and Research* (eds) J.A. Burack, T. Charman, N. Yirmiya and P.R. Zelazo, 131–148. Mahwah: Erlbaum.

Mottron, L., M. Dawson and I. Soulieres. 2009. Enhanced Perception in Savant Syndrome: Patterns, Structure and Creativity. *Philosophical Transactions of the Royal Society B: Biological Sciences* 364, no. 1522: 1385–1391.

Mottron, L., M. Dawson, I. Soulieres, B. Huber and J.A. Burack. 2006. Enhanced Perceptual Functioning in Autism: An Update, and Eight Principles of Autistic Perception. *Journal of Autism and Developmental Disorders* 36: 27–43.

MSNBC. 2004. Can Animals You Eat Be Treated Humanely? Temple Grandin's Decent-Life, Humane-Death Crusade. <http://www.msnbc.msn.com/id/5271434/ns/business-us_business/t/can-animals-you-eat-be-treated-humanely/#.T69dHlH3B-k> (accessed 1 March 2011).

Murray, S. 2008. *Representing Autism: Culture, Narrative, Fascination*. Liverpool: Liverpool University Press.

Nazeer, K. 2006. *Send in the Idiots: Stories from the Other Side of Autism*. New York: Bloomsbury.

Ochs, E., and L. Capps. 2001. *Living Narrative: Creating Lives in Everyday Storytelling*. Cambridge, MA: Harvard University Press.

Page, T. 2009. *Parallel Play: Growing Up with Undiagnosed Asperger's.* New York: Doubleday.

Park, C.C. 1967. *The Siege: A Family's Journey into the World of an Autistic Child.* New York: Little, Brown and Co.

——— 2001. *Exiting Nirvana: A Daughter's Life with Autism.* New York: Back Bay Books.

Park, C.C. and Park, J. 2006. Living with Autism: A Collaboration. In *Stress and Coping in Autism* (eds.) M.G. Baron, J. Groden, G. Groden, and L.P. Lipsitt, 82–94. New York: Oxford University Press.

Perner, L. 2012. *Scholars with Autism: Achieving Dreams.* Sedona: Auricle Books.

Prince, D.E. 2010. An Exceptional Path: An Ethnographic Narrative Reflecting on Autistic Parenthood from Evolutionary, Cultural, and Spiritual Perspectives. *Ethos* 38, no. 1: 56–68.

Prince-Hughes, D. 2002. *Aquamarine Blue 5: Personal Stories of College Students with Autism.* Athens, OH: Swallow Press.

——— 2004. *Songs of the Gorilla Nation: My Journey through Autism.* New York: Doubleday.

——— 2005. *Expecting Teryk: An Exceptional Path to Parenthood.* Athens, OH: Swallow Press.

Reilly, M. 1962. Occupational Therapy Can Be One of the Great Ideas of 20th Century Medicine. *American Journal of Occupational Therapy* 16, no. 1: 1–9.

Ruddick, S. 1980. Maternal Thinking. *Feminist Studies* 6, no. 2: 342–367.

Sacks, O. 1970. The Twins. In *The Man Who Mistook His Wife for a Hat and Other Clinical Tales*, 195–213. New York: Touchstone.

Savage, D. 2003. Matthew's Story. In *Treating Autism: Parent Stories of Hope and Success* (eds) S.M. Edelson and B. Rimland, 287–292. San Diego: Autism Research Institute.

Solomon, O. 2009. Giftedness and Creativity in Autism. In *Encyclopedia of Giftedness, Creativity, and Talent* (ed.) B.A. Kerr, 82–83. Thousand Oaks: Sage.

——— 2010. Sense and the Senses: Anthropology and the Study of Autism. *Annual Review of Anthropology* 39: 241–259.

Treffert, D.A. 1989. *Extraordinary People: Understanding Savant Syndrome.* New York: Ballantine Books.

Trevarthen, C. 1996. *Children with Autism: Diagnosis and Interventions to Meet Their Needs.* London: Jessica Kingsley.

Wall, G. 2010. Mothers' Experience with Intensive Parenting and Brain Development Discourse. *Women's Studies International Forum* 33, no. 3: 253–263.

Wiltshire, S. 1991. *Floating Cities: Venice, Amsterdam, Leningrad – and Moscow.* New York: Summit Books.

Yanow, D. 1999. Public Policies as Identity Stories: American Race-Ethnic Discourse. In *Telling Tales: On Evaluation and Narrative* (ed.) T. Amba, 29–52. Stamford: JAI Press.

7

Achievement and Private Equity in the U.K.

A Game of Abstraction, Sociality and Making Money

*Sarah F. Green**

What counts as achievement in private equity for those who founded the sector in the U.K.? The question has one obvious answer: making as large amounts of money as possible. Rather less obvious is what the money stands for as an achievement: given that private equity makes money out of money, as is the case for all financial techniques, and that the quantities of money made by successful practitioners are many orders of magnitude larger than could be normally accounted for in terms of the effort put into the activity, the kind of achievement indexed by the money is not altogether obvious. It is clearly not the same as a wage received in return for a given amount of work; but equally, it is also not randomly made, like winning the lottery. As Maurer notes in his summary of anthropological debates about money: 'money has been a metaphor for and exemplar of the problem of the relationship between sign and substance, thought and matter, abstract value and its instantiation in physical and mental labours and products' (Maurer 2006: 27). This means there is no self-evident answer to the question of what making money out of money achieves. In the same article, Maurer notes that these relations between things that money stands for, or of which money is an exemplar, do not remain stable but are contingent, changing both across time and according to different vantage points. What is more, since the end of the gold standard in the 1970s, when political control over money was loosened and fragmented – what Chris Gregory famously called the rise of 'savage money' (Gregory 1997: 1–2) – there has been a marked increase in the frequency with which the meaning and value of money, let alone its asserted relationship to anything 'real', has been questioned (Maurer 2006: 28). So while there have been extensive debates about the relationship between political power and markets in determining the value of money in a wider sense,[1] this chapter focuses instead on what kind of achievement making money out of money constitutes for those involved in one part of the financial sector in the U.K.: private equity.

The moral aspects of this question are of course pervasively present, and could even be argued to be a key element of what counts as achievement in this sector. This is not only because classic debates about money-making, especially in a capitalist context, often suggest that social damage is caused by the activity; nor is it only because of the argument that money in general, at least within a market-based economy, acts as a kind of acid, corroding social relationships (Parry and Bloch 1989: 6); it is also because certain forms of money-making come in for a lot more critical commentary than others. As an activity, private equity has attracted its share of negative media attention, even before the financial crises that gripped large parts of the developed world in 2008. For example, in 2007, there was an outpouring of criticism in the U.K. when a consortium of private equity firms attempted to buy out Sainsbury's, one of the best known supermarket chains in the country. A headline in *The Economist* read: 'Sainsbury's: A Trolley Too Far. Barbarians at the check-out as private equity prepares to pounce'.[2] Richard Wachman, writing about a second potential buyout of Sainsbury's, this time by a Qatari private equity firm called Delta Two, noted that in recent months the debate in the U.K., 'has seen private equity leaders pilloried as asset strippers and quick buck merchants' (Wachman 2007). The Sainsbury's bid, which eventually failed, had followed the successful buyout of Alliance-Boots, one of the best known pharmacy and toiletry businesses in the U.K., for an estimated £11.1 billion; that purchase attracted high levels of public attention to this previously rather obscure part of the financial sector.[3]

The negative coverage was by no means limited to the U.K. In 2005, Franz Müntefering, who was then head of Germany's SPD party, described private equity firms as 'swarms of locusts that fall on companies, stripping them bare before moving on'.[4] Much earlier than that, in the late 1980s in the U.S.A., the history of one particularly large private equity deal, the buyout of RJR Nabisco, became the subject of a book entitled *Barbarians at the Gate* (Burrough and Helyar 1990); a film by the same name was released in 1993. The 'barbarians' epithet coined by Burrough and Helyar has since stuck with headline writers, as have phrases such as 'predatory capitalism', 'corporate stalkers' and 'vulture capitalism'. Academic commentators have also joined in the debate, arguing that private equity practices have potentially deeply damaging implications, both for the companies that are the objects of these practices and in wider social and economic terms (e.g., Froud and Williams 2007; Nielsen 2008).

There is no doubt, then, that private equity is one of those financial techniques currently in the public dock for having contributed to the economic mess in which much of the developed world in the northern hemisphere finds itself, and is also suspected of helping to develop a form of capitalism – (neoliberal, globalised) finance capitalism, as opposed to industrial or managerial capitalism – that wreaks havoc with wider social, political and economic relations.[5] The recent Occupy movement is the latest of a long series of attacks against what many suggest is the moral vacuum, serious financial instability and widening economic inequalities that such techniques have apparently generated.[6]

It is in that wider context, one that questions both the moral value of financial practices after the collapse of the gold standard, as well as questioning the economic logic of such practices even within their own terms, that this exploration of what constitutes achievement within private equity is couched. The five men who founded private equity in the U.K. whom we interviewed (and who accounted for approximately one-third of all founders of private equity in the U.K.) were acutely aware of these critical commentaries, though they never explicitly referred to them in their interviews with us. I will be suggesting that these men both ignored and occasionally even implicitly mocked the values that would condemn private equity as a practice. They certainly expressed no defensiveness about it, nor attempted to redeem the practice using the same moral standards that critically challenged such financial techniques. So rather than adding another voice to the well-rehearsed debate about what is morally objectionable about finance capitalism, this chapter focuses instead on how the founders of one aspect of it provide an alternative logic to their practice through an understanding of it as a highly intellectually complex skill that is practised in the 'real world' but that derives its meaning and justification from within its own field, a field temporarily separated from the wider context in which it exists. A particularly provocative aspect of this is the very high quantities of money these men made personally, which unsurprisingly turns out to be a key index of achievement in the field: these quantities seemed to take the activity out of normal scales for evaluating the relationship between activity and monetary reward. Indeed, some have suggested that there was such a big mismatch between the amounts of money generated and any positive effect on the companies involved, let alone wider economic and social conditions, that private equity as a practice was labelled a 'moral hazard', liable to generate economic crisis by encouraging behaviour that was ultimately unsustainable and damaging to economic relations as a whole (Bernile et al. 2007; Nielsen 2008). Even in classical economic terms, the quantities do not appear to make sense. Nevertheless, these quantities were the key measure of achievement, the visible trace of having succeeded in the field of private equity. Yet that still leaves open the question of what was achieved, and that is the underlying focus of this chapter.

Some anthropologists have already carried out extensive studies on what was going on within a variety of financial institutions, and for the financiers themselves, during the development and rising use of these techniques in other parts of the financial sector, most particularly in investment banking and large trading floors. Those studies have offered a wide range of perspectives on the cultural logic that has informed those practices (Maurer 2002, 2005a; Zaloom 2006; Miyazaki 2007; Ho 2009), on the social inequalities that they both reflect and reproduce (Ho 2009), and on the historical moments that drew people inexorably into social relations and practices that subsequently proved to make little financial sense at all (Tett 2009; Ouroussoff 2010). This contribution on private equity is both more modest, being based on a handful of interviews with some of the key people who developed private equity in the U.K., and more focused on the interface that was simultaneously created and imagined between the practice of private equity and the purchased companies that had private equity financial techniques applied to them. Through the descriptions these men gave of their activities, which unsurprisingly made no mention of locusts, vultures, stalkers or barbarians, a picture emerged of a high risk, highly complex game that operated outside the boundaries of other financial practices and mildly mocked the more familiar values of work, while at the same time being apparently deeply rooted in principles of integrity in financial dealings, yet also made a virtue of regularly firing even the closest of colleagues. In short, these interviews seemed to constitute a kind of running critical commentary on the more familiar moral principles of the relations between work, money, people and commercial enterprise that private equity practices appeared to be up-ending. At the same time, the commentaries managed to side-step the wider moral implications of the practices of private equity by framing its activities within a self-contained and short-term field: the period during which companies were bought, leveraged, restructured and then re-sold. What follows is an attempt to explore how that worked and the paradoxes it involved, beginning with a description of how private equity works, providing the context for the commentaries of its founders in the U.K.

Private Equity as a Practice

Private equity firms begin their activities by attracting private and institutional investors to build up a large fund: in the 1980s and 1990s, this was typically several hundred million pounds; in the early 2000s, it was often several billion pounds.[7] This fund is then used to purchase one or more publicly listed companies, which, by being bought out with private funds, then become privately owned – that is, the company is no longer listed on the stock exchange. Usually, the purchased company is then heavily leveraged; this means the debt of the company is increased substantially, by between five and eight times more debt than it had before it was bought (Nielsen 2008: 381). This substantially increases the company's debt repayment obligations, which regularly leads to cost-cutting measures, typically including branch closures and compulsory redundancies. But those loans also provide large quantities of available cash that can be used for restructuring the purchased company, and for paying special dividends to the private equity firm's investors. As Nielsen notes, it is highly unusual outside the private equity business to use newly acquired debt to pay dividends to investors; yet the majority of the new debt in private equity leveraged buy-outs is used for this purpose, with a much smaller proportion used for restructuring the business (ibid.). The partners of the private equity firm also extract payments for management of the private equity fund, typically 1 to 2 per cent of the fund's total value. A fund of £1 billion (quite modest in 2000s standards) would thus generate an annual management fee of £10 to £20 million.

The ultimate aim of private equity practice is to sell the company back into public ownership (or to another private equity firm) within a maximum of five years after its acquisition, and ideally at a considerable profit. This is called the 'exit strategy', which is put into place the moment the company has been bought. Typically, private equity firm partners retain 20 per cent of the profit on the sale, on which they pay a considerably lower tax rate than normal income tax, as this is classed as income from capital investment rather than from employment.

During the period before the financial crash, between 2002 and 2007, debt was relatively cheap and easily obtained, so private equity funds used exceptionally large amounts of leverage (often 70 per cent of the entire value of companies) to increase both their ability to buy more companies and to pay higher dividends. During that period, it was possible to build up private equity funds of tens of billions of pounds, which made it possible to buy up companies such as Debenhams, Boots and the Automobile Association. It also became possible for individual private equity practitioners to personally make tens of millions of pounds a year from the activity. All five men interviewed for this research were included in the select group that did regularly make that amount of money.[8]

In the simplest terms then, private equity is a money-making technique: private equity firms borrow others' money to make more money, and they apply a variety of financial techniques while companies are in their ownership to generate money for themselves and the fund's investors. The main difference between the activities of private equity practitioners and people working in stock exchanges or in investment banking, and this is an important difference, is that private equity practitioners purchase whole companies that exist in what is usually called the 'real economy'. The idea of a 'real economy' of course depends upon the existence of a financial sector that is considered to be separate from the companies that produce goods and services. Assuming the existence of that separation for a moment, this was the key financial innovation of private equity, developed in the U.K. in the 1980s: rather than contain the complex financial arrangements involving derivatives, high levels of leverage, hedge funds and so on within the banking system and stock exchanges, private equity took all those techniques out of the trading floor and applied them to factories and shops directly. This difference is also what generated high levels of moral indignation within the media and some political circles about private equity: the only purpose of buying a company was to extract money from it while it was owned and to sell it off at a profit as soon as possible. This appeared to many to be even worse than making money out of money in the banks and stock exchanges, as it was directly altering the operations of the bought-out company and the lives of its employees (many of whom lost their jobs) in the process of making money out of money, and also adding enormous levels of new debt to the company. In Froud and Williams's terms, what was going on was 'financial engineering' whose sole purpose was the extraction of monetary value from the company: 'In our view, private equity represents a rearrangement of ownership claims for value capture which then allows value extraction, particularly for the benefit of the few who are positioned as private equity principals or senior managers in the operating businesses' (Froud and Williams 2007: 407). Of course, the word 'value' in this statement is being used as a synonym of money. Froud and Williams go on to discuss the work of some academics, most famously Michael Jensen (1989),[9] who welcomed the development of what was increasingly called finance capitalism during the 1980s, and who argued that applying financial techniques such as leveraged buy-outs to companies resulted in a 'purer, more efficient' form of capitalism (Froud and Williams: 407).

There are many who would argue that the development of finance capitalism effectively erases the distinction between the 'real' economy and financial markets,[10] and if that is the case then private equity could be said to have provided the direct bridge that allowed such a blending. However, this is a question of semantics, for in order for there to be a 'real' economy, there must be some economic activity that is imagined to be outside it and that is somehow less 'real' – and that is the financial sector. What makes it less 'real' is the making of money out of money without making anything else (such as shoes or a railway journey).[11] The underlying key idea here is that making money out of money is an abstraction, that it is less involved with the experienced world than making shoes or providing a train journey. Karen Ho has argued that even amongst investment bankers within Wall Street, there is an asserted, rather than an actual, separation or abstraction going on, which conceals a complex interplay between virtual and real (Ho 2009: 34–37). I will return to this later, in suggesting that private equity practitioners did not imagine a separation between the virtual and the real, nor even an articulation between them: they placed their activity entirely within the real, emphasising that practitioners needed to have the social skills to deal with the complex relations involved in buying and selling companies which they managed for up to five years, as opposed to the much shorter time frames used in investment banking – these days, often microseconds.[12]

More importantly, the separation private equity practitioners made was between two different kinds of real: the period during which companies were owned within private equity, and the periods outside that time. While owned, these companies entered into the private equity field of activity and were managed within its rules. This separation, rather than one between a 'real' economy and something more abstract, was the crucial one for private equity practitioners: within this time-limited field, the techniques, rules, structures and values were all defined by private equity logic which was designed to do one thing: generate as much money as possible and have a successful 'exit' (that is, the end of the game). There were many players involved: the major investors who contributed to the funds; the partners in the private equity firm, who were relied upon to spot, develop and make good deals; and even the managers of the companies that the private equity firms bought out. But during the period of private equity ownership, all of these were under private equity management and control.

What follows is an outline of how the private equity practitioners we interviewed described that field, which draws out how the relations between the people, the money, the activity and the companies were all framed within this field during the period that companies were owned. This underlies the whole logic by which achievement was understood by these men. Because of the small number of people involved in the development of private equity in the U.K., I am unable to give detailed descriptions of these men, save to note the following: all five are British citizens, ethnically white, aged between their late 40s and early 60s, and all gave us a minimum of ninety minutes of their time for the interviews. They were interviewed in 2007 in their offices in London. No ethnographic research was done, so the material in this chapter is necessarily limited to these men's descriptions of their activities in response to questions during the interviews.

Absurdities

In response to a question about his thoughts about money, Tony commented:

> I discovered that as I was doing this incredibly exciting job that I love, that people kept paying me more and more and more money to do it [*sic.*]. Beyond any sane logic. Investors have decided that this is the place to be but none of us who started in the early days in this business had any contemplation that it could be as absurdly profitable as it is.

Tony's emphasis on the degree of fun involved in this activity was shared by all interviewees. Richard, in discussing what got him into the business in the first place, commented: 'compared to sitting in some office somewhere off a long corridor in corporate Britain, it seemed more fun'. All depicted the development of private equity as a kind of maverick activity, outside what they described as being rather safe and boring jobs within the financial sector. And as all our interviewees were founders of private equity firms, all of them also emphasised that they enjoyed not having an employer.

In addition to emphasising the enjoyment, all were also struck by the quantities of money they made. As outlined earlier, during the 2000s, those amounts were remarkably large. Some sense of the level of this also comes from another interviewee, Gary, on being asked whether he keeps track of how much he is worth. He replied: 'I would worry about my net assets nowadays if they went down to single millions because I'm well beyond that point. I wouldn't worry about it before then. The difference between being worth 10 million and a 100 million is nothing'. 'Nothing' initially seemed to me to be an excessive remark, absurd even: to say that the difference between 10 million and 100 million was nothing appeared to challenge the value of money, the very object, subject and product of private equity activity. Yet as the conversation continued, the comment began to make sense. The word 'worth' in Gary's statement referred only to quantities of money; there was no moral or qualitative evaluation here, a point emphasised by Gary's statement that there is no difference between being worth 10 million and 100 million. The sheer quantities of money made it difficult to associate the money with the value of persons, relations, things, activities: the quantities were too large for that, they went beyond any scale for comparison. Recall Maurer's comment about money: that it involves 'the relationship between sign and substance, thought and matter, abstract value and its instantiation in physical and mental labours and products' (Maurer 2006: 27). It would appear that something slightly different happens when the quantity of money rises beyond a certain level.

I am borrowing Strathern's understanding of scale here (Strathern 1991): in Strathern's view, scale not only measures quantitative differences (scale of magnitude); it also measures the quality of something, for every yardstick also defines what it measures (scale of domain). Thus money could be used as a scale to compare a diamond and an orange, but it would not make much sense to use calories as a scale for that comparison. I am suggesting that the quantities of money made by some private equity specialists went literally 'off the scale' and meant that its use as a comparative measure of the qualitative worth of the person who owned the money seemed absurd, even if it was possible to quantify the amount that a person was worth in purely numerical terms. As I mentioned earlier and will discuss further below, the quantities of money were depicted by these men as an index of (qualitative) achievement, but the quantity of money was not a direct index of qualitative worth of the person, only their quantitative worth. Thought of in that way, the difference between being worth 10 million and being worth 100 million is indeed nothing, zero.

Of course, zero is one of those numbers that has attracted especially close attention, both by numerologists and accountants. As Maurer notes, zero is crucial to double-entry book-keeping: the whole point of the double entry is to ensure that every transaction in the credit column has a matching one in the debit column, so that the final sum always adds up to zero, which is nothing. Maurer suggests that during the historical development of modern book-keeping and finance, certain numbers were associated with magic, monsters, the imaginary, and all kinds of moralising (Maurer 2005b: 115–21); zero was chief amongst these special, somewhat dangerously strange, numbers. Maurer argues: 'the troubling lack conveyed in zero ... the creation of nothing out of nothing for no (holy) purpose – called forth a new and terrible beast: the person as an empty cipher, the subject as its own negation and absence' (ibid.: 118).

The absence being pointed to in Gary's remarks was an absence of any direct connection between the activity of private equity and the quantity of money generated, and there is a moral commentary here as well. The simultaneous recognition and denial of the moral charge carried by such enormous quantities of money within a capitalist context is palpable here. Of course it is hubris, but there is an important negation in the statement: the quantities of money generated not only mocks the relationship which ideally ought to exist between levels of effort and a just reward; it also suggests that beyond a certain quantity, the whole system of measurement in those terms becomes meaningless – literally nothing, just more zeros. In that sense, Gary's statement not only negates the labour theory of value (there is zero relationship between work done and the payment made for it), it appears to mock the logic of the (Protestant) work ethic as well: that is, the idea that people should work hard as a moral principle in order to be good citizens, comrades, bourgeoisie, believers or whatever, in return for which they will receive their just desserts, whether in this world or the next. The practice of private equity was nothing like that, and yet it was better at making money than just about any other activity.

Earnings and Achievement

Given that the money generated from private equity is defined as capital gains rather than employment income for tax purposes; that there appeared to be no relationship between the quantities of money generated and the activity; that the activity was defined by its top practitioners as 'fun'; and that those same practitioners pointed to the apparent absurdity of the level of profitability of private equity practices, it is perhaps not surprising to find that none of the interviewees described the money they had made as 'earned'. While there was a close relationship between the quantities of money and the activity of private equity, earnings did not come into it.

Although all interviewees emphasised that they were extremely disciplined, dedicated, often worked long hours and were competitive in their activities, the reason they gave for doing all of this was that it was enjoyable and they wanted to win, and not that they were following some sense of obligation to work hard, or because they wanted to achieve some higher moral or spiritual aim. There was no higher purpose or dedication to something beyond the game of private equity: the game was all. Indeed, all emphasised that they took regular holidays (six a year on average) and John even suggested that those who did not do so were 'mugs'. David noted that one of the advantages of being a partner in the firm rather than one of the firm's lawyers was that he never had to be on call at weekends or unsociable hours.

The apparent paradox here is self-evident: the whole stated aim and purpose of private equity was to make money; yet the money was not regarded as 'earned' and nor was it an adequate index of the activities that led to the profits made. However, the achievement was indexed by quantities of money: not only the money extracted from deals successfully managed and concluded (that is, the profits made, both personally and for investors), but also the size of the funds that could be raised in order to carry out new deals. Being able to attract investors was as much a measure of achievement as being able to successfully complete deals. In short, the quantities of money might be better regarded as an index of the skill of the private equity practitioner at playing the game of private equity, rather than as a reflection of the qualitative value of the activity itself. Within this game metaphor, the only limits to the quantities that can be 'won' is the skill of the player. To return to the point made by Strathern about scale here: the scale used to measure success in this context was not based on a labour, exchange, gift or commodity theory of value, but instead on measuring levels of skill in playing the game. This achievement was indexed by the quantities of money generated by playing it, which could be limitless. In this sense, the value attached to the achievement is integrally part of the time-limited private equity field described above, because the measure of the value is dependent upon the skills that are defined by, and which make sense within, that field. I should note that this is not a 'spheres of exchange' argument, as it was not the ascribed value of the objects (the companies) or the products (the money) involved that was the focus of the achievement;[13] rather, the value of the money extracted, within the private equity field, was taken as an index of the skill with which the game was played.

This might sound akin to Graeber's definition of value, as 'the way people represent the importance of their own actions to themselves: normally, as reflected in one or another socially recognised form' (Graeber 2001: 47). Graeber's explicit intention, borrowing from the work of Nancy Munn and combining it with some particular interpretations of Mauss and Marx, is to make the concept of value political, in the sense of rendering it contingent, active and potentially transformative: value is generated from creative and socially meaningful actions, he suggests. The difficulty in borrowing this idea to understand the relation between the money and private equity practice in terms of achievement is that it was the underlying skill at practising private equity that was indexed by the quantities of money generated, not the actions themselves as such: given that the quantities of money generated were 'off the scale', there was no relation between the actual activities (actions) and the quantities of money. Indeed, Froud and Williams note that some of the fees extracted for managing private equity funds 'provides a reward which is completely unrelated to performance' of the fund (Froud and Williams 2007: 412), something that has become more familiar in recent years in relation to investment bankers' bonuses.

If it is the skill of playing the game that was a measure of achievement, then it is worth taking a brief look at what the interviewees understood to be the game, and how they went about creating the field in which it was played.

Attractions of the Game

As already discussed, the objective of the game is to make as much money as possible, and all the interviewees were open about that. Brian, for example:

SARAH: Several times you said that money is the main motivation for people in this business ...

BRIAN: The purest of motives.

Brian repeated this statement on a couple of occasions: that the key motivation in private equity is to generate money, and that this motivation is the 'purest' of motives. As the interview went on, it became clear that what he meant by this reference to purity was again, like Gary with his comment on nothing, an oblique critique of those who would challenge private equity's apparent complete absence of a moral sense. Later on in the interview, he said:

> One of the great purities of our business is that the overwhelming majority of people working in this business focus on making money. Now you might say that that's not a very pure objective. But in the classical definition of, you know – 'What am I here to do?' – I am here to make money for my investors. And on the way through, by the way, I make a bit too, for myself. But if I do my job, I make a satisfactory return for my investors. Lots and lots of other criticisms that you get in other businesses and other industries just fall by the way side.

Here, Brian was explicitly contrasting an implied moral purity ('what am I here to do?') with a clarity and singularity of purpose: a purity generated by the single-minded motivation of making money, an activity achieved through placing companies bought out by his firm within the field of private equity activities and applying a variety of complex financial practices to them. The important point to note here is that the purity of the motivation requires that the company is taken temporarily out of its usual domain and placed within a circumscribed, highly logical private equity field, with its own rules and dynamics, so as to be able to generate money from it using financial techniques.

There is a somewhat tricky relation to abstraction here. Neither Brian nor any of the other interviewees implied that placing a company in private equity control for a fixed period of years constituted a separation from the 'real world'. While the financial techniques used were described as highly mathematically complex, and also that they had a certain abstract beauty to them, there was no suggestion that private equity activity itself was an abstraction from reality. This contrasts somewhat with Karen Ho's description of American investment bankers on Wall Street (Ho 2009). In her ethnography, Ho spends some time debunking the cloak of abstraction that surrounds their financial activity. Along with a number of others now, she argues that the notion of the reified abstraction of finance is deliberate mystification, that the appearance of the mystery of finance is actually the operations of power, hidden behind this idea of numerical wizardry (ibid.: 37). Using the work of Michel Callon,[14] she rejects the dichotomy between the abstract and the real, and suggests: 'economic ideals are neither wholly performed and instantiated into reality nor virtual substitutions for "real life complexity". Analysing what Wall Street investment bankers actually enact necessitates attention to the interface between the virtual and the real, model and effect, as well as the existence of other key cultural contexts that would influence this interaction' (ibid.: 36–37). In other words, Ho is pointing to the way that the concept of abstraction is a political and social artefact, rather than an objective reality, and she also suggests that the model can create the reality that it describes. Nevertheless, she also notes that the financial practitioners she studied made a clear distinction between the virtual and the real, so it was important to ethnographically study how that imagined separation was put into practice. She argues that this occurred in a cultural context that was shot through with inequalities of race, gender and class, and that these differences were deeply embedded within the abstractions of financial calculation.

In contrast to this, the private equity practitioners we interviewed made no attempt to separate their financial techniques from 'reality' in commenting on the abstract character of those techniques. Rather, it seemed to me, their comments on the complexity of the techniques used was part of creating the parameters of the field of the game: generating a distinction between one kind of reality and another, as a means to mark a difference during the temporary period that companies were under private equity ownership. There was no suggestion that this was a pure abstraction. On the contrary, most interviewees asserted that this was a complex and fascinating technique that required immense skill to practise well, and that the outcome, if successful, altered the shape of the companies to which these techniques were applied, and in the course of this, created a great deal of money.

In this respect, all our interviewees emphasised what, in their view, was the beauty in the complexity and abstraction of the calculations involved in private equity financial arrangements (that is, the various leveraging and other financial techniques used to generate money), and they emphasised this as one of the main attractions of the business for them.[15] All had done exceptionally well in their higher education, most particularly in studies that involved a deep understanding of, and ability to deal with, mathematics. Three of the five had also achieved at the top level in other academic disciplines (philosophy, physics and chemistry). Less surprisingly, four had MBAs from top universities such as Harvard, and all insisted that anybody they employed in their private equity firms had to have attained the same, if not better, levels of academic achievement, most particularly in dealing with the abstractions of number. In short, there was an insistence that people should have reached an exceptionally high level of intellectual achievement before joining private equity firms.

So one of key skills required to be good at private equity practice was exceptionally high abilities in quantitative calculation. But in order to create the field in which private equity can be practised, funds need to be raised and companies need to be purchased, and for those two activities the crucial skills are, according to all interviewees, good judgement and high levels of social skills, or what Bourdieu rather famously called a 'feel for the game':

> the 'feel for the game' is what gives the game a subjective sense – a meaning and a *raison d'être*, but also a direction, an orientation, an impending outcome, for those who take part and therefore acknowledge what is at stake (this is the *illusio* in the

> sense of investment in the game and the outcome, interest in the game, commitment to the presuppositions – *doxa* – of the game). (Bourdieu 1995: 66)

The 'feel for the game' in this definition is also what defines it as a game, one that involves certain expectations and intentions (making money was in this sense the *doxa* of the game), and an idea about the best way to go about it. Brian's discussion of the purity of the motivation of making money made clear that this was not some other-worldly activity but that the whole point of the activity was performative: the activity had to leave its material trace and also be integrally a part of the world, or there was no point in doing it. The money was partly an index of achievement of skilfully manipulating the world of finance, precisely quantified in numbers. But there was more to it than that. Being able to generate or extract money also required effective, and apparently quantitatively non-measurable, social skills. Most interviewees emphasised that while a certain number of people could achieve the highest levels of technical ability in financial calculation, a much smaller number could, in their view, combine this with the additional skills required to spot a 'good deal', to have the social skills required to bring all the people needed in a deal together in order to make it into a reality, and to see the whole project through to the end. In short, an essential part of achievement in this field was an ability to be in the thick of things, to deal with all the messiness of everyday life, and to have the persuasive skills to draw both investors and potential companies into the private equity field. The alchemy of the financial techniques, and their ability to define the private equity field in which companies could be restructured, was only part of both the enjoyment and the achievement: even more important, in many ways, was the way these activities were both bound up with, and also changed, things in the world. That was a big part of the fascination: the combination of calculation with the ability to pull it off in terms of both changing companies and generating money.

All interviewees emphasised that an extraordinarily small number of people could achieve at the highest levels in this activity, and that what distinguished the successful people from the failures was a really excellent understanding of the social context in which they were working. This was one reason why, Gary suggested, Americans had not been initially very successful in the private equity field in the U.K. Although private equity was developed in the U.S.A., the Americans did not initially have the appropriate 'feel for the game' in the U.K., in Gary's view. This was not because they could not learn the game, he said; indeed, by the late 1990s and early 2000s, the Americans were making significant headway in the private equity business in London. It was rather that when they first arrived they were unaware of significant social differences and expectations in the U.K. compared to the U.S. To quote Gary's views on this, speaking of the late 1990s: 'The Americans came back and really speeded it on. But when the Americans had come before at the end of the 80s, they soon retreated with their genitals in tatters'.

Putting aside the distinctly gladiatorial and deeply gendered commentary (Gary was distinctive in that respect amongst our interviewees), the overall sense these practitioners gave was that years of experience in business relations within the U.K. initially gave British private equity practitioners the edge over the Americans. For example, David commented that it would be unthinkable, in the U.K., to question a verbal agreement from a representative of a financial institution who had the authority to give that agreement; Americans usually insisted on having such agreements in writing. Americans were also, according to two of the interviewees, more aggressive, more corporate and less diplomatic than their U.K. counterparts, but they learned rapidly to adjust to the different conditions. This was a relatively weak assertion of national differences; my point, in any case, is that all interviewees emphasised the need for a fairly deep understanding of social relations and appropriate interactions in order to be able to succeed in private equity: this was not an other-worldly activity in any sense.

Interestingly, this is one area where all interviewees did evoke a fairly strong assertion of moral integrity in their practices, and even contrasted themselves with others in the financial sector. This was Richard's response to a question about trust within the private equity field:[16]

> You start lying, cheating or treading on people, you don't last long. With the possible exception of investment banking where treading on people as they go past is considered fine. You only need to make three or four years of bonuses, then you're off in the big wide world to do something else. Probably not very happy souls. I bet if you took your average investment banker and private equity lad, any reasonable measure of contentment would go to the private equity guy.

The comment here refers specifically to integrity in relations between private equity practitioners, and the contrast with investment bankers was made by several interviewees. The difference, all suggested, was the amount of time private equity practitioners had to commit to each deal: the building up of a fund, the purchasing of companies (sometimes as hostile takeovers, but it was much easier if company directors could be persuaded to sell out willingly), the management of the company, and then the final 'exit', which could take up to ten years. That was an unimaginably long time in investment banking; and that relative longevity, despite also always being time-limited, is one of the elements that made the private equity field part of the 'real' world. If the financial sector as a whole had lost its 'moral bearings' in terms of social relations, the private equity sector, at least in this sense, had not.

The implication of this is that private equity practitioners are not denying the value of integrity in personal social relations per se, nor the importance of maintaining and sustaining that integrity consistently and over long periods of time; and in fact, they identified some others within the financial sector as failing in this regard. Instead, these interviewees were denying that the absence of a relationship between the quantities of money made and earnings somehow axiomatically made the activity morally suspect. At the same time, none of the interviewees made any comments about the wider social effects of private equity practice, and nor was that part of a sense of the achievement or otherwise of private equity: this issue fell outside the field of the game.

A High Risk Game

So, successful achievement in this field was about the intellectual and social skills needed to both attract and then generate theoretically limitless quantities of money (as it involves making money out of money, so there is no material limit to how far this game can go). The final element to consider is what constituted failure for these men, and how that was confronted. I am limited here, as the five interviewees were selected precisely because they were spectacularly successful, so their views on what constitutes failure was probably more of a rule book than any kind of self-reflection.

There were two kinds of failure described by the interviewees: the first was a failure to achieve at the highest levels, which indicated a personal incapacity and led to instant dismissal; and the second was any kind of failure of social integrity, honesty or reliability, which also led to instant dismissal from the firm. The first requires little comment, as it is a characteristic of many financial institutions: the skills (high levels of intellectual and particularly numerical ability; an ability to make good judgements; extremely good social skills) had to be constantly re-demonstrated – any drop in standards would lead to instant firing. The one notable aspect of this in the view of our interviewees was that the regular firing of senior colleagues was described as an essential and healthy aspect of the private equity business rather than being an unfortunate but necessary aspect. Brian: 'If we don't lose a partner every two years, I would suggest that would be an unhealthy environment'; Tony: 'We fire partners. Lots of partners. Not one every three years, more than that.'

The parallels with high-risk sports that can involve sudden death are obvious here, and the association is possibly an explicit one, given that all our interviewees, without exception, were also actually involved in high-risk sports, such as heli-skiing (skiing using a helicopter to transport you up mountains), car racing, rock-face climbing and so on. The links with the tendency to lay off workers from the companies bought out by private equity are also quite clear. The 'feel for the game' also involved an expectation that the game could end disastrously at any moment.

In this respect, these private equity practitioners reflected Callon's ideas about 'economics in the wild' (Callon 2007): the relationship between a given financial technique, the companies to which it was applied, and the wider context in which the game was played out, was always one of mutual dependence. So while private equity practitioners went a good way towards generating a distinction between the field in which the company has been purchased by a private equity fund and the field beyond that, the interface is always porous. That always introduced elements that might result in failure: a feel for the game might give a good private equity practitioner a means to create the field and to have a good guess at what might happen next – or what Bourdieu calls 'a proleptic adjustment to the demands of a field' (Bourdieu 1995: 66) – but much could happen that was entirely unpredictable. And this brings me to the second aspect of failure: failure of social integrity, honesty and reliability. All interviewees could easily forgive a partner whose deal had gone terribly wrong, even if it lost the firm tens of millions of pounds (so long as the failure was not too frequent); such things happen, apparently. What they could not forgive was any kind of deceit – an important issue in a business that is trying to create new realities through rearranging old ones and adding a few zeros in the process.

This approach towards the risks of private equity – risks generated by the logic and rules of the game that had been created by these founders of the business in the U.K. – was the final element that shaped the manner in which achievement was understood by them: just as the time that a company was in private equity hands was limited, the amount of time that someone might survive in the business was also usually limited, dependent upon the maintenance and constant development of the skills needed to keep playing.

Conclusion

I have suggested that what the founders of private equity in the U.K. understood as achievement was the demonstration of immense skill required to generate as much money as possible from private equity activities. And in this game, the quantities of money generated – both the money made personally by the partners and the sheer size of deals and funds built up – acted as a constant numerical monitor of this achievement. The money as such did not act as a measure of the activity in any direct sense because there was no perceived equivalence between the actions of the practitioners and the amount of money generated: apart from the point that the quantities of money that could be made went way beyond any scale that is normally used to establish such an equivalence, there was also a good chance that the effort expended could generate no money at all on occasion, and in a way that was unpredictable. The one area where the quantities of money *were* regarded as being an index of achievement was as an indicator of the skill of the practitioner: that skill did not guarantee success, but without it the money would not be generated. Having said that, the sheer quantities of money limited what the money could indicate about the qualities of the people involved in the activity: beyond a certain level, all that could be measured is quantity, and nothing else, because there was no means of bringing these quantities into relation with anything else.

In addition, private equity practices were deliberately circumscribed within a private equity field limited by the short time period during which bought-out companies remained within private equity control, and by the financial techniques applied to them during that period. This depiction of private equity activity gives the practice more the characteristics of a game with circumscribed rules that do not necessarily map onto the logic that informs external moral judgement of the activity as an activity. The time-limited character of the private equity practice in that sense both sidesteps any direct consideration, within the field, of what the implications of the game are for a given company once it has been returned to public ownership. The whole process is a shape-shifting one, during which the entity is taken out of its previous context, reorganised, and then returned, yet what happens next is not part of the field.

Notes

* The research for this paper was based on a joint project with Karel Williams and Julie Froud (both of the Centre for Research in Socio-Cultural Change), who jointly carried out the interviews for this paper and who are the real experts in private equity and financialisation in the research team; my contribution was to explore the social contexts in which these financial practices occurred, and to try to understand something of the descriptions its practitioners gave for their activities. All the names of the interviewees have been changed.

1. Some of the more notable anthropologists debating the issue include Hart (1986, 2009), Graeber (1996, 2001) and Gregory (1997).
2. *The Economist*, 8 February 2007 <www.economist.com/node/8675257> (accessed 24 March 2013)
3. BBC News Channel, 31 May 2007 <http://news.bbc.co.uk./1/hi/business/6708245.stm> (accessed 24 March 2013).
4. *The Economist*, 5 May 2005 <www.economist.com/node/3935994> (accessed 24 March 2013). It should be noted that the article heavily criticised Müntefering's remarks, and even suggested they were unfortunate, coming as they did from a German politician.
5. Boltanski and Chiapello (2005) have provided a sweeping account of these transitions in what they call 'spirits' of capitalism (borrowing from Weber). This most recent version, they suggest, is the one that is networked, non-hierarchical, flexible, fragmented and highly individualistic, with no overall moral compass by which people should judge themselves.
6. David Graeber provides an interesting perspective on this, arguing that not only finance capitalism but also postmodern theory suffers from this moral vacuum. Indeed, he goes so far as to argue that postmodernism (not quite the same thing as postmodern theory) shares the same ideology as the ideology of this market (Graeber 2001: xi, 89).
7. This description of the practice of private equity is necessarily brief. More detailed descriptions can be found in Nielsen (2008) and Froud and Williams (2007).
8. Five is a small number for most social science research; however, this represented about a third of the total number of people who developed private equity in the U.K. As noted by Savage and Williams, the study of elites has suffered from a statistical approach towards social research that developed in the twentieth century in the U.K. (Savage and Williams 2008: 5).
9. See also Jensen and Meckling (1976), which was the earliest articulation of this approach, extending the work of Milton Friedman.
10. See, e.g., the contributions to Mackenzie et al. (2007).
11. The concept of a 'veil of money' as somehow obscuring the 'real' economy in which genuine goods and services are made, somehow hidden by the monetary transactions that are built upon them, is an important part of this perceived distinction (Boianovsky 1993). The obvious practical difficulty with this view of economy – i.e. that it presumes the prior existence of goods and services (the real part) before the existence of the market (the veil or virtual part) hardly needs rehearsing here (Graeber 2011: 345). In any case, I do not intend to enter into the debate about whether there is a distinction; my point is that people behave as if that distinction is real, and that has important social effects.
12. The speed of trading that is automated by software is truly impressive, as is described by Mackenzie (2011).

13. Graeber makes the point that the spheres of exchange idea depended primarily on looking for the value in objects (Graeber 2001: 44).
14. Callon has also written a more recent and further developed argument of his view that economics creates the reality that it describes (Callon 2007).
15. It is worth noting that this fascination with intellectual skill was not, I think, an expression of some kind of Aristotelian ethics, a notion of what is 'good' (*kalo*, sometimes translated as 'beautiful') based on the notion of 'intellectual virtue' (see Aristotle, *Nichomachean Ethics*, VI). Aristotle indelibly related his notion of good to the question of virtue, and that was explicitly absent in these men's descriptions.
16. Julie Froud, Karel Williams and I have discussed the question of trust within private equity elsewhere (Froud et al. 2012).

References

Bernile, G., D. Cumming and E. Lyandres. 2007. The Size of Venture Capital and Private Equity Fund Portfolios. *Journal of Corporate Finance* 13, no. 4: 564–590.

Boianovsky, M. 1993. Bohm-Bawerk, Fisher, Irving, and the Term Veil of Money: A Note. *History of Political Economy* 25, no. 4: 725–738.

Boltanski, L., and E. Chiapello. 2005. *New Spirit of Capitalism*. London: Verso.

Bourdieu, P. 1995. *The Logic of Practice* (trans. R. Nice). Cambridge: Polity Press.

Burrough, B., and J. Helyar. 1990. *Barbarians at the Gate: The Fall of R.J.R. Nabisco*. New York: Harper and Row.

Callon, M. 2007. What Does It Mean to Say That Economics Is Performative? In *Do Economists Make Markets? On the Performativity of Economics* (eds) D.A. MacKenzie, F. Muniesa and L. Siu, 311–357. Princeton: Princeton University Press.

Froud, J., S. Green and K. Williams. 2012. Private Equity and the Concept of Brittle Trust. *Sociological Review* 60, no. 1: 1–24.

Froud, J., and K. Williams. 2007. Private Equity and the Culture of Value Extraction. *New Political Economy* 12, no. 3: 405–420.

Graeber, D. 1996. Beads and Money: Notes toward a Theory of Wealth and Power. *American Ethnologist* 23, no. 1: 4–24.

——— 2001. *Toward an Anthropological Theory of Value: The False Coin of Our Own Dreams*. New York: Palgrave.

——— 2011. *Debt: The First 5,000 Years*. New York: Melville House.

Gregory, C.A. 1997. *Savage Money: The Anthropology and Politics of Commodity Exchange*. Amsterdam: Harwood Academic.

Hart, K. 1986. Heads or Tails: Two Sides of the Coin. *Man* 21, no. 4: 637–656.

——— 2009. The Persuasive Power of Money. In *Economic Persuasions* (ed.) S. Gudeman, 136–158. Oxford: Berghahn.

Ho, K.Z. 2009. *Liquidated: An Ethnography of Wall Street*. Durham, NC: Duke University Press.

Jensen, M.C. 1989. Eclipse of the Public Corporation. *Harvard Business Review* 67, no. 5: 61–74.

Jensen, M.C., and W.H. Meckling. 1976. Theory of Firm: Managerial Behavior, Agency Costs and Ownership Structure. *Journal of Financial Economics* 3, no. 4: 305–360.

Mackenzie, D. 2011. How to Make Money in Microseconds. *London Review of Books*, 19 May, pp.16–18.

MacKenzie, D.A., F. Muniesa and L. Siu (eds). 2007. *Do Economists Make Markets? On the Performativity of Economics*. Princeton: Princeton University Press.

Maurer, B. 2002. Repressed Futures: Financial Derivatives' Theological Unconscious. *Economy and Society* 31, no. 1: 15–36.

——— 2005a. Due Diligence and 'Reasonable Man', Offshore. *Cultural Anthropology* 20, no. 4: 474–505.

——— 2005b. *Mutual Life, Limited: Islamic Banking, Alternative Currencies, Lateral Reason.* Princeton: Princeton University Press.

——— 2006. The Anthropology of Money. *Annual Review of Anthropology* 35: 15–36.

Miyazaki, H. 2007. Between Arbitrage and Speculation: An Economy of Belief and Doubt. *Economy and Society* 36, no. 3: 396–415.

Nielsen, R.P. 2008. The Private Equity-Leveraged Buyout Form of Finance Capitalism: Ethical and Social Issues, and Potential Reforms. *Business Ethics Quarterly* 18, no. 3: 379–404.

Ouroussoff, A. 2010. *Wall Street at War: The Secret Struggle for the Global Economy.* Cambridge: Polity Press.

Parry, J., and M. Bloch (eds). 1989. *Money and the Morality of Exchange.* Cambridge: Cambridge University Press.

Savage, M., and K. Williams. 2008. Elites: Remembered in Capitalism and Forgotten by Social Sciences. *Sociological Review* 56 (supplement 1): 1–24.

Strathern, M. 1991. *Partial Connections.* Savage, MD: Rowman and Littlefield.

Tett, G. 2009. *Fool's Gold: How Unrestrained Greed Corrupted a Dream, Shattered Global Markets and Unleashed a Catastrophe.* London: Little Brown.

Wachman, R. 2007. Qataris' Sainsbury Bid Risks Flying into Private Equity Storm. *Observer*, 22 July, p.3.

Zaloom, C. 2006. *Out of the Pits: Traders and Technology from Chicago to London.* Chicago: University of Chicago Press.

8

For Family, State and Nation
Achieving Cosmopolitan Modernity in Late-Socialist Vietnam

Susan Bayly

The economic and political challenges of marketisation in 'late-socialist' Vietnam have generated many new and remarkable understandings of achievement. Drawing on recent fieldwork in Hanoi, my concerns in this chapter are with the often painful complexities of those perceptions, including the dilemmas of moral life and selfhood now widely referred to as 'achievement disease' (*bệnh thành tích*).

My study's context is what is referred to as 'renovation' (*đổi mới*), a process defined as a post-planning or post-'subsidy' transformation, rather than the death of socialism.[1] Vietnamese attach great importance to the story of the country's leap from extreme poverty in the high-socialist era to today's life as one of the world's leading 'transition societies'. That story is now told as one of self-propelled attainment tracked and validated through such global ranking exercises as the Grant Thornton Emerging Markets Opportunity Index, with its celebration of unshackled markets, thrusting entrepreneurs and industrious workers refining their skills in a fast-growing international production and knowledge economy.[2]

In their reactions to this much-propagated success narrative, Vietnamese engage notions of achieving selfhood, both echoing and contesting the more familiar versions of goal-driven 'Asian values'.[3] Yet also widely shared is the sense of an enduring though greatly reconfigured Vietnamese socialist heritage, in which achievement – the most common term for which is *thành tích* in Vietnamese – is defined as attainment by and on behalf of the collective. (Other terms for achievement, attainment and success are discussed below.) Vietnamese citizens still grow up with experience of schoolroom-achiever culture, with its Soviet-style rewards and prizes for those mastering the disciplines of socially active moral citizenship. So too for adults in the still massive state sector, with its obligatory merit schemes rewarding contributions to the work unit and wider community. And as I show below, the materiality of socialist-style achievement culture with its productivity banners and attainment citations is still a conspicuous presence in contemporary Vietnam, within and beyond the home and workspace.

These are diverse yet dynamically interacting regimes of attainment, as can be seen in newly prosperous households engaging conspicuously with the ideal of the modern home as an arena for the nurturing of achievers. Large sums are expended on such things as children's crammer classes and martial arts tuition. Such personal development provision is yet another setting for competitive ranking and indexing exercises. Those involved show little if any sense of disjuncture in moving between these disparate achievement realms. Thus on domestic ancestor altars where householders display items reflecting family members' past and ongoing attainments, a child's award badges from baby-karate competitions will be as prominently displayed as those conferred for exam success and Young Pioneer (Communist Party youth wing: *Thiếu niên tiền phong*) service.

For mothers particularly, such items embody their own successes as achievers on the home front. In addition to their workplace obligations, women must be successful as domestic nurturers. Yet they are also enjoined not to be ferocious 'tiger mothers' like those derided in press accounts of countries like Singapore, where achiever cultures are held to be far more prone to the immorality of 'achievement disease' than in humane and caring Vietnam.[4] Tiger mothers (*mẹ hổ*) are widely conceptualised as Chinese-descended citizens of the 'tiger economy' states, hence products of what is often said to be the pressure-cooker values of the capitalist Pacific Rim countries which are now Vietnam's most important trade and investment partners.

Paradoxically, these new ties have produced dilemmas much like those of the old socialist world: that is, how to benefit from close relations with richer resource-providing 'sibling' powers, without sacrificing the moral fundamentals of Vietnameseness. This generates a dual pressure on women. While struggling to avoid tiger mother excesses, they are still supposed to keep abreast of new ways to sustain their households as mini-achievement bastions. There is always more to learn about making homes into production sites of what is required for a meritorious modern life: health, educational success, selfless patriotism, the drive to excel in the 'modern globalised knowledge economy' (*kinh tế tri thức toàn cầu*, a term familiar to many Hanoians from national media use).[5]

What I am pointing to here is thus the dynamic and mutable qualities of achievement experience: that is, achievement as continually evolving, contested and reconceptualised, and generating intense concern about the basis on which to define or rank a particular pursuit as being either a worthy or unworthy reflection of personal or national capability. Key dimensions of this dynamism include the often painful moral concerns inflecting Vietnamese understandings of achievement. These can be seen in the interplay between notions of individual, familial and other forms of collective attainment at a time of intensive state-led drives to make Vietnam a world-class powerhouse economy, one peopled by high achievers equipped and motivated to become high-quality 'human resources' for the nation's development concerns (Nguyen and Johanson 2008; Fry 2009). What is also notable here are those aspects of achievement experience entailing massive change in the sense of terrain or landscape in which national and personal success have come to be marked and indexed.

Spaces and Horizons of Achievement Experience

At the level of public culture, state-initiated achievement drives are still framed in the old socialist vocabulary of 'struggle movements' and 'patriotic emulation campaigns' (*phong trào thi đua yêu nước*), though in ways suitably updated for a globalised age. This can be seen in the case of the country's National Patriotic Emulation Congresses (*Đại hội thi đua yêu nước toàn quốc*). The 2010 Emulation Congress was held in Hanoi, and attended by 1,500 delegates from the Vietnam Women's Union and other bodies still under the authority of the country's supervisory agency for official mass organisations, the National Fatherland Front. Press accounts noted that these convocations were a creation of the country's pre-independence revolutionary proto-state and have been regularly held since 1948. But what was on show in 2010 was a much transformed conception of what a good citizen should exemplify in a marketised world. Business people were the Congress's most prominent emulation models, even though there were also awards for achievers from the more familiar recipient categories: students, soldiers and workplace 'labour heroes' (*Anh hùng lao động*).[6]

'Emulation' images are still widely used in the state campaign iconography to be seen in public places throughout Vietnam, as in the official poster issued for street use in 2011 (see Figure 8.1). The poster's caption reads: '[Let's all] strive to better [our] record achievements in honour of the fifty-seventh anniversary of

Figure 8.1 Poster exhorting Vietnamese citizens to better their achievements in honour of the fifty-seventh anniversary of Hanoi's liberation.

our capital city's liberation'. Its use of the most familiar Vietnamese term for achievement, *thành tích*, in combination with the expression *thi đua*, is very common in such contexts. *Thi đua*, often translated as 'emulation', is widely used in mobilisation campaigns exhorting workers, students and other key groups to exceed established productivity and excellence norms.

The exaltation of entrepreneurs as citizen-achievers is not a total break with Vietnam's socialist legacy. The tradition of praise for the trader-patriot dates back to the 1946–54 anti-French Liberation War, with its construction of a revolutionary economy in which the skills of trade in wholesome 'home produce' were legitimate and even honourable attainments for a socialist citizen in the making (Dang Phong 2002: 204–8; Bayly 2007: 159–63).[7] It is the anti-colonial context that makes the difference here. Not even all socialist sites and settings define achievement in the same way, still less the wider world. There is thus a real need to note the wide variety of achievement's personifications and languages, as well as the ways these interact and co-construct one another in all the contexts where we seek to understand the nature and significance of attainment as a domain of experience and moral life.

Clearly this view of the trader as a patriotic achiever has made for a surprisingly smooth transition from the high-socialist era's attainment norms to today's understandings of national economic and strategic need. Furthermore, the exaltation of entrepreneurs as role-model achievers rests on a vision of business sense harmoniously combined with patriotic virtue in its various modern forms: concern for the environment, love of community, due deference to authority. So while achievement in Vietnam is far more than a matter of what the state and its agencies define or decree, there is no question of marketisation licensing achievers to embrace attainment goals at odds with those of a still strong and controlling party-state.[8]

Yet as I explain below, there is one particular arena in which attainment criteria are being forged in an area that might appear to be greatly at variance with high-socialist thought. This entails the efforts being made by high-profile individuals and institutions to identify Vietnam as a land of unique gifts in a domain formerly vilified in official ideology, that of psychic spirituality (*tâm linh*). What we see here is clear evidence of the remarkable breadth and range of present-day achievement thinking in Vietnam, as well as a striking transformation in the experience of family life as a critical nexus of achievement goals and strategies.

In Vietnam as elsewhere, attainment is more than the successes or gains of a lone striving individual, as often assumed in studies focusing on the psychological traits and 'goal structures' conducive to high or low achievement.[9] To note the interpenetrating ways in which attainment may entail both single-person and collective concerns and actions means seeing achievement as something other than the capacities and motivations of individuated subjects, either alone or in the aggregate. Achiever collectivities are thus as important for the study of achievement effects as the experiences of the individuated subject who may seek to engage, challenge or reconceptualise a compelling achievement regime.

Within and beyond present-day post-socialist contexts, there is much to learn from exploring points of interface between individual and collective attainment experiences.[10] Of particular interest in Vietnam is the sense of importance attached to a knowledge that one's affective collectivities of family, nation, school and workplace are under perpetual scrutiny: measured, marked and evaluated by either past or current criteria of targets achieved and competitive performance sustained.

It must also be recognised that significant achievement markers do not take shape within exclusively local or even national terms of reference. Vietnam is a site of very active reflection about the wider world of competing achiever nations and comparative scrutiny exercises, both global and those more specific to the Pacific Rim 'tiger' zone. This sense of being a nation under perpetual scrutiny and assessment relates very closely to individuals' personal attainment stories. Such reflections are not necessarily stressful, despite the many expressions of anxiety about how to sustain the momentum of today's increasingly positive success indicators. There is real gratification attached to the knowledge that Vietnam has come to be so strongly ranked in the world's great broad-brush world-scale inventory exercises: the World Economic Forum's Global Competitiveness Index, the World Bank Poverty Reduction scale, the UN's HDI reports, and many more besides.[11]

Of course there is considerable cynicism about reports of exercises such as the U.K.-based New Economics Foundation's Happy Planet Index (HPI), in which Vietnam regularly scores in the top tier.[12] But in the Hanoi neighbourhoods where I do my fieldwork, there is much interest in these matters. This is certainly the case among those residing in my main current field site, a former gated village for which I use the pseudonym Hồ Tây (West Lake), now a populous *phường* (ward or precinct) near the still-active market area known as the Old Quarter (*Khu phố cổ*).

Hồ Tây has moved in less than a generation from an impoverished lakeside fishing and artisanal locality to a high-growth, mini-boom micro-region, fuelled initially by the carefully husbanded capital of its socialist-era overseas labour-draft returnees. In 2010 I found that student-age as well as older Hồ Tây residents are strikingly knowledgeable about the fanfare surrounding Vietnam's recognition as virtually the only non-Western aid-receiver officially recognised as having met its United Nations Millennium Development Goal targets.[13] In this case, it was the fact of their President being applauded at a UN summit that had registered with my informants. They had a general impression of Vietnam being acclaimed for 'doing well' or 'overcoming backwardness', rather than anything more precise about the scheme's goals, such as poverty reduction or gender equality.

Indeed, when Vietnam is rated high on any international index, people tend to notice. Another case in point was the announcement in 2010 that the *Economist* magazine's Intelligence Unit had ranked Vietnam as the world's top CIVETS economy – that is, the strongest of the six emerging fast-growth, non-commodity-dependent, second-tier powers (Colombia, Indonesia, Vietnam, Egypt, Turkey, South Africa) – classed just behind the super-emerger BRICs (Brazil, Russia, India, China) in terms of globalised development potential.[14] Again, what had registered was something fairly general about the country's appearance in yet another worldwide league table. Even so, CIVETS is a known term in Hanoi, like the more established acronym BRIC.

What these exercises thus convey is the notion of Vietnam as a success story on the world stage, booming in ways that impress the great arbiters of national progress in a globalised age. Hồ Tây is still a site of home-based family enterprises, some doing very well in today's volatile business climate. But interest in the nation's attainment indicators is more than a matter of those struggling with a risky market environment focusing on news relating to their profit margins. To be known abroad, especially to Vietnam's Asian 'tiger' neighbours, as citizens of a go-ahead achiever nation generates a real affective charge. This is apparent when Hanoians reflect on the commodity-starved 'subsidy' years when, despite all the country had achieved as a land of victorious freedom fighters, it was the Communist superpowers and Soviet 'satellites' that were hailed as socialism's lands of plenty. Even worse are the memories of these countries' shaming condescension as aid givers, and their claims that China and the USSR had engineered socialist Vietnam's victories against colonial France and the U.S.A. These victories are still hailed as the country's greatest feats of valour, clear proof of collective will and virtue, and emphatically not to be thought of as the achievements of 'elder sibling' benefactors.

In today's Vietnam, the global achiever's landscape looks very different. There is known to be both a worldwide stage and a more specific Asian regional arena for ambitious nations to achieve in, and the country's admission to ASEAN (1995), APEC (1998) and the WTO (2007) are widely perceived as landmark successes through which Vietnam has secured its presence in a greatly expanded geopolitical attainment arena. 'Not like the Russians. So much trouble there now', said Mr Vu, a Hồ Tây resident who had been a labour-draft Siberian pipeline worker in the 1980s, finishing his stint shortly before the Soviet Union's collapse. He went on: 'We couldn't have imagined it when I was there'.

Like many Hanoians, Mr Vu thinks of Putin's Russia as a land of skinhead violence and urban anomie, with elderly Soviet war heroes reduced to beggary and selling their Lenin medals for bread. He had been telling me about friends and relations caught up in the disintegration of the state contract-labour systems in which so many Vietnamese had experienced well-paid if gruelling employment in the great worker-export schemes of the pre-marketisation era. Mr Vu was thus someone for whom the old USSR had been Vietnam's infinitely powerful if not always beloved 'elder brother' role model.

Mr Vu was thus making a point I heard from many Hanoians: with the end of the Cold War, Vietnam had rapidly become habituated to the evaluation norms of a far bigger world than those of what I have referred to elsewhere as the global socialist ecumene (Bayly 2007). And when Mr Vu and his wife took me through their family's photo albums, they were reliving journeys across the dramatically changed spaces of their own and the country's wide-ranging achievement map. There were pictures of the recent ceremony held to inter the hitherto lost remains of Mr Vu's father, a hero of the anti-French Liberation War who had received his military training in Mao's China.[15] There were also photos of his brother, rewarded for exemplary service in the anti-U.S. War with a posting in 1978 as a construction worker on one of Hanoi's first great high-socialist architectural projects, the Soviet-designed Friendship Cultural Palace. We then traversed Mr Vu's own achievement history: his work-unit merit certificates, and souvenir photos of his works outings in the USSR. There were also cherished pictures of his children today: a doctor and private-sector accountant, the family's first graduates and first participants in the new world of capitalist Asia's high-powered professional environments.

Together with China, South Korea and the ASEAN countries are key sites of Vietnam's new economic achievement life. When I met Mr Vu in December 2009, his younger son was about to set off on a hospital exchange tour to Thailand, and the elder had just returned from training in Singapore. There is a striking spatial dimension to the sense of achievement being marked here. Becoming part of today's much bigger evaluation landscape compared to that of the old socialist ecumene has greatly changed the ways Vietnamese perceive personal and national success, particularly its tabulation and recognition criteria. Yet equally notable about these evaluation experiences is what they have in common: a hard-science positivism exalting statistical tools and targets as sources of unimpeachable super-truth. Under high socialism, official thinking decreed that all human activity was amenable to scientific scrutiny and the generation of data through which to measure the progress of a revolutionary society. The conceptual underpinnings of today's evaluation exercises are very different from those of high-socialism's statistical target-setters, not least because in Vietnam certain kinds of statistics are emphatically not for public consumption. In the ultra-sensitive area of economic indicators, the distinction between scientific findings and state secrets is currently a matter of considerable debate and uncertainty.

Yet it is still notable that when the World Bank or *Wall Street Journal* report on yield curves, competitiveness or even 'social wellness', few commentators challenge the notion of numbers as theory-neutral and truth-telling, or question the scientising of social and moral analysis, whether the spaces under scrutiny are those of the old socialist world or today's capitalist arenas. Indeed it is notable that in December 2010, officials responding to a World Bank report on Southeast Asian countries' effectiveness in statistical reportage announced a new national target for Vietnam. This was to make Vietnam a better producer of statistical knowledge. Here too the spatial context for this new achievement goal is that of the Pacific Rim 'tiger' arena: the new target is to make Vietnam one of marketised Southeast Asia's top statistics producers by 2025.[16]

The Temporality of Heroic Exemplarship

From issues of emplacement and spatiality, I turn now to temporality as a key dimension of achievement experience. Here my concern is with the ways Hanoians narrativise the pressures and rewards they encounter as participants in Vietnam's deeply resonant new success story as a globalised market-economy achiever nation. There is a complex and plural temporality in such accounts, one still reflecting the power and pervasiveness of official narratives exalting the country's life as a revolutionary role model within the worldwide socialist ecumene. My informants' knowledge of these disparate yet closely entwined achievement narratives raises tricky questions about how a country with a history of fostering revolutionary achievers can nurture strong performers in the hotly competitive global knowledge economy.

The achievements exalted in Hanoi household settings are those of the individual whose attainments serve the needs of the wider collective. But they are also the achievements of community and nation, actively registering the forging of a new social order imbued with the enlightened qualities for which the term *văn minh* (civilised) is widely used, as well as the triumph narrative of the country's victories in its two protracted liberation wars (Bradley 2004).

This then is a perspective defining success in terms of the exemplarship of such idealised actors as war heroes and what are called 'Heroine Mothers' (*Mẹ Anh Hùng*), with a clear distinction to be made between the opportunist and the selfless achiever-citizen. The career-minded young Hanoians I know are anything but dismissive of this historic past with its revolutionary's morality deploring those who use talent and attainment for personal gain, in contrast to true achievers who strive so that their capabilities may be refined and put to productive use, excelling at whatever tasks they may be set in order to serve the greater good.

Mẹ Hoa is one of the Heroine Mothers I have in mind as embodiments of this temporally dynamic achievement thinking. This energetic octogenarian marks the loss of her husband and only son in the 1961-73 anti-U.S. War through a striking display on her household family altar of her loved ones' medals, photos and regimental honours banners. These are the focus of her daily incense-lighting (*thắp hương*) ritual with its offerings of flowers and food items.

The two young graduates who accompanied me regarded our visit as a gratifying privilege, and Mẹ Hoa herself as a very special kind of achiever, not a victim or sufferer but a giver of life, an active agent living and deserving of special exaltation and respect by virtue of their exemplary sacrifice for the nation's good. Those awarded the title *Mẹ Anh Hùng* are addressed as *Mẹ* (Mother), not with the ordinary personal pronouns which vary according to the speakers' relative ages.[17] While signalling significant distinctions between the achievement domains appropriate to male and female patriots, this still puts Heroine Mothers on a plane with that most exalted of personages, the nation's revolutionary war leader, President Ho Chi Minh, whose status as a quasi-devotional exemplification of revolutionary virtue is reflected in the same hallowing way.

Especially in contexts treating him as an undying model for the modern achieving young, President Ho is 'Uncle' (*Bác Hồ*), father's elder brother to all citizens, never to be spoken of as ordinary people are, even other great leaders – that is, as relationally senior and elder to some but to others a relational junior. These practices thus constitute exemplarship as qualities entailing a highly specific achievement ideal, one that shines inspiringly across a complex temporal field and evading or glossing over its contradictions between past and present attainment ideals. What it thus exalts is a striving, active agent who attains exemplary virtue by dint of doing and acting with ceaseless moral force in both past and present contexts: the mother who carries on with a life of service and dedication despite her losses; the selfless leader who still inspires and galvanises his valiant modern citizenry.

In the families I know, there are usually older people with something comparable to Mẹ Hoa's achiever-citizen experience from the wartime or postwar 1970s–80s high-socialist era. Mr Cuong, for example, is the son of a Red River rice-farmer decorated for valour as a teenage recruit to the anti-French Viet Minh liberation army in 1950. He himself was one of the carefully selected Hanoi school-leavers sent to study mining technology in Poland shortly before the end of the anti-U.S. War. Thousands of such people were talent-spotted during and after the war years, and if deemed both gifted and politically clean like Mr Cuong, sent to be vested with suitable credentials at key sites of the wider socialist world (Bayly 2007). Their mission as young trainees in Poznan, Prague or Magdeburg (in former East Germany) was conveyed to them by their Ministry minders. Abjuring love, sex and frivolity when overseas, they were to devote themselves single-mindedly to acquiring expertise. They were then to return home with a clutch of prize certificates and other attainment markers, their subsequent careers in fields like medicine, engineering or even cinema design to be determined on the basis of national need, not personal or family preference.

These credential-holders were national assets, their accomplishments qualifying them to be sent abroad yet again to earn much-needed hard currency remittances for the national exchequer under the official 1980s–90s *đi chuyên gia* ('go be an expert') schemes, which sent thousands of technically qualified Vietnamese to act as aid and development providers in countries such as Algeria and Guinea-Conakry (ibid.). To have amassed and deployed such experts in the decades when Vietnam was still at war, and to carry on doing so during the grim postwar austerity years, is still a matter of great pride. Under Mao and the Khmer Rouge, people say, China and Cambodia wantonly destroyed their valuable human capital. In marked contrast, the story of the overseas expert initiative is one of loving friendship forged with the African postcolonies to which Vietnam gave aid and tutelage in the modern arts and sciences.[18]

Everyone knows that the ideal often did not match the reality, and that the quest for credentials might be viewed even by close kin as bourgeois and corrupting, too 'Soviet' in the eyes of those enthused by the example of China under Mao, their achievements reviled as products of unmerited privilege. I know elderly Hanoians who say that as red scarf-wearing teenage Pioneers they believed that Mao's China held the key to that critical attainment goal of the post-independence period, the achievement of revolutionary self-transformation for a land and people not yet fully liberated from a feudal past. Such individuals now applaud their high-achieving grandchildren with MBAs and impressive public- or private-sector job titles, having made peace in later life with the elders they had reviled in the 1960s and 1970s as careerist and bourgeois. At the time, they say, they had believed that the credential-hating values of China's Cultural Revolution offered a more inspiring model of socialist achievement than that of the COMECON states, with their reverence for professional qualifications and technocratic expertise.[19]

But there is also much personal investment in the other key version of these narratives. This one represents the COMECON-trained experts as heroes and patriots, their attainments proof that Vietnam has always been a land of learning and modernity, its poverty in the central-planning years thus a consequence of war and colonial oppression rather than unremedied 'backwardness' (*lạc hậu*). With its post-independence mass literacy campaigns, its near-universal school attendance and stock of accredited experts, Vietnam could proclaim itself a land of enlightenment and civility within and beyond the old socialist ecumene.

What then about today, when Vietnamese must now engage with the very different assessment exercises of the globalised contemporary world? Here there are some striking continuities with past experience. The fear of losing the knowledge-economy competitiveness race against other Pacific Rim achievers leaks constantly into other anxieties, notably those involving inadequate physicality – dark skin, weak physique and small stature in children. These concerns echo early twentieth-century eugenicist pronouncements about the supposed differences between nations with greater or lesser qualities of 'race health'. Small stature is even more a concern in today's era of global 'human development' indices than in the colonial period.[20] Height anxiety, which is closely related to concerns about skin and complexion, is widely experienced as an achievement issue. The yearning for stature gain pervades advice columns and teen chatroom posts: 'Help me! I'm from viet nam. I'm 14 and my height is 1.67m? ... Can I tall maximum 1.90m. [sic] Is it possible?' And adults are well informed about such policy moves as the recently affirmed official commitment to a ten-year deadline for the achievement of children's height norms comparable to those of Japan and the other rich Asian states.[21]

The fallout from this kind of target-setting is especially painful in the domestic sphere. Young mothers with know-it-all in-laws can be placed under relentless pressure to dose their children with internet-sourced hormones promising fast-track 'stunting' cures. My friend Tuyet, an energetic young businesswoman in her early thirties, finds this a particularly harrowing form of 'achievement disease': 'Never mind that my daughter is happy and has good health. It's like those body counts in the war'. This is a shocking allusion in Vietnam: Tuyet had in mind the Americans' notorious battlefield kill statistics, a vision of dehumanising quantification gone mad. 'We're body-counters now', she said, a grim and graphic way of representing this intimate aspect of contemporary target-mindedness, something she sees as immoral and damaging in deeply worrying ways.

The Discourse of 'Achievement Disease'

What I am calling attention to here is the everyday experience of achievement's diverse and interacting affective registers; these constitute both harmonious and inharmonious relations and balances between distinct forms and modes of successful agency. Recognition that the applauding and marking of attainment can be other than exalting and productive is what is meant by the notion of Vietnam as a site not only of true and honourable achievement (*thành tích*) , but of 'achievement disease' (*bệnh thành tích*).

This much-discussed phenomenon reflects the sad recognition that Vietnam has become a country where a region's poverty-reduction statistics may be inflated or fabricated by merit-hungry officials, or a school's impressive exam results a product of shady practices like expelling underperformers and selling essential curriculum information.[22] When Hanoians discuss *bệnh thành tích,* many have in mind selective high-achiever schools that pressurise pupils over exam results and ruthlessly expel those thought likely to damage their league-table standings. How different, they say, from the schoolroom atmosphere of their own childhoods, when teachers were expected to nurture all children in their care.

Householders also speak of discreditable things other families do. Stories abound of parents paying bribes so their children get top-of-the-class attainment status, rather than helping them gain proper study skills so they can join the marketable 'human resources' pool the country is known to need for its continuing growth and welfare. So 'achievement disease' is the possibility of what is thought good and moral about attainment-marking becoming unbalanced and disordered like a body in the grip of the humoural and psychic energy or *qi* disturbances which manifest themselves as ill health. People say the *bệnh* – that is, the disease – is a disorder of bodies in need of rebalancing and reharmonising, as understood in Sino-Vietnamese traditional medicine (*Đông y*) rather than Western medicine (*Tây y*), where the idea is to blast the evil of infection with toxic super-drugs. 'If we thought of it [faking returns, target-obsessing] the way Western medicine thinks about disease, we'd say "social evil" [*tệ nạn xã hội*] – things like drug addiction and prostitution [i.e. irredeemably bad things]'.

Attainment indexing and achievement targets are therefore good things, at least in moderation. Hanoians are quick to defend all sorts of league-tabling and achievement exercises outsiders might regard as competition mania, such as martial-arts contests for five-year-olds. In Vietnam, such things are only bad when they are allowed to become overheating and unbalancing, like the excesses that disharmonise and thus sicken an individual body: much like eating too many humourally heating mangoes, or encountering the kind of etheric flow usually referred to as a noxious wind (*gió độc*) – the corruptions they bring are bad and even shaming, but correctable by doing them in moderation, not by ceasing to count, reward and enumerate.

Achievement and its Spiritual Arenas

It is in these realms of spirituality and engagement with supra-mundane forces and entities that the complexities of present-day Vietnamese achievement experience entail some of the keenest challenges and opportunities. The state media still signal that Vietnam's revolutionary life is to be thought of as the highest realm of national achievement morality. Furthermore, the potent materiality of the country's revolutionary attainment history still pervades domestic as well as public spaces. Hanoians still see all around them the tokens and reference points of what it means to be a creditable achiever by standards set within the old socialist ecumene, even as they find themselves subjected to the universalising measurement and ranking regimes of today's international investors and aid providers.

The documentation of meritorious service is emphatically not a matter of state practice only, despite the emphasis on official memory sites in studies of Vietnam's still massively elaborated commemoration culture (Hue-Tam Ho Tai 2001). But there is much to learn about Vietnamese achievement experience by noting the display of such things as regimental citations and other party-state documentary materials on the domestic ancestor altars (*bàn thờ tổ tiên*) where householders perform their daily *thắp hương* (incense lighting). This act of provision and communication is an accessing of the agentive presence of the dead by material means. Its efficacy is achieved through the sight and smell of the incense, and the provision of sustenance through material offerings: these include foodstuffs and translocally burned 'hell money' (*tiền âm phủ*), together with other comforts which sustain the deceased in the afterlife (Kwon 2007).

In Hồ Tây, families who have rebuilt their homes with the profits of renovation-era business success often have altars occupying a whole upper-storey room. But whether large or small, the installation and tending of a *bàn thờ* altar are profoundly important in family life. It is before the altar that householders make their prayerful incense presentations, thereby making contact with the departed kin in whose responsive presence they aspire to lead a purposeful and achieving life. Like graves, altars are sites where past, present and future can be brought into dynamic co-presence. These interpenetrations are achievements in their own right, to be energetically initiated through the accessing practices of families, often with the aid of specialist psychic adepts (*nhà ngoại cảm*).[23]

Photographs of the deceased are the most common focal point around which altars are arranged as spaces of interaction with the active and conscious dead. But as in the case of Heroine Mother Mẹ Hoa, and especially where the remains of a soldier or other loved one have not been found and interred in a family grave, householders may use items such as military death certificates as their altar's focus. With their hammer and sickle emblems and vivid official logotypes spelling out the national motto *Độc lập, Tự do, Hạnh phúc* ('Independence, Liberty, Happiness'), such documents enshrine the party-state's claims to enduring revolutionary life. Thus they are not thought of as an incongruous referencing of party-state atheism premised on a trajectory of crudely linear time – that is, a superstitious pre-modern past expunged or overridden by a disenchanted socialist present and future. On the contrary: in the households I know, such state-issued merit markers are active conduits to an achieving past, hence an effective means of siting and instantiating the dead as a conscious, experiencing presence among their kin.

These household altar rituals thus bring together material things and people acting as dynamic assemblages even more extensive in form and temporality than the hybridised human-object collectivities now commonly thought of as characteristic modes of association in the contemporary world (Latour 2007). What such Vietnamese contexts entail are networks of both humans and objects in which the realm of achievement experience extends to include not only the living but the dead as agents and actors. When these interactions occur, they do so in settings where the temporalities of past, present and future can be brought into fruitfully productive contact. Such contacts are achievements in their own right, and are also a means of directing and shaping the fields of force and causality enabling other forms and instances of achievement on the part of those aspiring to succeed in the modern age.

A family's ancestor altar is thus one of the many sites of Vietnamese personhood that both situate and celebrate the properly balanced embodiments of a striving, experiencing life, one that experiences achievement in the multiple forms and registers described above, engaging and interacting with the many beings and forces within and beyond the corporeal human world that shape everything that individuals and their collectivities may do, plan or will. The notion of achievement, whether identified as ordinary accomplishment (*thành tích*) or a more exalted attainment (*thành quả*; *thành tựu*) implies a striving agent recognising that multiplicity of realms in which personal projects and attainments are initiated and experienced by the self and others. I do not mean something clichéd and Orientalist about an absence of individuated self in the way people conceptualise initiative, agency and success or failure in Vietnam. But there is an important and often problematic complexity and plurality in the business of having goals and initiating action in the world. This is reflected in the host of things people conventionally say and do when someone sets off to accomplish something: sitting an exam, taking a trip with an important purpose in mind, starting a business, building a house.[24]

Everyone knows that a child must study to pass an exam and that a business will not prosper without hard work and good commercial strategies. Yet in Vietnam as elsewhere, outcomes rest on far more than personal will and diligence, and in keeping with this multi-sited or 'distributed' perception of agency and achievement potential, one of the most common things Hanoians do when undertaking important enterprises is to seek aid and counsel from ancestral kin. This is a far from straightforward process because the deceased are not alike in their willingness and capacity to facilitate achievement. To improve one's chances of securing aid from the departed for ongoing or potential achievements, it is now common to seek an appropriate expert. The question is how to find the right person when wishing to fulfil one's intricately intertwined achievement obligations to the living and dead: someone reliable, skilled and honest in the use of the appropriate psychic arts; in short, an achiever in the realm of supra-mundane achievement fostering.

The services of psychics (*nhà ngoại cảm*) are now regularly made use of because, while everyone recognises the importance of striving and achieving for family, self and nation, a successful outcome for the would-be achiever is a product of something more complex and challenging than the efforts of a striving, goal-defining individual subject. A personal or familial failure to achieve in such pursuits as the search for a deceased relation's remains is a distressing and even shaming matter to have to report at a family's end of year accounting before their household ancestor altar.

I do know sceptics who say 'I don't believe in all that' in regard to the role of psychics, ghosts and spirit mediumship in the fostering of human attainment. But I know many more Hanoians for whom an awareness of living in the presence of efficacious non-mortals with the capacity to foster their goals and projects is not perceived as a failure to appreciate the truths of modern science. A graduate friend in her fifties explained that twenty years ago, if suffering from an otherwise inexplicable affliction causing failure in one's aims and enterprises, 'we'd say it was a ghost'. She used the word *ma*, which denotes a malign succubus-like entity. 'Now of course we know more', she said, going on to describe the wealth of available information from sources to which Hanoians did not have access in the war and 'subsidy' years.

Today when her high-achieving family has a new goal or project in hand she consults Thầy (Master) Hai, a geomancy (*phong thủy*) expert whom she believes to be both learned and honest, thus not like the cheating pseudo-adepts of whom everyone has a cautionary tale. And like most people I know, she has geomancy manuals at home to guide her in such matters as the placing of beds, cooker, altar and computer monitors. If wrongly sited, such items can damage family members' well-being and attainment prospects through their effect on the subterranean flows of astro-biological energy known as *qi*.[25]

Science and the Psychic Achiever

In contrast to the 1980s, there is now much that scientifically aware householders feel they can and should ascertain about the forces that may enhance or endanger their achievement potential, whether what they have in mind are the projects of self, family or their larger collectivities, including those of classroom, workplace or even nation. Geomancy is a key element of this knowledge. It is widely described as a Chinese-derived but fully Vietnamised knowledge system, a key addition to the scientific resources to which modern citizens now have recourse, thus akin to the much improved medical technologies now available to those in need. Anyone can consult a reputable geomancer (*thầy phong thủy*) about the blocked or misdirected *qi* energies that may be the cause of one's ill health or children's poor exam results, just as one can readily purchase an almanac or instruction manual explaining how to address the Buddha or conduct a death-anniversary rite. Geomancers regularly serve as advisors to major state and private construction projects; they also act as diviners in the search for missing graves.

In recent years an array of high-profile public figures have let it be known that they have used the services of 'special capacity' seers and geomancers to fulfilment 'heartfelt' quests to locate the remains of deceased loved ones lost in the carnage of the anti-French and anti-U.S. Wars. The sympathetic tone of state media reports of these undertakings has been a striking feature of the much-discussed resurgence of spirituality entailed in Vietnam's renovation process (Taylor 2008). Two things should be noted here. One is the framing of such uses of psychic power for purposes of virtuous *việc gia đình* (literally 'family work'; that is, ancestral care or veneration) as instances of morally creditable achievement uniting patriotism, authentic Vietnameseness and a laudable love of family and nation.[26] The second is their siting in a dynamic, open-ended time frame uniting the high-socialist past and market-minded present and future.

It is a vision of science as a realm of exalted achievement goals that provides the essential conduit linking past and contemporary temporalities in these accounts. As far back as the early 1970s, a few daring Hanoi scientists tried to initiate lab-based research on the kinds of psychic activity now achieving quasi-official standing as a domain of national science. Their hope was for Vietnam to be proclaimed a land of psychic aptitude, its seers recognised through the truth-seeking skills of science as national assets whose gifts could be put to use in the meeting of national need. But the establishment hard-science materialism of the day defeated their efforts: diviners and other supra-mundane adepts continued to be denounced as charlatans and enemies of scientific truth.[27]

Today these old campaigners feel at least partially vindicated, though they bemoan the slowness of the science establishment to respond to their insights. After all, they say, in the high-socialist years so-called Eastern medicine was officially endorsed and became a well-funded domain of institutionalised national expertise. Much the same was true of Mao's China, though in Vietnam it was a matter of special pride that there were certain healing arts that could be claimed as specifically Vietnamese.[28]

The idea that there can be measurable attainment in the realm of psychic capacity is a remarkable expansion of the notion of personal and national success. And while far from universally accepted, today's attempts to represent Vietnam as a land of uniquely gifted psychic achievers – that is, a country equipped to compete on the world stage in ways many richer and more powerful countries are not – have generated vigorous public debate of a kind unimaginable in the 1970s. This has taken the form of press and online battles over whether attempts to set attainment markers for psychics are an affront to more established forms of credentialising, such as the defining of Heroine Mothers and the physically and morally perfected young as national role-models. Yet no one would say today that in matters of collective achievement morality it is easy to handle the differences between being a credible achiever by the standards of high-socialist revolutionary merit-marking, and those now more applicable to the age of the globalised competitive knowledge economy.

I believe this helps significantly in explaining why the debates focusing on achievement issues relating to psychic spirituality (*tâm linh*) and the powers of clairvoyants and other adepts have become so vigorous and sensitive in Vietnam. This is certainly the case in Hanoi, where many well-known psychic service providers have their consultancy practices, and where the controversial Human Capacity Research Centre (*Trung tâm nghiên cưu tiềm năng con người*) has its headquarters (Endres and Schlecker 2011).

This much-discussed quasi-official institution provides extensive facilities including a booking service and consultation space for psychics and their clients. It also has a widely publicised research division staffed by late-career biologists and other scientists with higher degrees and other advanced qualifications from leading Vietnamese and former COMECON state universities. The professed goal of these researchers is to scientise the Centre's provision of psychic *tâm linh* expertise by setting credible attainment markers for practising psychics including geomantic diviners (*thầy phong thủy*) and other specialists in the spiritual arts. The aim of the Centre is thus to legitimate and some say to commercialise the exercise of psychic powers as a realm of measurable modern achievement, comparable to those of the nation's other classes of doers and attainers.

Of course there are other ways for Hanoians to access the many forms of psychic practice now widely performed in Vietnam. But the growing popularity of the Human Capacity Research Centre for initiatives such as 'soul-callings' (*gọi hồn*) and 'grave searches' (*đi tìm mộ*) is a reflection of the extent to which the meeting of psychic needs has become an achievement regimen in its own right. This can be seen most clearly in the case of Hanoians' often anguished yearnings for a successful outcome to a long-running family grave search.[29]

It is an extremely common plight in Vietnam to lack knowledge of the sites of ancestral remains. This can be because one's kin are among the countless war dead without a recorded burial site, or because tombs or grave markers were destroyed by bombs or displaced by road-building or the innumerable other changes that continually transform the country's urban and rural landscapes. Such situations are experienced as intensely distressing achievement problems. It matters enormously in Vietnam to be in a position to honour and tend the graves of kin, both affinal (related by marriage) and agnatic (paternal kin). Given the widespread conviction, much substantiated by the media and word of mouth anecdotal accounts, that a geomantically well-sited burial place is a potent source of material and spiritual benefits, and a forebear whose remains are not properly cared for can afflict an entire kindred, male householders often take as keen an interest in achieving a successful outcome to their wives' family grave searches as in their own blood kindred's 'ancestor work'.

Nowadays it is common for family grave searches to be undertaken in consultation with psychics, as with other major undertakings such as building a house and launching a new business. All are part and parcel of what an achieving family does for those in their care. Children are routinely equipped with amulets endowed with efficacious power by a trusted geomancer. And in cases of illness, the opinion of a clairvoyant is often sought to determine whether the source is biomedical or a consequence of spirit attack or malign *qi* energy configurations (Nguyen Thi Hien 2008).

A successful grave search is a yearned-for landmark in collective familial life, a success that householders particularly long to report at their ancestor altar on conclusion of a productive year as a dynamically achieving family unit. Yet all too commonly, the finding of lost ancestral remains is a goal painfully difficult to achieve. And when a grave search fails in its objective, attainment in a host of other spheres and arenas will be threatened or undermined.

People often decide to initiate a grave search for a parent or other relation following an oracular dream or consultation with a spirit medium or soul-caller. There are other factors too which may prompt a decision that the time is right for such undertakings. Once a search is agreed on by family members, those involved will muster the resources required to make successful contact with the un-housed soul's remains, through divination, oracular vision and/or mediumship. But they do so in the knowledge that they may well experience inconclusive manifestations or otherwise unsatisfactory outcomes to a strenuous trip to a far-off graveyard or battlefield site.

After a bad experience of this kind, frustrated seekers tend to blame themselves for failing to lay the necessary foundations for achievement. Their accounts of such occasions have much in common with what is said about the meeting of attainment goals in any other walk of life. 'Things don't just come out right when you want them to – you have to prepare, you have to spend money sometimes and do so much, learn so much about what's right to do'. Those of sufficient means often book with a big-name seer like the celebrity medium Mrs Nga consulted by a number of the Hồ Tây households I know. Like other prominent clairvoyants, this psychic is a specialist grave finder with a long waiting list. Clients pay a fee for an initial consultation. Mrs Nga then provides site-finding instructions by mobile phone to family parties pursuing searches in distant areas. She can handle several calls at once from groups seeking their kin's remains in different locations, impressing seekers with the explicit detail she can relay from her distant vantage point: 'Go another hundred steps to the left of the big tree – you'll see a small hill: the grave mound is just next to it. Dig down now – you'll find the bones.'

Yet even with a celebrity psychic, searchers often fail and after repeated frustrations may then turn to the Human Capacity Research Centre. My management-consultant friend Quyen told me that this is what she and her civil servant mother had done, having initially been reluctant to try the Centre. Her mother and army officer father were of rural origin, both incomers to the city who had overcome the powerful disadvantage of 'bad-class' family antecedents to achieve notable career successes, working hard to support their children's even more impressive array of academic and career attainments.

The bones they were seeking were those of Quyen's maternal great-grandfather. Being unable to rebury and tend his remains was a predicament keenly felt, distressing her mother particularly with a nagging sense of objectives not met, a dereliction of familial duty not to be tolerated in the life of an otherwise dutiful and productive achiever family. But they had heard that the Centre was expensive; her great-grandfather had been an early French-educated member of Vietnam's pre-revolutionary intelligentsia, and they feared that he might have disapproved of the Centre as a site of superstition promoting an improper understanding of causality and attainment in the modern world.

Having taken the plunge, they liked what they found there. Like other clients, especially those with degrees and professional credentials, they were reassured by the Centre's ambience, reminiscent of an official institution where documents are checked and qualifications validated – 'like my mother's office', Quyen said. Another friend mentioned a visit to South Korea where he had seen psychics operating in what looked to him like commercial outlets in a shopping centre. The Centre is thought of in very different terms, its style much more that of an official agency with gatekeepers and forms to fill in than a glossy consumer space.

So Quyen and her mother went ahead, using the Centre's services to arrange a soul-calling (*gọi hồn*). At the Centre, family groups arrive, wait their turn to be seen and present their needs to the kind of brisk reception staff familiar from other interactions with service providers. In due course they will be assigned a psychic from those available on the day's consultation rota. Quyen said this was all reassuringly like going to some other mundane space of public provision, a ward office or health centre. They had lost confidence in the psychic they had found by word of mouth who had repeatedly failed to achieve a successful soul-calling for them. 'My mother saw a television programme about the Centre; that's how we knew about it.' It was not so much that state media coverage made it seem more reliable than a psychic recommended by friends, but what they found did appeal to their sense of how modern citizens make informed choices to achieve desired ends.

'Of course we had to pay, but that's what happens when you go to the hospital', Quyen said. This too made the Centre feel familiar, a space of ordered professional care. The fee aspect was not problematic for them. In the past, her mother pointed out, state anti-superstition drives had to be simple and uncompromising: payment for ritual services was morally repugnant and a mark of feudal backwardness. But today's globalised market life requires an updating of moral categories. There is sophisticated science at hand to help careful householders distinguish fakes from true providers. And while they know that some Hanoians think the Centre is too commercial and profit-oriented, they are content that its supervision keeps payment fair and reasonable, and that psychics who take money need no longer be thought of as charlatans blocking the path to modernity.

This is a view I have encountered quite widely in Hanoi: today's citizens need a highly flexible understanding of how modernity may be successfully achieved in every walk of life, including that of psychic provision. People must learn how to distinguish between good and bad achievements, as in the case of telling worthy forms of merit-marking from the evil of 'achievement disease'. And as in other attainment realms, there will be ample evidence for those who look for it. The greedy money-grubbing seer may start out as a possessor of authentic skills and powers, and it will be perfectly legitimate for these to be made use of by those in need, as in the case of families seeking resolution in cases of unachieved 'ancestor work'. But psychics who cheat and extort will soon be punished by the weakening or loss of their powers. And again, it is an important achievement in its own right to learn to recognise the signs of a bad or fraudulent adept. Much like acquiring the skills of a world where the market rather than the state provides much that an achieving family and nation require for contemporary success, the modern goal-oriented citizen must know what it takes to make productive use of authentic achievers in the realm of the psychic knowledge and skills economy.

Conclusion

My friend Quyen's story sums up much that I have been seeking to establish in this exploration of past and contemporary Vietnamese achievement experience. My focus has been on the often problematic plurality to be seen and experienced in the complex business of having goals and initiating action in the world. What is evident in contemporary Vietnamese contexts is that the aspiration to attain and mark the successes of a striving self, and of the important affective collectivities to which one is bound by ties of familial and patriotic love, involves elements of very great diversity and dynamism.

These elements of achievement experience entail powerful moral challenges that play out in far-reaching and compelling ways both spatially and temporally, and also in terms of the remarkable forms of materiality and institutionalisation through which achievers may register some of their most notable successes. In this respect as in others there are both good and bad realms and indices of achievement. This can be seen in the country's ongoing battles about the iniquities of 'achievement disease', which can be especially painful for women in their role as achievement facilitators for home and family. Yet this does not mean that the empirical and positivistic aspects of achievement-marking are necessarily experienced as dehumanising and tyrannical. Hanoians often find comfort and warmth of affect amid the trappings of science, bureaucratised care and state-issue merit-marking. It would thus be wrong to think of the state merit banners and hammer and sickle emblems to be found on so many domestic ancestor altars as something necessarily alien to the spirit of loving intimacy through which achievement experience can be made part of both individual and collective moral life.

There are also complex geographies of achievement. This can be seen in the disjunctures as well as continuities that have been experienced as citizens have learned to make the leap from the achievement indices of the high-socialist and revolutionary era to the novel experiences of achieving and striving for the needs of a globalised but also more specifically regional super-achieving capitalist knowledge economy.

Finally, and perhaps most remarkably, Vietnam offers a striking instance of something I believe to be far from unique in the contemporary world, though not widely recognised in other studies of attainment experience. This is the extent to which the spaces and temporalities of achievement can be lived and expanded on in ways uniting not only the living and the dead, but also the realms of the empirical, the scientific and the commercial with those of the spiritual, the spectral and the supra-mundane.

Acknowledgements

I am grateful to this volume's editors, the anonymous readers and a number of my Cambridge colleagues, including Caroline Humphrey and James Laidlaw, for valuable comments on earlier drafts of this chapter. I also gratefully acknowledge fieldwork funding provided by the Economic and Social Research Council (grant number RES-000-22-4632) for a joint comparative project with Dr Nicholas Long on 'The Social Life of Achievement in Indonesia and Vietnam'.

Notes

1. The austerity years following the anti-U.S. War and 1976 reunification of the two Vietnams is known as *thời kỳ bao cấp*, the 'subsidy' period.
2. For the Grant Thornton Emerging Markets Opportunity Index, see <http://www.internationalbusinessreport.com/files/gti_ibr_emarkets_2010final.pdf> (accessed 3 April 2012).

3. On the debate about whether the Pacific Rim 'tigers' owe their successes to so-called Asian values such as order, consensuality and selflessness, see Subramaniam (2000).
4. Although the phenomenon of the pressurising parent has been long debated in Vietnam, the term 'tiger mother' has been popularised more recently through media coverage of the Chinese-descended U.S.-based author Amy Chua's (2011) controversial account of her rigorous 'Asian values' parenting regimen.
5. See, e.g., Drummond and Rydstrøm (2004).
6. State media give high-profile coverage to such events: see, e.g., <http://vtv.vn/Article/Get/Dai-hoi-thi-dua-yeu-nuoc-toan-quoc-lan-thu-VIII-14a0dbb173.html> (accessed 3 April 2012). For a rich account of the construction of pre-independence and high-socialist emulation models, see de Tréglodé (2003: esp. 131–78).
7. This is not to deny the party-state's long-standing hostility to those it defined as capitalists or 'bourgeois elements'; the mobilisation campaigns of the post-independence, high-socialist period did not treat traders as emulation heroes. Even so, there are important distinctions to be made between Vietnam and its socialist 'siblings' (the USSR and China) in such matters as the inclusion of the little trader with his itinerant vendor-provisioner's balance or weighing-scale in propaganda images depicting the five class-based embodiments of the Vietnamese revolutionary/resistance spirit (the others being the worker, the scholar, the soldier and the peasant). For detailed discussion, see Bayly (2007: 153–78).
8. *Viet Nam News*, 27 December 2010, p.4. One of the Congress's resolutions was to enhance the country's array of role-model campaigns – i.e., holding more achievement events is an achievement target in its own right.
9. See, e.g., Diener and Dweck (1980), Elliot and Harackiewicz (1994) and Elliot (2005).
10. As in the U.S.A. and U.K. achievement contexts explored by, e.g., Fordham (1996) and de Rond (2009).
11. E.g., the Legatum Prosperity Index for 2011, which placed Vietnam at number 62 out of 110 countries surveyed: <http://www.prosperity.com/country.aspx?id=VN> (accessed 4 April 2012). Vietnam was ranked 28 out of a total of 187 countries on the UN's 2011 Human Development Index, placing the country in the 'Medium Human Development' category, together with the Philippines, Egypt, Indonesia and China. See <http://hdr.undp.org/en/statistics/> (accessed 4 April 2012).
12. See <http://www.happyplanetindex.org/public-data/files/happy-planet-index-2-0.pdf> (accessed 3 April 2012). There was also widespread coverage of a 2011 Gallup poll of citizens' views of national economic prospects, which found Vietnam to be 'the world's most optimistic nation'. See, e.g., <http://www.tuoitrenews.vn/cmlink/tuoitrenews/society/vietnam-is-world-s-most-optimistic-bva-gallup-1.18446> (accessed 3 April 2012).
13. See <http://data.worldbank.org/country/vietnam> (accessed 3 April 2012), <http://www.wpro.who.int/vietnam/mdg.htm> (accessed 3 April 2012) and <http://veryvietnam.com/2010-12-30/2010-replay-top-10-news-stories-from-vietnam/> (accessed 3 April 2012).
14. Defined as possessing high-grade 'human resources', thus making the CIVETS attractive to G7 investors. See <http://vietnamtodayonline.typepad.com/blog/2011/04/viet-nam-cements-ranking-as-ideal-investment-location.html> (accessed 3 April 2012).
15. Mr Vu and his family had commissioned a psychic to find his father's bones, an achievement practice I discuss below.
16. See 'Statistics crucial to economic future' at <http://www.dztimes.net/post/business/statistics-crucial-to-economic-future.aspx> (accessed 3 April 2012).
17. See Hy Van Luong (1990); on Heroine Mothers, see Hue-Tam Ho Tai (2001: 177).
18. For a more detailed account, see Bayly (2007).
19. COMECON (the Council of Mutual Economic Assistance, or CMEA) was the Soviet-centred economic alliance system created in 1949 to coordinate ties with allied socialist states. Vietnam became a full member in 1978; the scheme was formally dissolved in 1991.

20. See, e.g., <http://un.org.vn/en/feature-articles-press-centre-submenu-252/339-maternal-and-child-nutrition-in-viet-nam.html> (accessed 3 April 2012).
21. A government spokesman for the agency charged with initiating growth rate improvement (the Viet Nam Sports Science Institute), quoted in a report of 2 April 2009 at <www.irinnews.org/Report.aspx?ReportId=84079> (accessed 3 April 2012). The year 2010 marked the start of a five-year programme to spur childhood growth rates so as to add four centimetres to the average citizen's height by 2020.
22. Reminiscent of Demerath's critique of U.S. school achievement culture (Demerath 2009; this volume), Vietnamese media regularly carry headlines such as 'SOS: "Achievement Disease" Prompts Schools to Expel Bad Students' (<http://english.vietnamnet.vn/en/education/3354/sos---achievement-disease--prompts-schools-to-expel-bad-students.html>, accessed 3 April 2012). The cartoon accompanying this item shows a hard-faced school principal roasting a sweating student over a fire labelled *thành tích* (achievement).
23. Jellema (2007); cf. Thompson (1988), Scott (2007) and Toulson (2012).
24. Exam success is the kind of achievement for which my informants routinely use the word *thành tích*; its connotations are of things quantifiable: targets met, routine wins or gains. For nobler attainments such as building or renovating one's home (an act of significant spiritual resonance for Vietnamese families, signalling much more than mere material gain or advancement), *thành tựu* is preferred. This is a term known to be Chinese-derived: school textbooks teach children to identify the many Sinic loan-words deemed suitable for formal speech and writing. *Thành tựu* is therefore not the word for ordinary accomplishments, even of a very positive kind. However ardently prayed for, a child's top exam score or a business deal profitably concluded is mere *thành tích*. *Thành quả* is even more respectful, a word also used in official language; rather than referring to the 'achievements' of Vietnam's revolution, one would say *thành quả cách mạng*, literally 'the revolution's fruits' or 'fruitful outcome'. For achievement of a positive outcome in a search for a lost family grave (as described below), one uses *thành công* ('success', usually of a meritorious kind). I was told that even the more exalting terms for attainment are inappropriate for this most yearned-for of goals because it is so important to avoid the suggestion of a selfish claiming of credit on the part of those undertaking such quests. *Thành công* is thus more in keeping with the key issue for family members: the doing of selfless service for departed kin, without concern for gain or self-advantaging. This is highly important to establish because it is so well known that ancestors left uncared for in the after-world have the power to sicken or otherwise afflict their neglectful mortal kin, while those convinced of their descendants' sincerity and generous care can enrich or otherwise aid and comfort them.
25. On geomancy in Vietnam and China (*feng shui*), see Feuchtwang (2002), Bruun (2003) and Thien Do (2003).
26. Costlier and more extensive forms of such care are referred to as *việc họ*, a term generally signalling involvement of an entire lineage rather than the more modest scope of 'familial' care (*việc gia đình*).
27. The logic of this was that Eastern medicine was a science amenable to provision on a basis of social equity. Geomancy was thought to benefit the rich at the expense of those unable to pay for such things as well-sited graves and tombs. Spirit mediumship, soul-calling and other such activities were also condemned for exploiting the credulous and fostering 'feudal' class division (Malarney 2002).
28. A key landmark of Vietnam's pre-marketisation life was the recognition accorded to electric acupuncture, an innovation pioneered in Hanoi and widely disseminated abroad through the 'go be an expert' initiatives as an exemplary hybrid of ancient Vietnamese science and modern biomedicine. The medic who demonstrated it during an operation broadcast live on Soviet television became a much-praised socialist-era role model.
29. Soul-callings are widely performed in Vietnam, as are spirit possessions (*lên đồng*). In soul-calling the psychic facilitates the deceased person's manifested presence through

possession (*nhập*, literally 'joining, merging with') of someone else, usually a close family member. In spirit possession, the psychic practitioner is possessed by the deceased individual. See, e.g., Fjelstad and Thị Hiền Nguyễn (2006), Nguyen Thi Hien (2007) and Endres (2011).

References

Bayly, S. 2007. *Asian Voices in a Postcolonial Age: Vietnam, India and Beyond.* Cambridge: Cambridge University Press.

Bradley, M.P. 2004. Becoming 'Van Minh': Civilizational Discourse and Visions of the Self in Twentieth-Century Vietnam. *Journal of World History* 15, no. 1: 65–83.

Brayboy, B.M.J. 2004. Hiding in the Ivy: American Indian Students and Visibility in Elite Educational Settings. *Harvard Educational Review* 74, no. 2: 125–152.

Bruun, O. 2003. *Fengshui in China: Geomantic Divination Between State Orthodoxy and Popular Religion.* Honolulu: University of Hawaii Press.

Chua, A. 2011. *Battle Hymn of the Tiger Mother.* London: Bloomsbury.

Dang Phong. 2002. *Lịch Sử Kinh Tế Việt Nam, 1945–2000* [Economic History of Vietnam 1945–2000]. Hanoi: NXB xã hội.

Demerath, P. 2009. *Producing Success: The Culture of Personal Advancement in an American High School.* Chicago: University of Chicago Press.

De Rond, M. 2009. *The Last Amateurs: To Hell and Back with the Cambridge Boat Race Crew.* London: Icon.

De Tréglodé, B. 2003. *Héros et Révolution au Viêt Nam, 1948–1964.* Paris: L'Harmattan.

Diener, C.I., and C.S. Dweck. 1980. An Analysis of Learned Helplessness (II): The Processing of Success. *Journal of Personality and Social Psychology* 39, no. 5: 940–952.

Drummond, L., and H. Rydstrøm (eds). 2004. *Gender Practices in Contemporary Vietnam.* Singapore: Singapore University Press.

Elliot, A.J. 2005. A Conceptual History of the Achievement Goal Construct. In *Handbook of Competence and Motivation* (eds) A.J. Elliot and C.S. Dweck, 52–72. New York: Guilford Press.

Elliot, A.J., and J.M. Harackiewicz. 1994. Goal Setting, Achievement Orientation, and Intrinsic Motivation: A Mediational Analysis. *Journal of Personality and Social Psychology* 66, no. 5: 968–980.

Endres, K.W. 2011. *Performing the Divine: Mediums, Markets and Modernity in Urban Vietnam.* Copenhagen: Nordic Institute for Asian Studies.

Endres, K.W., and M. Schlecker. 2011. Psychic Experience, Truth, and Visuality in Post-War Vietnam. *Social Analysis* 55, no. 1: 1–22.

Feuchtwang, S. [1974] 2002. *An Anthropological Analysis of Chinese Geomancy.* Bangkok: White Lotus Press.

Fjelstad, K., and Thị Hiền Nguyễn (eds). 2006. *Possessed by the Spirits: Mediumship in Contemporary Vietnamese Communities.* Ithaca, NY: Cornell University Press.

Fordham, S. 1996. *Blacked Out: Dilemmas of Race, Identity and Success at Capital High.* Chicago: University of Chicago Press.

Fry, G.W. 2009. Higher Education in Vietnam. In *The Political Economy of Educational Reforms and Capacity Development in Southeast Asia: Cases of Cambodia, Laos and Vietnam* (eds) Y. Hirosato and Y. Kitamura, 237–261. New York: Springer.

Hue-Tam Ho Tai (ed.). 2001. *The Country of Memory: Remaking the Past in Late-Socialist Vietnam.* Berkeley: University of California Press.

Hy Van Luong. 1990. *Discursive Practices and Linguistic Meanings: The Vietnamese System of Personal Reference*. Philadelphia: John Benjamins.

Jellema, K. 2007. Everywhere Incense Burning: Remembering Ancestors in Đổi Mới Vietnam. *Journal of Southeast Asian Studies* 38, no. 3: 467–492.

Kwon, H. 2007. The Dollarization of Vietnamese Ghost Money. *Journal of the Royal Anthropological Institute* 13, no. 1: 73–90.

Latour, B. 2007. *Reassembling the Social: An Introduction to Actor-Network Theory*. Oxford: Oxford University Press.

Malarney, S.K. 2002. *Culture, Ritual and Revolution in Vietnam*. London: RoutledgeCurzon.

Nguyen Thi Hien. 2007. 'Seats for Spirits to Sit Upon': Becoming a Spirit Medium in Contemporary Vietnam. *Journal of Southeast Asian Studies* 38, no. 3: 541–558.

——— 2008. Yin Illness: Its Diagnosis and Healing within Lên Đồng (Spirit Possession) Rituals of the Việt. *Asian Ethnology* 67, no. 2: 305–321.

Nguyen, T.T., and G. Johanson. 2008. Culture and Vietnam as a Knowledge Society. *Electronic Journal on Information Systems in Developing Countries* 33, no. 2: 1–16.

Scott, J.L. 2007. *For Gods, Ghosts and Ancestors: The Chinese Tradition of Paper Offerings*. Seattle: University of Washington Press.

Subramaniam, S. 2000. The Asian Values Debate: Implications for the Spread of Liberal Democracy. *Asian Affairs* 27, no. 1: 19–35.

Taylor, P. (ed.). 2008. *Modernity and Re-enchantment: Religion in Post-Revolutionary Vietnam*. Singapore: Institute of Southeast Asian Studies.

Thien Do. 2003. *Vietnamese Supernaturalism: Views from the Southern Region*. London: RoutledgeCurzon.

Thompson, S.E. 1988. Death, Food and Fertility. In *Death Ritual in Late Imperial and Modern China* (eds) J.L. Watson and E.S. Rawski, 71–108. Berkeley: University of California Press.

Toulson, R. 2012. The Anthropology of a Necessary Mistake: The Unsettled Dead and the Imagined State in Contemporary Singapore. In *Southeast Asian Perspectives on Power* (eds) L. Chua, J. Cook, N. Long and L. Wilson, 93–106. Abingdon: Routledge.

9

Practising Responsibilisation
The Unwritten Curriculum for Achievement in an American Suburb

Peter Demerath

When Ann Rice opened the door to her house for our interview I could see that she set her jaw in the same way as her eldest daughter, fifteen-year-old Julie.[1] She was White, in her mid-thirties, and was dressed business casual. She lived with her husband and three children in an attractive well-maintained, two-storey home on a quiet curving street in one of the most appealing neighbourhoods of Wilton – the suburb of a large Ohio city in the Midwestern U.S.A. where I had begun my study of class culture and academic competition the previous autumn. Julie was about to finish her freshman (ninth grade) year at the local public high school. She was one of the high-achieving White students in my sample of eight focal students, and over the previous nine months she and her peers had taught me a great deal about what was involved in the pursuit of their academic and professional aspirations. Now, as the school year was drawing to a close, my research assistants and I were talking to their parents.

Mrs Rice invited me to sit on the sofa in the tastefully decorated living room, and asked if I would like a cup of coffee or tea. The room had a large picture window looking out on the freshly mown lawn and street beyond. She told me that she and her husband were both originally from Ohio and had met at a selective college in the south-western region of the state. After earning their Masters degrees in Texas they decided to move back to central Ohio. Her husband, an architect, had had five job interviews and received three offers. They moved into the neighbourhood ten years earlier, and during that time Mrs Rice worked three days per week as an audiologist. Mrs Rice explained that they had been attracted to Wilton largely by the 'quality of the education', and liked living in it a great deal. They had initially lived in a smaller house on the same street, but when this house had become available a few years earlier 'we just moved right up'. She then directed a sharp glance out the front window and said the only problem with their street was that there were a few 'renters' who were 'not always the best', largely because they did not have the same 'commitment' to the neighbourhood and the upkeep of their homes as the other residents.

I asked Mrs Rice what kinds of concerns she and her husband had about their children's future. Her brow furrowed, and she began to talk about the prospects of their admission to selective colleges:

> A lot of schools are saying you've got to be in the top – colleges are saying we want top ten percent or better. And I can have Julie with a 4.0 [a grade-point average equivalent to an 'A'] who might not be in the top ten percent of her class ... Another thing that irks me. I mean these kids have to produce basically a résumé to get into college, you know: 'I did Key Club for four years. I ran track for four years'. And colleges want it loaded. But what's being sacrificed at the cost of loading a schedule, you know? Are they being given a chance to be a kid? Are they given a chance to go over to the pond at Brookside and hunt for snapping turtles? Are they being given a chance to hang out with their friends?

Mrs Rice also said that she and her husband worried about financing their children's college education. 'You know, we make good money, but college is expensive', she said, pointing out it was an especially concerning issue for a family like theirs with three children. Nevertheless, she said she wanted Julie to, 'stay with the flow, caught up with the pack, even with all those other kids'.

Mrs Rice went on to explain that she had always been an 'involved' or 'hands on' parent in her daughters' schools (Julie's sisters were twelve and eight). She had served on the Parent and Teacher Association (PTA) board during the entire time they lived in Wilton, and was currently serving as PTA president. She said that she was in frequent communication with other parents regarding how best to support their children in school. 'I'm always picking', she said, 'Tell me what's going on. What I can expect'. Mrs Rice had questioned Julie's teachers several times about how they had assessed Julie's work: she had recently sent back a paper on *Romeo and Juliet* that Julie's teacher had 'marked incorrectly'. The teacher's grade had kept Julie from getting an A in the course. 'I called her on it', she said, 'I sent the paper back and said I know for a fact that this question is correct'. She never received a response from the teacher. (Two months earlier this teacher had shared with me a similar note she had received from Mrs Rice.)

Finally, Mrs Rice revealed that the weekend before our interview she had 'put in' fifteen hours on Julie's science group project. She was aware, however, that there was one girl in Julie's group that 'didn't pull her weight'. 'And I was talking to another mother in the other day and I said if they don't get an A on this project, I'm on the phone so fast to that teacher', she said.

Julie herself was a religious young person, and had told me earlier that year that she hoped to one day establish a school in a developing country for underprivileged children. 'I have it all planned out', she had said. A year later, Julie's grades had begun to slip and she had had to re-orient her life around her schoolwork. At an interview around that time, she had told me, 'I am a lot more focused on what I need to be focused on and I need to be focused on that'. During her twelfth grade (senior) year, Julie struggled to balance the demands of school, the college application process, extracurricular activities (especially her involvement in the school's theatre programme) and her job (she had recently got her driver's license and was waitressing at a local restaurant). Julie began to experience changes in her menstrual cycle at this time, and her mother took her to see a gynaecologist, who prescribed birth-control pills as a remedy.

Julie and Ann Rice's educational efforts were typical of achievement-oriented families in Wilton. Like many local residents, the Rices had moved there for the quality of its schools – and life. They were on an upwardly mobile trajectory themselves, having since moved into a larger home and been conscious of the extent to which 'renters' diminished the appeal of their neighbourhood. Mrs Rice in particular was anxious about the competition her daughters were facing in order to be admitted to good colleges, as well as her family's ability to pay the costs of tuition. One way that Mrs Rice had found to support her daughters' schooling was by becoming an 'involved' parent. Her involvement was far-ranging: from serving as president of her younger daughter's PTA, to spending a considerable portion of a weekend on Julie's science project, to having knowledge of the work habits of Julie's peers, to regularly contesting the assessments made by Julie's teachers. Yet Mrs Rice also expressed ambivalence about this achievement orientation within her family, saying that she worried about her daughter having a chance to 'be a kid'.

When Julie herself talked about her academic goals, she tended to set her jaw in a determined way. She herself was an 'involved' student at the high school, being a member of the track team, the select a cappella choir, the student government, the young Christian association, student government, and theatre programme. She had developed an unfailing ability, in her words, to 'focus' on what she needed to accomplish. However, in her senior year, these total efforts had finally caused her body to complain.

I argue in this chapter that Julie and her mother were both following and co-constructing an unwritten curriculum for what Nikolas Rose refers to as 'responsibilisation' (Rose 1992: 149): internalised pressure to take responsibility for themselves and their future class status. This unwritten curriculum in Wilton was comprised of a class-cultural assemblage and ideological bearing deeply rooted in American competitive individualism, but with striking new features that had seemingly arisen because they provided its youth with the additional advantages they would need in a neoliberal era. These new features were oriented primarily around giving students the image, if not the substance, of competitive success in order to improve their appeal on the education and employment markets.[2] One of the primary reasons this unwritten curriculum became apparent to me and my research team was that it was partly institutionalised when Wilton Burnham High School, the community's second high school, was built in 1991.

This chapter draws on a four-year study of middle-class culture and schooling in Wilton conducted between 1999 and 2003, and maintains that as the social world of Wilton has become more market-oriented, local competitive individualism has intensified.[3] The central focus of the chapter is on the educational beliefs and practices the community has developed to maximise the market appeal of its youth so that they may at the very least remain in the middle class. In illuminating these social foundations of personal advancement, the chapter aims to contribute new insights to the anthropology of achievement; specifically, to how individual achievements are in fact produced systematically, relationally and ideologically, as much as they are individually, yet are fetishised such that these conditions are rendered largely invisible.

An 'Elite Suburb' Facing Change

Wilton itself has long been a favoured residential spot for the area's professional class. It has well-maintained parks and libraries, two country clubs, an expansive public recreation centre and excellent public (government-funded) schools. At the time of the study, approximately 60 per cent of adult residents had a bachelor's degree or higher (the U.S. average is 24.4 per cent). Of its population of approximately 50,000, nearly half of all employed adults were in managerial and professional occupations, and just over a third were in technical, sales and administrative support (U.S. Census Bureau 2000).

Furthermore, Wilton lays claim to a 'New England heritage' in that it was originally established over 200 years ago by settlers from the north-eastern United States. The distinctiveness that Wilton attributes to itself and its citizens is apparent in many ways, including the glossy publications and events that were produced to mark its bicentennial in 2003. The motto on the bicentennial brochure was: 'Wilton – 1803-2003 – Building the Future with Pioneering Spirit.' According to Dorst (1989), 'elite suburbs' that devote this much effort to maintaining such a historical identity are motivated in part by an awareness of the commoditised value of their promotional efforts.

Finally, Wilton had a reputation for an outstanding school system. One of the local metropolitan magazines consistently ranked it as one of the top three suburban districts in the area. The average standardised test scores for students in grades 3, 5, 7 and 10 were between the eightieth and eighty-fifth percentiles nationally (Wilton School District 2002). Like the Rices, virtually all of the parents interviewed for the study that were not originally from Wilton said they had moved there explicitly for the quality of its schools – and life. The father of a high-achieving White, male Wilton student said, 'It was supposed to be great schools and just a great community.' A school librarian mentioned that she had moved to Wilton because the district would pay for her Master's degree. Most Wilton parents were well off, and many were able to provide a variety of enriching opportunities for their children, such as private music lessons, trips to England with the select soccer team, and family vacations to far-flung locations.

However, socio-economic diversity has increased in Wilton over the last three decades – more low-income people have moved to the suburb largely to

Figure 9.1 The Wilton 'village green.'

take advantage of employment and educational opportunities not found in the city centre. Parents, students and teachers all commented that there were poor people in Wilton; some expressed concern that there had been an increase in rental properties in the community (in 2000 of the 5,845 homes in Wilton, 904 were renter-occupied). During the 1999/2000 school year, 4.7 per cent of students in the Wilton district qualified for free and reduced-price lunches (U.S. Census Bureau 2000). In the school itself, class status was sometimes a basis for harassment.

Indeed, as Varenne and McDermott (1998) noted in their comparative study of suburban schools, students and parents in Wilton generally evinced a keen awareness of being in competition with others. For example, when we asked students in an Advanced Placement (AP) U.S. History class,[4] 'What drives you – to work so hard?', a sophomore Asian American student responded, 'It's harder for our generation to live the same lifestyle as our parents do.'

The 'Anxious Class' Goes to School: Intensifying Competition, Credentialism and Risk

This compulsion towards individual advancement in Wilton and communities like it certainly has an origin in the great uneasiness felt by many people in this socio-economic group – a demographic that Robert Reich labelled several years ago as the 'anxious class' (Reich 1994). Indeed, current economic restructuring and the 'flattening' of global markets make it likely that middle-class children will have a lower standard of living than their parents (Lareau 2003; Friedman 2005), and several authors have commented on middle-class parents' preoccupations with the possibilities of 'downward mobility' or 'fear of falling' for their children (Newman 1988; Ehrenreich 1989). While young Americans themselves are more ambitious than ever before, they seem to be increasingly aware of their status relative to others and to be preparing themselves at ever earlier ages for the sort of individualistic competition that is more and more central to American life (Schneider and Stevenson 1999; Rosenfeld and Wise 2000; Elkind 2001). Labaree (1997) pointed out several years ago that such market pressures and the social and class anxieties they foster encourage a view of education as a private good that facilitates individual advancement: a stance that ultimately leads to intensified educational credentialism.

Anthony Giddens observed over twenty years ago that Western modernity is a risk culture: individuals must think in terms of risk and risk assessment more or less constantly as they attempt to 'colonise the future for themselves as an intrinsic part of their life-planning' (Giddens 1991: 125). To be sure, risk societies are those that have undergone significant degrees of neoliberalisation, which, in Harvey's words, seeks to 'bring all human action into the domain of the market' (Harvey 2005: 3). There is a certain precariousness, then, in the future as regarded by middle-class youth, as the worth of themselves, as well as their accomplishments, are subject to the vicissitudes of the market (see Mole 2010).

Jean and John Comaroff argue more specifically that neoliberalism calls for a 'more radically individuated sense of personhood', which leads to new calculations regarding what sorts of exertions and practices are deemed ethical (Comaroff and Comaroff 2001: 15). More recently, Katharyne Mitchell, Sallie Marston and Cindi Katz have characterised the formation of the 'neoliberal subject' as marked by 'the devolution of more and more choice to a seemingly ever more autonomous individual who must rationally calculate the benefits and costs of all aspects of life' (Mitchell et al. 2003: 418; see also Katz 2001). The summary implication, Apple argues, is that neoliberalism demands, 'the constant production of evidence that one is in fact making an enterprise of oneself' (Apple 2001: 420). It is in this vein that Larner recently called for researchers to examine neoliberalism in everyday practice, especially the 'complex and contested processes through which new spaces, socialities and subjectivities are being constituted' (Larner 2005: 9). She advised researchers to contextualise such processes in specific 'neoliberalising political economies' (ibid.: 12). In this way, schools are becoming primary sites for a complex of achievements: not only the acquisition of essential academic knowledge and skills but also for the development of the sort of self that has market value in the contemporary neoliberal world.

Accordingly, an emerging literature in the U.K., the U.S. and Australia is focusing on the lived experiences of parents, students, teachers and administrators as they negotiate the contemporary education market. Several researchers, for example, have studied the practices of middle-class families as they seek to advocate and procure advantages for their children in school (see Ball 2003; Brantlinger 2003; Lareau 2003). Diane Reay commented that the practices of these families are 'part of a moral agenda of putting one's child first. Any notion of common good is subsidiary to getting the best for one's own child' (Reay 2004: 556). Other studies in education have recently investigated how a school leader's attempts to make a school more 'entrepreneurial' in a choice environment can undermine its historic commitments to equity, and lead to staff and community revolt (Forsey 2008), and the student resistance an urban school encountered when it attempted to explicitly transmit elements of cultural capital inherent in middle-class professionalism (Brown 2010). Most recently, Elsa Davidson has shown how middle-class youth in Silicon Valley respond to their 'increasing responsibility for middle class status' by learning to 'package or market authentic personal traits to showcase their exceptional qualities' (Davidson 2008: 2814; see also Davidson 2011).

Understanding Socialisation Processes of Schooling: The 'Unwritten Curriculum'

For over forty years, researchers have used the concept of the 'hidden curriculum' to effectively focus such inquiries on the relationship between schooling and the social order. The notion, an elaboration of Dewey's concept of 'collateral learning' (Dewey 1997), was first fully articulated by Jackson in his study of 'hidden consequences of life in classrooms' (Jackson 1990). His research focused on what students must 'master' in order to make their way satisfactorily through school. The hidden curriculum has since been defined as the 'messages imparted by the classroom and school environment ... not publicly set forth in official statements of school philosophy or purpose or in course guides and syllabi' (Cornbleth 1984: 29), or more succinctly, 'the socialization process of schooling' and how, as part of this, students experience an 'unwritten curriculum' (Kentli 2009: 83).

Given what I have learned from my study of Wilton, in this chapter I am broadening this conception of the unwritten curriculum in two ways. First, due to its ideological nature, it reaches beyond students, to include parents, teachers, administrators and other community members. Second, according to the tenets of practice theory, while it shapes the beliefs and behaviours of all of these actors, it is also co-constructed by them through their everyday practices (Bourdieu 1977; Ortner 1984). In this way, the unwritten curriculum encompasses the process of learning the middle-class logic of personal advancement in this setting (see Demerath 2009).

Figure 9.2 provides a display of the key beliefs and associated practices of the hidden curriculum for achievement in this community, and serves as a guide to the content of the chapter. The figure identifies the extent to which the practices of the hidden curriculum are dependent upon economic, social, cultural or psychological capital (Bourdieu 1998; Ortner 2002).

An Unwritten Curriculum for Achievement: Key Beliefs and Associated Practices

With Identification of Those Requiring Economic, Social, Cultural or Psychological Capital

- Competition is pervasive and is a natural process
- The primary purpose of schooling is instrumental: to facilitate social class security or mobility
    - Parents 'push' their students to achieve at high levels
    - Parents and community members support educational efforts and projects with private resources *EC, SC*
    - Parents intervene with and manipulate school and district policies on behalf of their children (depends on P cultural capital) *CC, SC*
- Positive self-worth is necessary for competitive success
    - Parents, the community, and school enhance the self-worth of young people by granting them significant authority and by recognising their achievements *CC*
    - Institutions generate their own symbolic capital which then may enhance the self-worth of their members *CC*
- Students expect to exert significant control over their own social and educational experiences – they are the authors of their own lives (within constraints, and depending on their own class habitus)
    - Students should have deep attachments to personal success *PC*
    - Students should develop high levels of confidence *PC*
    - Students should identify specific aspirations early in their school career *CC, SC*
- Intelligence is primarily innate, though once recognised can be capitalised upon with hard work (hard work beats talent when talent doesn't work hard)
    - A work ethic must be self-consciously cultivated *SC, CC, PC*
- Deceptive communication styles should be adopted in order to hide certain achievements, avoid harsh moral judgment, and preserve potential for solidarity *PC*
- Stress and fatigue are natural
    - It is adaptive to habituate to stress and fatigue *PC*
- Academic assessments may be negotiated with teachers *CC*
    - Self-advocacy skills should be developed *CC, SC, PC*
- Cheating is natural

Figure 9.2 An unwritten curriculum for achievement: key beliefs and associated practices.

The 'Wilton Way': A Middle-Class Guide to Individual Competitive Success

The hidden curriculum for achievement in Wilton was shaped by multiple social actors, organisations and ideological forces. The chapter seeks to show the central role these external factors play in the enterprise of producing individual youth's achievements – and thereby how the cultural emphasis on framing these achievements as individual accomplishments renders this social machinery largely invisible.

It is important to note at the outset that the class-*cum*-cultural achievement ideology in this community actually had a name: the 'Wilton Way'. The Wilton Way was a trope related to personhood and success, and comprised more or less shared beliefs concerning the primacy of the individual, the distinctiveness of the community, and competitive strategies for individual and community advancement. This trope was understood in various ways by White parents and teachers. A White AP history teacher described the 'Wilton Way', as, 'the upper middle-class way: how your capacity for consumption determines your worth'. An African American teacher, on the other hand, interpreted the 'Wilton Way' as meaning, 'Just keep your mouth shut, do what you're told, and you'll go far'. Indeed, some students were a bit cynical of the 'Wilton Way'. When asked what it was on the survey, one replied, 'They push us harder, make us work longer, and try and make us learn faster to keep up this "tradition of excellence". How stuck-up can you get?'

There were pervasive and pronounced community expectations for success in Wilton. The school district motto was 'Where Excellence is a Tradition', and signs affixed to district schools noted that they were in one of the state's 'Best Communities'.[5] David Sterling, a high-achieving White focal student said in his first interview in ninth grade, 'It's just, Wilton, everyone has to do well in Wilton. It's like, you can't *fail* [original emphasis] if you live in Wilton. And that's what you see'.

These expectations for success shaped conceptions of personhood as well. A key component of the Wilton Way was the importance of the maintenance of self-worth and that children ought to 'feel good' about themselves. This tenet seemed to have its basis in unspoken beliefs about the role of positive self-regard in competitive success.

Institutionalising Responsibilisation in a New High School

These community beliefs regarding the requirements for success in an increasingly competitive world were made visible in the planning process for Wilton Burnham High School (WBHS), founded in 1991. A 'Climate Committee' was formed of parents, teachers and students to decide on various school policies and structures. The Committee's work seemed to be guided in part by two locally accepted means of developing self-worth in students: granting them authority and recognising them (discussed below). Accordingly, school policies and pedagogies tended to grant students great latitude and input as to the nature of their school experience.[6] A WBHS science teacher who was a member of the school's original planning committee said of their deliberations, 'We wanted to work with kids on managing their time, so it is more like when they go away to college'. So the school adopted a 'blended schedule' with some blocks and some regular class periods. Moreover, juniors and seniors carrying a minimal grade-point average (GPA) were afforded 'options' wherein they could leave the campus during their free periods.

By the time I started my study, WBHS itself had become quite successful.[7] In 1998 it was recognised by the U.S. Department of Education as a 'Blue Ribbon High School'. Of the graduates of the class of 1999, 88.2 per cent planned to attend a college, university or technical school. The school offered a series of Enriched classes for all students, as well as a comprehensive array of AP classes that were open to sophomores, juniors and seniors (generally aged 16–18) – some of which had fewer than eight students in them. In addition, the extracurricular activities included award-winning programmes in music, theatre and the arts, and a wide variety of varsity[8] athletic programmes, clubs and societies.

The school's successful athletics teams were a particular source of community pride. When I asked Bobbi Taylor, the school's athletics director, how important winning was to parents, she replied:

> It's important to some, it's just teaching your kids, or letting them feel what it's like to win ... Once you have that sense that, 'Hey we can win', and you have that little natural arrogance which comes with it, I think you, I mean, kids can really do some incredible things when they have the confidence and the sauce, and the trust in their team-mates to be able to win.

The athletics director here goes beyond parents' desires to have their children play on winning athletics teams. She states the intrinsic importance of experiencing winning to a person's 'natural' sense of self-confidence.

Indeed, the school itself went to considerable efforts to make its students and staff feel that they were on a 'winning' team – largely through its production of various kinds of symbolic capital. The capacious Commons area had flags from nations around the world draped from the ceiling, with the school's Blue Ribbon banner featured prominently in the centre of them. Throughout the school's hallways, framed artwork adorned the walls, and classical music emanated quietly from speakers. When the class of 1999 graduated, 86 per cent of the students received a 'Certificate of Excellence', and all received a WBHS key ring and a wallet-sized copy of their diploma which stipulated, 'bearer entitled to all rights and privileges' of being a WBHS graduate. For the school's tenth anniversary, Principal Cunningham had postcards printed with a photograph of the school on the front. The caption on the back read:

> Founded in 1991, Wilton Burnham High School achieved Blue Ribbon status in 1998 as a Nationally Recognised School of Excellence. WBHS has a faculty, administration, and staff acclaimed by state, national, and international professional organisations for overall excellence, dedication, and commitment to students and learning. Wilton Burnham High School celebrated its ten-year anniversary by commissioning an original piece of music by Dr. Fitzpatrick for its annual Arts in Action celebration.

Finally, the school introduced a new letterhead in 2001 that included the names of all staff members in tiny print all around the border of the page. Indeed, when Principal Callahan welcomed the class of 2003 to WBHS, she concluded her remarks by saying, 'Welcome to an outstanding national treasure'.

Hypercredentialing

The WBHS Planning Committee decided early on that 'the achievement of each student is important and should be recognised'. It was this philosophy that led the school to develop so many ways of recognising students and their accomplishments. These included: an Honour Roll, Student of the Month award, Academic Honour Awards (Bronze Key, Silver Key, Gold Key), an Award of Merit, an Honours Diploma, Junior Book Awards, a Senior Recognition Program, a Key Club, a Socratic Society, a National Honour Society, a Scholar Athlete Award, a Celebration of Excellence Medal, twelve Seasons of Greatness, a Hall of Fame, and Valedictorian(s). Most of the winners of these awards were on display in the central school Commons, where students ate lunch, along with photographs of National Merit finalists. Photographs of pupils who had been identified as 'Student of the Month' were also featured in the Commons. One teacher explained the origin of this award as follows: 'Because some students may not get any recognition. But if a teacher catches a student doing something good, then they can give them that recognition'. Celebration of Excellence Medals were awarded at an end-of-year assembly to students who had achieved a measure of success in extracurricular competitions (for example, it might be given to a member of the Concert Band that had come in third place in the District Music Festival). It was essentially an award for getting an award.

The school had another way of recognising students that bordered on credentials fraud: school policy dictated that all students who graduated with a 4.0 GPA or higher were 'Valedictorians'.[9] The high school class of 2000 had 28 valedictorians, the class of 2001 had 41, the class of 2002 had 42, and the class of 2003 had 47: 10 per cent of the class. One of the focal students in the study was one of those 47 valedictorians in the class of 2003, and they received a 'Valedictorian Scholarship' to a highly competitive university. This is a trend in the U.S. at present: a recent survey showed that 40 per cent of high schools have begun to report the general grade distribution for graduating classes instead of the class rank of individual students (NACAC 2007). While some have done so to mitigate pressure on students, others have done so, in the words of the WBHS director of counselling, to 'not penalise' students with high GPAs. A school district in Maryland recently adopted a grading system where students could earn GPAs in excess of the usual maximum of 5.0. The district superintendent commented: 'This opens it up much more and it gives more recognition to more kids and that's the crucial thing. We want to recognise as many kids as possible' (Dahl 2010). The logic here is not unlike that of the fictive rock group Spinal Tap's lead guitarist when he explains to a bewildered reporter that his amplifier is louder than others because it 'goes to eleven'.

In sum, I argue that these practices constitute a process of 'hypercredentialing': the production of artificially high credentials intended to strengthen students' positions on education and job markets. This had its basis in how many of the teachers saw their work at the school: as enabling students to compete. One teacher of both Enriched and regular classes said, 'Our job is to get these kids into the best college they can possibly get in to'. Teachers like this one foregrounded competition in their classes: discussions of assessment criteria and grades almost always occurred at the beginning of class and could take ten to fifteen minutes.

Grade inflation was certainly present in the school and opportunities to earn extra credit were commonplace. One science teacher gave each student three 'bathroom passes' for each nine-week marking period. If the passes went unused, the student could turn in the passes at the end of the marking period for extra credit. Some teachers took steps to counter the school's emphasis on credentialing. At the end of each school year an AP history teacher gave those students whom he felt demonstrated true intellectual curiosity tee-shirts with Aeschylus' epigram, 'Wisdom through suffering'.

WBHS's policies of freedom, discourses of excellence, logics of competitive success, technologies of recognition, and hypercredentialing were all mutually reinforcing components of the unwritten curriculum of the school: they further shaped what people in Wilton believed about schools, their children's activities there, and appropriate futures for them. The resulting institutional culture naturalised competition, built up students' confidence, framed their efforts as successes, and constructed them as adult successes-to-be.

The Role of Parents: Private Support, 'Pushing' and Policy Manipulation

In addition to WBHS's institutional efforts to sponsor students, the hidden curriculum in Wilton called on parents to play specific roles as well. For example, parents could expect to leverage their own private resources to support particular school programmes and mitigate the uncertainties of government funding for public schools. WBHS had an array of parent-led 'booster' organisations to support extracurricular and academic programmes. The largest was Bears, Inc., a registered non-profit organisation devoted to supporting the school's athletics teams. Between 1997 and 2003, Bears, Inc. raised several million dollars for the construction of a 4,000 square foot 'Strength and Power Room' adjacent to the school's gymnasium – the largest privately funded project in the history of Wilton's schools (one visitor compared the weight training room to a 'health club'). The athletics programmes quickly developed a new stress on weight training, which Bobbi Taylor, the athletics director, explained:

> I think the second thing we have done, and I think Bill Watson [the varsity football coach] has really spearheaded this, is that we had to be – strength training had to almost be a part of *all* of our programs. We *had* to have our athletes conditioned. In the last ten years, you've noticed that kids are bigger, stronger. We *had* to be able to compete ... So I think that's really – if you look at Bob Jefferies [the boys' varsity soccer coach], I think he would say that, his conditioning helped him win that state title.

Here Taylor refers to the state championship won by the boys' varsity soccer team in 2000. In the years prior to that championship, Jefferies had instituted an off-season strength-training programme for his players where they were expected to lift weights four days a week in the spring. The boy's football team won a conference championship in 2002.

One of the more ironic themes developed in this collection is the importance of the big or well-developed body – even in an information age (see Bayly, this volume). Indeed, three years after the Strength and Power Room opened, the school adopted a student wellness strategy of opening it to all pupils and making a strength coach available to them.

Wilton parents supported and sought to enhance their children's academic achievement in a variety of ways. Parenting styles in the community were characterised by a distinctive combination of affective support, high expectations and pressure. As mentioned at the outset of the chapter, parents also routinely intervened with individual teachers, and some of them used their class-cultural know-how and social and professional networks to appropriate educational resources for their children. The one example of support I will share here is what some teachers referred to as parental 'pushing'. This discourse was evident in yearbook vanity ads (advertisements of various sizes in the school yearbook that parents could purchase), and was simultaneously encouraging, congratulatory and pressure-inducing:

> Congratulations Sean on your success at WBHS! Remember, supersuccess is not a matter of talent, it's character. It's what kind of person you are. You have to choose a winning attitude, and in order to succeed you must first affirm and then believe ... May all your dreams come true. You just have to T-R-Y. Trust and Respect Yourself.[10]

Community Beliefs Regarding Intelligence and Achievement

Another important thread that runs through this volume concerns relationships between theories of intelligence and achievement. Most achievement-oriented parents and students in Wilton seemed to subscribe to what Dweck would refer to as an 'entity' or 'fixed' theory of intelligence (Dweck 1999). A Wilton School District special education supervisor said that a guiding assumption for parents in the community was that, 'There are no average kids in Wilton. You are either gifted or special ed [i.e., special needs]. And that's taken from the mindset that the average IQ is 115.' The supervisor went on to explain that Wilton students functioning at an IQ of 97 or 100 were often seen as having a disability because they could not compete. Students themselves shared some of these beliefs about the innateness of intelligence. They often referred to students who took Enriched or AP classes as the 'smart' kids. Our research team once overheard one White male student say to another in the cafeteria, 'I hate geniuses. They get an easy break. They don't work for it.'

One important consequence of these beliefs was that many parents who believed their children were not competing well sought Other Health Impaired (OHI) diagnoses for them in order for them to have extra time on school-based as well as ACT and SAT (college entrance) tests.[11] During the third year of the project I learned of two sets of parents of students carrying 4.0 GPAs who were seeking to have their children classified as OHI (cf. Solomon, this volume). The district special education supervisor expressed her view that it was part of Wilton parents' efforts to ensure that their children had 'optimum performance.' She went on to explain that this could include the use of pharmaceutical enhancements: 'You know, fix the kid. If they need medication, fix the kid.' The U.S. Department of Education reported that between 1990 and 2001 the number of students receiving OHI services grew by 397 per cent (Wodrich and Spencer 2007). In the next section, I discuss what students themselves seemed to infer about the purposes of school and how to achieve both academically and personally.

The Role of Students: Developing Psychological Capital

The inferences WBHS students made about what was needed for competitive academic success and personal achievement seemed to be largely evident in their identities, which were made up of an assemblage of characteristics oriented toward control and individual advancement. I have argued elsewhere (Demerath and Lynch 2008) that these identities make up new forms of what Sherry Ortner calls 'psychological capital': 'the production of the kind of social self a person emerges with from childhood ... the things that make for different social effectiveness' (Ortner 2002: 13). I will focus here on the four components of psychological capital that are especially relevant to the unwritten curriculum for achievement in Wilton: having strong attachments to personal success; self-consciously developing a work-ethic; adopting politically correct ways of talking about individual achievements; and habituating to stress and fatigue.

One of the striking characteristics of the high-achieving students in Wilton was the extent to which they saw their selves as ongoing projects, ones which necessitated a high degree of control. One of the survey items asked students to rank the following influences in determining a person's future: individual effort, parents' background, social support, and quality of education. Of the respondents, 71.5 per cent ranked effort at the top. Indeed, in a lively discussion on the origins and perpetuation of social inequality in an Enriched Global History/English class, two European American female students made the following comments:

> TIFFANY: Our parents have worked very hard to send us to good schools, but some of them haven't tried as hard.
> SUSAN: Some of them don't have the will.

Such a comment does not account for factors outside the personality resources of parents in the neoliberal context which could affect residency and where parents are able to send their children to school, such as employment, socio-economic status and social and cultural capital.

Attachments to Success

Several students said openly in interviews that everyone's goal was to be 'the best', and that they themselves wanted to be 'the best' or 'the top'. What student voices illuminated, though, was the depth of these attachments to personal success. In an English class, several student speeches dealt with 'success' in some way. Most notably, a wrestler brought in a framed Hallmark-type card with a printed message of support about success and learning from failure. He explained that his mother had given it to him his freshman year , at age 15, when he had first started wrestling at the varsity level, and was losing a lot of matches. He began his speech by holding up the framed card and saying, 'I love my mom, and I love success, so I love this'.

Another theme that cuts across the contributions to this volume is how many achievements 'chase each other' without endpoints, and how this can lead to, for example, 'achievement disease' (see Bayly, this volume) or 'addictions to success' (see Long 2007). In Wilton, hypercredentialing seemed to fuel the desire of many young people for these relative markers of success. One day in 1999, the Enriched Global History/English class mentioned above watched a WBHS news announcement regarding the posting of student names who had received merit awards. One White female student said to another, 'There it is! How do you get it'? After ascertaining that none of the students sitting near her knew, she went up and asked the teacher.

Nevertheless, in Wilton, some achievement-oriented students adopted veiled ways of talking about their own success. David Sterling said his father had once told him, 'Not everyone feels wonderful about your success because some people feel bad that it's not their success'. Indeed David said that, 'No one wants to admit that they're better than anyone else'. Hence, many students, especially as they moved through the grades in high school, talked instead of wanting to 'do well'. Foley would refer to this as 'impression management' (Foley 1990: 1) – learning situational speech performances and adopting deceptive communicative styles that enable middle-class young people to re-inscribe their social prominence (see also Goffman 1974). But using such speech devices also suggests a concern for hiding certain achievements from the judgement of others, in part, perhaps to preserve that very American veneer of equality and affiliation (see Varenne 1977, 1986).

The Self-Conscious Cultivation of a Work Ethic

As the voices of some of the Wilton high-achieving students have already made clear, another central component of these identities for success was the self-conscious development of a strong work ethic. The consensus was that most students worked very hard to get good grades. The motto on the back of the 2000 WBHS men's volleyball team's tee-shirts was epigrammatic of this belief: 'Wilton Men's Volleyball: Learning Success Through Hard Work'. Several of the high-achieving 'enriched' focal students mentioned staying up until 1.00, 2.00 or even 3.00 AM in order to study for tests. David Sterling described his approach as follows: 'I told myself long ago that, you may not be the smartest guy, you may not be the fastest runner, but if you work hard, there's a lot of people who you'll go past'.

Work ethics are nothing new, but the degree to which these young people rationalise them and self-consciously cultivate them may be. The deeply seated adoption of this work ethic married to a success orientation seemed to be behind the constant compulsion of the high-achieving students to be, or do something, 'productive'. Above all, they embodied the grim determination with which, as de Tocqueville noted nearly 200 years ago, Americans seem to go about 'acquiring the good things of life' (de Tocqueville 2003: 161; see also Henry 1963: 7).

Habituating to Stress and Fatigue

Finally, it is appropriate to mention that the entire study could have become an ethnography of stress. Most students at WBHS went through their daily lives with great stress and fatigue – female students more so. Survey data indicated that 70.2 per cent of students reported being 'stressed out' either 'frequently' or 'all the time', and that there were important gender differences in this area: while female students had significantly higher cumulative GPAs than male students, they were also much more likely to report being 'stressed out' either 'frequently' (64.9 per cent of females; 45.5 per cent of males) or 'all the time' (17.9 per cent of females; 12.3 per cent of males), and to identify their schoolwork as the most important source of stress (48.3 per cent of females; 31.6 per cent of males; χ^2=44.56, p=.0001). At the school's annual Arts in Action day there was always a

Figure 9.3 Liz Cross, [Untitled] (2003). Source: *Solstice*, Vol. 12.

considerable amount of student artwork that powerfully expressed themes of anxiety, stress, failure, loss, desolation and emptiness.

The voices and experiences of Wilton students as a whole suggested that the most successful were those that were able to habituate themselves to these conditions. Indeed, when asked on the survey how he coped with stress, a White male ninth-grade student responded, 'I deal with it by playing sports and filling my need for competition because it relaxes my mind.'[12]

The class-cultural identities of these youth seem to be strongly shaped by what they infer will be needed for personal success in an uncertain yet highly competitive future. What is notable about these young people is the extent to which their total selves are oriented towards individual achievement, and their seeming awareness that particular identity characteristics have value as psychological capital.

Instrumental Strategies for Academic Achievement and Advancement

While many achievement-oriented Wilton students developed strong work ethics and exerted themselves in school, others adopted strategies to, as one senior said, 'get the best grade with the least amount of work' – an approach that suggests a cost–benefit calculation. These students often negotiated with their teachers for extra points, easier assignments or extra credit. One available category for understanding these practices, and especially these students' preoccupation with extra credit, is shopping. 'Thrift' is central to an anthropological logic of shopping in the West (see Miller 1998), and in this view

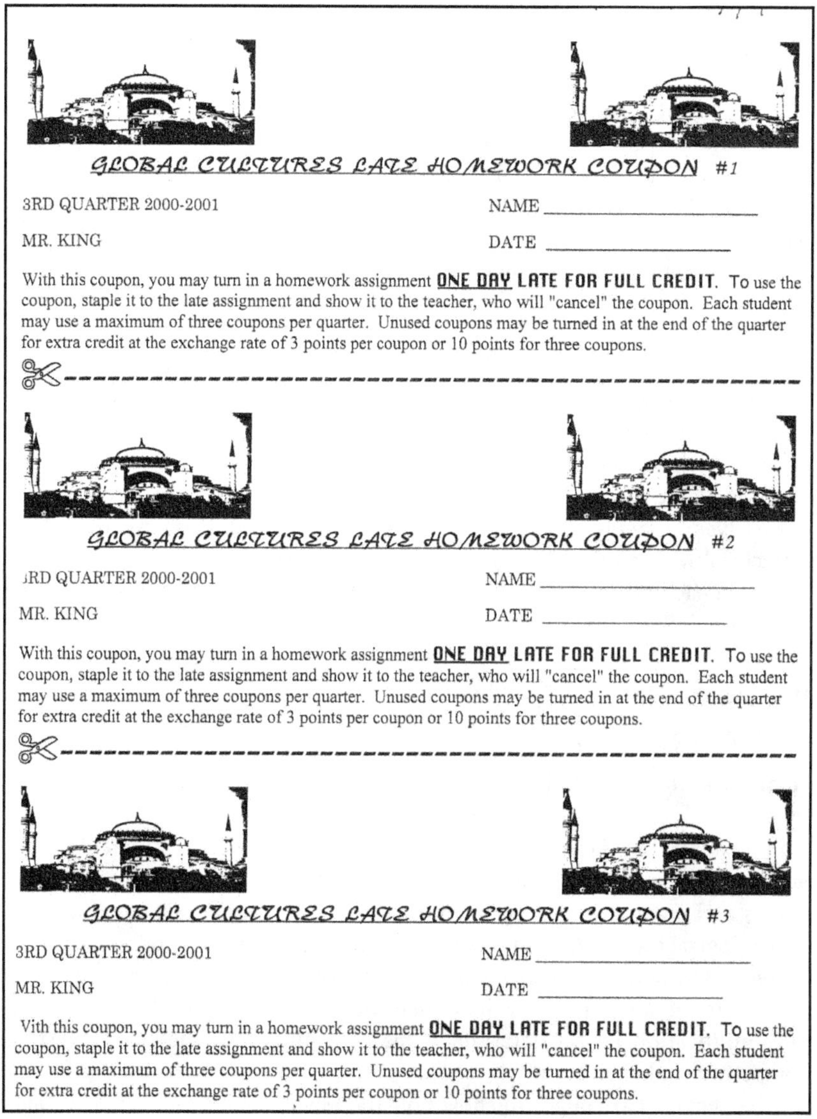

GLOBAL CULTURES LATE HOMEWORK COUPON #1

3RD QUARTER 2000-2001 NAME ______________________

MR. KING DATE ____________________

With this coupon, you may turn in a homework assignment **ONE DAY LATE FOR FULL CREDIT.** To use the coupon, staple it to the late assignment and show it to the teacher, who will "cancel" the coupon. Each student may use a maximum of three coupons per quarter. Unused coupons may be turned in at the end of the quarter for extra credit at the exchange rate of 3 points per coupon or 10 points for three coupons.

✂- -

GLOBAL CULTURES LATE HOMEWORK COUPON #2

3RD QUARTER 2000-2001 NAME ______________________

MR. KING DATE ____________________

With this coupon, you may turn in a homework assignment **ONE DAY LATE FOR FULL CREDIT.** To use the coupon, staple it to the late assignment and show it to the teacher, who will "cancel" the coupon. Each student may use a maximum of three coupons per quarter. Unused coupons may be turned in at the end of the quarter for extra credit at the exchange rate of 3 points per coupon or 10 points for three coupons.

✂- -

GLOBAL CULTURES LATE HOMEWORK COUPON #3

3RD QUARTER 2000-2001 NAME ______________________

MR. KING DATE ____________________

With this coupon, you may turn in a homework assignment **ONE DAY LATE FOR FULL CREDIT.** To use the coupon, staple it to the late assignment and show it to the teacher, who will "cancel" the coupon. Each student may use a maximum of three coupons per quarter. Unused coupons may be turned in at the end of the quarter for extra credit at the exchange rate of 3 points per coupon or 10 points for three coupons.

Figure 9.4 'Late homework coupons' from WBHS's 2000/2001 social studies class.

'extra credit' is essentially a credential on sale – a 'bargain.' Many achievement-oriented WBHS students were expert at maximising their opportunities to obtain such bargains, and they pushed their teachers for as many of them as possible. Some teachers accommodated themselves to these requests. An example is provided in Figure 9.4: A set of three 'homework coupons' that students could affix to their homework and turn it in one day late without being marked down. They could turn in unused coupons at the end of the marking period for extra credit at the exchange rate of three points per coupon or ten points for three coupons.

In addition, many achievement-oriented students seemed to infer that cheating was 'natural'. On an anonymous school survey administered by WBHS's student forum during the 1998/99 academic year, 77 per cent of students in the school admitted to having cheated. Student comments on the survey were particularly illuminating: 'Cheaters always win. Bending the system is what makes the human race the most advanced'; 'Cheating is real life. People who are rich and successful lie and cheat every day'.

In this sense, the most powerful and unsettling messages of the WBHS unwritten curriculum were that education serves primarily instrumental purposes – to credential – and that a primary function of the school is to sort students accordingly. These emphases seemed to have a particularly deleterious effect on the academic engagement and self-worth of average and under-achieving students in the school. Indeed, students who did not perceive themselves as being among the 'smart' kids, and were not recognised as 'successes' within the school, commonly disengaged from their school work, degraded each other, told each other they 'sucked' or to 'shut up', and (among males) vandalised school property. It is possible that they were aware that they comprised the school's 'precariat' (Mole 2010), and that they were in danger of retaining that status into adulthood.

Conclusions: Conjuring Value in the Service of Responsibilisation

This chapter has sketched the contours of an unwritten curriculum for achievement in a neoliberal era, and more specifically identified constituent beliefs and practices that require measures of economic, social, cultural and psychological capital. A central argument here is that, just as neoliberalism may be seen as an amplification of core elements of market capitalism, the modal identity found among these achievement-oriented Wilton youth themselves is an amplification or acceleration of many of the components of Western competitive individualism.

The chapter has sought to show how the unwritten curriculum represents what must be learned for residents to participate in a highly synthesised, class-cultural system oriented toward educational credentialism, market orientation and personal advancement. One of the most important findings from the study is that personal achievements are produced as much by this highly evolved socio-cultural machinery as they are by individuals, yet they are fetishised in such as way as to make these external forces virtually invisible. Indeed, despite the existence of these external supports, nearly three-quarters of the students surveyed in the school still understood success as due primarily to their own personal efforts. Such students seemed to have a very faint understanding of how their parents' college degrees, SAT prep classes, the public library homework helpline, and their parents' transportation to and from curricular and extracurricular activities all comprised a set of advantages that underlay their efforts. The invisibility of this set of advantages is certainly part of the cultural logic of hiding from view strategies for achievement that might have morally questionable valences. The converse of this is also true: collective achievements, such as the school's standing and reputation, were framed in part as individual accomplishments (for example, by the inclusion of all staff names on the school letterhead).

It is also important to point out the self-reinforcing qualities of this class-cultural assemblage that underlie its durability. For example, certain kinds of resistance to the achievement ethos in Wilton were reframed as achievements in their own right: the students who demonstrated true 'intellectual curiosity' were rewarded with an Aeschylus tee-shirt; student artwork that expressed a kind of self-loathing brought on by the competitive atmosphere of the school was displayed in the Commons for its insight and creativity. These developments might be seen as a sort of 'counter-credentialing' that reframes resistance to achievement as another form of achievement. This is a somewhat insidious dimension to the hidden curriculum that helps explain how it brings more and more people into its orbit, and endures.

It is in this way that I hope that this research contributes to a broader project of 'writing against achievement as an individual act'.[13] I think Mary Douglas and Steven Ney's 'missing persons' critique is crucial to such an anthropology of achievement. Their concern that Western social science tends to have a 'non-social being at the centre of the so-called social sciences' (Douglas and Ney 1998: 18) helps to highlight the social foundations of individual achievements.

More specifically, the depth of individual and community attachments to 'success' in Wilton, and the manic embrace of competition of all sorts, raise the question of whether the community suffers from its own sort of 'achievement disease'. While parents like Ann Rice expressed discomfort with some of the costs of the hidden programme for educational success in Wilton – as did parents in Davidson's (2011) study in Silicon Valley – most did not go to great lengths to reign in their children's efforts. Indeed, the widespread inability of Wilton students, especially girls, to cope with stress could have been a contributing factor in the rising number of cases of 'school phobia' reported by the school psychologist during the study, which she defined as a condition characterised by experiencing debilitating anxiety upon entering the building. Though Julie Rice herself did not report symptoms of school phobia, she did tell me that as a self-professed 'Christian', the gynaecologist's remedy added to her stress.

More broadly, hypercredentialing calls attention to how such relative metrics of achievement articulate with more absolute or global ones. This is a core assumption of Wilton's highly developed practice of recognising student accomplishments – even those of questionable merit. It is possible that receiving an inflated credential may indirectly, perhaps through the temporary elevation of a person's confidence, enable them to achieve in more absolute terms. African American students in particular mentioned the important role confidence played in their academic success in the school (and they said that having more African American teachers would help with that). We did not ask explicitly about the extent to which receiving recognition enhanced confidence – this seems an appropriate avenue for future research.

Lastly, it is relevant to point out that the logic of the hidden curriculum in Wilton is reminiscent of 'casino capitalism' (Comaroff and Comaroff 2001). In their examination of the 'enigmatic' nature of millennial capitalism, the Comaroffs discuss the increasing prevalence of occult economies and related efforts conjure wealth from nothing. These include 'lottery mania', which has claimed several lives in Madya Pradesh, India; fortune-telling and e-mail divination in Thailand; ritual killing, witchcraft, zombie conjuring and tourism based on the sightings of 'fabulous monsters' in South Africa; hysteria across Asia, Africa, Oceania and Latin America about the secret theft and sale of the body parts of young people; and global Ponzi schemes and evangelical prosperity gospels. The Comaroffs refer to these as 'locally nuanced fantasies of abundance' which promise 'wealth without production, value without effort' (ibid.: 23). They point out that they share similar features with cargo cults. In light of these global developments, it does not seem unreasonable to ask whether American high-school guidance counsellors who countenance the naming of forty-seven valedictorians are conjurers, or alchemists, as well.

Notes

1. Pseudonyms are used throughout the chapter.
2. The broader study aimed to illuminate how the interconnected assumptions, beliefs and concerns regarding individual advancement shaped the everyday lives and approaches to schooling of the people of Wilton. A more detailed and elaborated interpretation of the entire cultural system is presented in Demerath (2009); on the role of student identity and the acquisition of psychological capital, see Demerath and Lynch (2008) and Demerath et al. (2008).
3. The project was designed as a four-year ethnographic study in order to understand the experiences and perceptions of a diverse group of students as they moved through high school (the school had two principals during this period: Principal Callahan during the 1999/2000 school year, and Principal Trent from 2000 to 2003). Data were collected by a diverse research team through participant observation and informal interviews in classrooms and other relevant settings in and out of school; over 60 tape-recorded interviews with teachers, administrators and students, including a diverse sample of eight high- and low-achieving male and female students from the class of 2003 and their parents; and consultation of school documents and popular-culture discourses and social narratives on youth, parenting and schooling. In addition, a grounded survey consisting of 44 forced-choice and 16 open-ended items was administered in March 2002 to 605 students.
4. Advanced Placement (AP) courses are especially rigorous and offer students the opportunity to earn college credits while still in high school.
5. Readers should be aware that I myself am White and my hometown is very much like Wilton: in the past it has referred to itself as a 'Center of Distinction'.

6. Some inadvertent effects of this stance are discussed elsewhere: see Demerath (2007).
7. During the 2000/2001 school year the school had 1,649 students, of whom 86 per cent were classified European American, 10 per cent Asian American and 4 per cent African American.
8. The principal team that represents the school in inter-scholastic athletic competition.
9. Traditionally, the student in a graduating class who has the highest academic rank. This student usually gives a valedictory speech at the school's graduation ceremony.
10. Taken from an advert in the 1998 WBHS yearbook.
11. OHI is a category of special educational needs in Ohio, and includes Attention Deficit Disorder and Attention Deficit Hyperactivity Disorder. The ACT (American College Testing) and SAT (Scholastic Aptitude Test) are standardised placement exams used for admissions by most colleges in the United States.
12. An important future research direction is understanding the use of pharmaceutical neuroenhancers to 'fix' young people in order to assure maximum performance. A truly multidisciplinary investigation of achievement in this day and age will need to examine the implications of what Anjan Chatterjee (2006) refers to as 'cosmetic neurology', including the 'off-label' use of neuroenhancers such as modafinil, methylphenidate, provigil/nuvigil and piracetam.
13. Signithia Fordham (personal communication, October 1, 2010).

References

Apple, M. 2001. *Educating the 'Right' Way: Markets, Standards, God, and Inequality.* New York: RoutledgeFalmer.

Ball, S.J. 2003. *Class Strategies and the Education Market: The Middle Classes and Social Advantage.* New York: RoutledgeFalmer.

Bourdieu, P. 1977. *Outline of a Theory of Practice.* Cambridge: Cambridge University Press.

——— 1998. *Practical Reason: On the Theory of Action.* Stanford: Stanford University Press.

Brantlinger, E. 2003. *Dividing Classes: How the Middle Class Negotiates and Rationalizes School Advantage.* New York: RoutledgeFalmer.

Brown, A. 2010. Pushing for Professionalism: Contesting 'Achievement' at a New York City Public School. Paper presented at 'The Social Life of Achievement', American Anthropological Association Annual Meetings, New Orleans, 17–21 November.

Chatterjee, A. 2006. The Promise and Predicament of Cosmetic Neurology. *Journal of Medical Ethics* 32, no. 2: 110–113.

Comaroff, J., and J. Comaroff. 2001. Introduction. In *Millennial Capitalism and the Culture of Neoliberalism* (eds) J. Comaroff and J. Comaroff, 1–56. Durham, NC: Duke University Press.

Cornbleth, C. 1984. Beyond Hidden Curriculum? *Journal of Curriculum Studies* 16, no. 1: 29–36.

Dahl, C. 2010. Honours System Proposed to Replace Class Ranking. *Maryland Coast Dispatch*, 22 January.

Davidson, E. 2008. Marketing the Self: The Politics of Aspiration Among Middle-Class Silicon Valley Youth. *Environment and Planning A* 40: 2814–2930.

——— 2011. *The Burdens of Aspiration: Schools, Youth, and Success in the Divided Social Worlds of Silicon Valley.* New York: New York University Press.

Demerath, P. 2007. Are Student-Determined Goods Good for Students? Unseen Effects of Student Identity, Policy, and Pedagogy in a U.S. Suburban High School. Unpublished manuscript, Columbus, OH.

——— 2009. *Decoding Success: Inside the Culture of Personal Advancement in an American Suburb and High School.* Chicago: University of Chicago Press.

Demerath, P., and J. Lynch. 2008. Identities for Neoliberal Times: Constructing Enterprising Selves in an American Suburb. In *Youth Moves: Identities in Global Perspective* (eds) N. Dolby and F. Rizvi, 179–192. New York: Routledge.

Demerath, P., J. Lynch and M. Davidson. 2008. Dimensions of Psychological Capital in a U.S. Suburb: Identities for Neoliberal Times. *Anthropology and Education Quarterly* 39, no. 3: 270–292.

De Tocqueville, A. [1838] 2003. *Democracy in America.* London: Penguin

Dewey, J. [1938] 1997. *Experience and Education.* New York: Free Press.

Douglas, M., and S. Ney. 1998. *Missing Persons: A Critique of Personhood in the Social Sciences.* Berkeley: University of California Press.

Dorst, J.D. 1989. *The Written Suburb: An American Site, An Ethnographic Dilemma.* Philadelphia: University of Pennsylvania Press.

Dweck, C.S. 1999. *Self-Theories: Their Role in Motivation, Personality and Development.* Philadelphia: Psychology Press.

Education Trust. 2001. *The Funding Gap: Low-Income and Minority Students Receive Fewer Dollars.* Washington, DC: Education Trust.

Ehrenreich, B. 1989. *Fear of Falling: The Inner Life of the Middle Class.* New York: Pantheon.

Elkind, D. 2001. *The Hurried Child: Growing Up too Fast too Soon.* New York: Da Capo.

Foley, D. 1990. *Learning Capitalist Culture: Deep in the Heart of Tejas.* Philadelphia: University of Pennsylvania Press.

Forsey, M. 2008. *Challenging the System? A Dramatic Tale of Neo-Liberal Reform in an Australian High School.* Greenwich, CT: Information Age Publishing.

Friedman, T. 2005. *The World is Flat: A Brief History of the Twenty-First Century.* New York: Farrar, Straus and Giroux.

Giddens, A. 1991. *Modernity and Self-Identity: Self and Society in the Late Modern Age.* Stanford: Stanford University Press.

Goffman, E. 1974. *Frame Analysis: An Essay on the Organization of Experience.* New York: Harper and Row.

Harvey, D. 2005. *A Brief History of Neoliberalism.* Oxford: Oxford University Press.

Henry, J. 1963. *Culture Against Man.* New York: Vintage.

Jackson, P.W. [1968] 1990. *Life in Classrooms.* New York: Teachers College Press.

Katz, C. 2001. Vagabond Capitalism and the Necessity of Social Reproduction. *Antipode* 33, no. 4: 709–728.

Kentli, F.D. 2009. Comparison of Hidden Curriculum Theories. *European Journal of Educational Studies* 1, no. 2: 83–88.

Labaree, D.F. 1997. *How to Succeed in School Without Really Learning: The Credentials Race in American Education.* New Haven: Yale University Press.

Lareau, A. 2003. *Unequal Childhoods: Class, Race, and Family Life.* Berkeley: University of California Press.

Larner, W. 2005. Neoliberalism in (Regional) Theory and Practice: The Stronger Communities Action Fund in New Zealand. *Geographical Research* 43, no. 1: 9–18.

Long, N. J. 2007. How to Win a Beauty Contest in Tanjung Pinang. *Review of Indonesian and Malaysian Affairs* 41, no. 1: 91–117.

Miller, D. 1998. *A Theory of Shopping.* Ithaca, NY: Cornell University Press.

Mitchell, K., S. Marston and C. Katz. 2003. Life's Work: An Introduction, Review and Critique. *Antipode* 35, no. 2: 415–442.
Mole, N. 2010. Precarious Subjects: Anticipating Neoliberalism in Northern Italy's Workplace. *American Anthropologist* 112, no. 1: 38–53.
NACAC. 2007. *How High Schools Use and Report Class Rank.* Arlington, VA: National Association of College Admission Counseling.
NCES. 2003. *The Condition of Education: An Annual Snapshot, 2003.* Washington, DC: National Centre for Education Statistics, Department of Education.
Newman, K. 1988. *Falling from Grace: Downward Mobility in the Age of Affluence.* Berkeley: University of California Press.
Ortner, S. 1984. Theory in Anthropology Since the Sixties. *Comparative Studies in Society and History* 26, no. 1: 126–166.
——— 2002. Subjects and Capital: A Fragment of a Documentary Ethnography. *Ethnos* 67, no. 1: 9–32.
Reay, D. 2004. Exclusivity, Exclusion, and Social Class in Urban Education Markets in the United Kingdom. *Urban Education* 39, no. 5: 537–560.
Reich, R.B. 1994. *The Revolt of the Anxious Class.* Washington, DC: Department of Labor.
Rose, N. 1992. Governing the Enterprising Self. In *The Values of the Enterprise Culture: The Moral Debate,* edited by P. Heelas and P. Morris. New York: Routledge.
Rosenfeld, A., and N. Wise. 2000. *The Over-Scheduled Child: Avoiding the Hyper-parenting Trap.* New York: St. Martin's Griffin.
Schneider, B., and D. Stevenson. 1999. *The Ambitious Generation: America's Teenagers, Motivated but Directionless.* New Haven: Yale University Press.
U.S Census Bureau. 2000. *American FactFinder.* Washington D.C.: U.S. Census Bureau.
Varenne, H. 1977. *Americans Together: Structured Diversity in a Midwestern Town.* New York: Teachers College Press.
Varenne, H. 1986. *Symbolizing America.* Lincoln: University of Nebraska Press.
Varenne, H., and R. McDermott. 1998. *Successful Failure: The School America Builds.* Boulder, CO: Westview Press.
Wilton School District. 2002. District Profile (Fact Sheet): Wilton, OH: Wilton School District.
Wodrich, D.L. and M.L.S. Spencer. 2007. The Other Health Impairment Category and Health-Based Classroom Accommodations. *Journal of Applied School Psychology* 24, no. 1: 109–125.

10

Competing to Lose?
(Black) Female School Success as Pyrrhic Victory

Signithia Fordham

> Loss looms large in women's culture ... women bond in pain, and then talk and sing about it.
>
> — Martha Ward and Monica Edelstein

Achievement is simultaneously the holy grail and the third rail[1] of America's claims to be a meritocracy, the double-sided centrepiece in the nation's assertions regarding equal opportunity for all and the structuring of social life so that fairness of outcome is rarely achieved. The state school system is where merit and achievement are initially defined, identified, measured and evaluated. It is also the first official site where race and gender differences are concurrently denied and reified. This chapter is based on ethnographic data obtained from an American high school in upstate New York, and reveals how intertwining ideas about achievement, gender and race profoundly mark the lives of the school's Black female students.[2]

Competing to lose sounds as strange to most Americans as competitive giving was to anthropologist Ruth Benedict (1934), who initially concluded that the Kwakiutl way of gaining status and prestige, which involved acquiring possessions with the sole purpose of giving them to others, was pathological. Benedict misunderstood the potlatch in large part because she was embedded in a Euro-American cultural frame in which status and prestige are earned through accumulating and hoarding wealth, not by giving what one owns to others.

Likewise, the American cultural frame assumes a model of achievement that values competition and makes winning the main, or even the sole, goal. Nevertheless, although the status system masquerades as gender-neutral, this model of achievement, enshrined in contemporary male-dominated culture, is not regarded as socially appropriate for women. Male achievers are able to proclaim unapologetically that they are winners. In striking contrast, female achievers cannot be so assertive or arrogant, at least if they want to retain the goodwill of the people they have defeated, and/or gain the support of the people they hope to lead. Because women are taught to be more collaborative than men in their quest for status (DiSesa 2006; Kochman and Mavrelis 2009), their roads to academic and professional success are paved with greater ambiguity.[3]

In this chapter, I argue that 'female achievement' includes two modalities: women compete to lose, and/or they experience 'achievement as loss'.[4] Consequently, enculturation is not just different for females but designed to assure and reward their subordination, or loss, as well.[5] In the male-dominated achievement game that exists in the American professional world, including the academy, many females are both uncomfortable and disillusioned with the hegemonic male practice of winning at all cost, and with the deliberate violation of a gender-specific cultural script they learned as effortlessly and unconsciously as they learned to breathe: the centrality of marriage and motherhood over virtually every other social position or professional accomplishment. In a political economy that places the burden of social reproduction on the individual household, many women and men are left to balance numerous competing real-life demands.

In an article titled 'The Opt-Out Revolution', Lisa Belkin (2003) highlights the centrality of idleness[6] as a marker of femininity and, by extension, the largely unconscious celebration of losing as female achievement. In her provocative analysis, which evoked the ire of millions of *New York Times Magazine* readers, Belkin chronicles how and why many academically successful upper-class women 'opt out' of the paid work arena – even when they have earned prestigious degrees from some of the nation's most vaunted institutions, such as Harvard, Yale, MIT and Princeton. These highly valued credentials do not alter this general practice. Ironically, these upper-class, elite women (the female template for all women) fight to be idle by reclaiming their mothers' housewife role with a different name: stay-at-home mom. The right to raise their children, they argue, is far more important than any professional achievement. The desire to be a good mother overrides the desire to be professionally successful.

> 'I don't want to be on the fast track leading to a partnership at a prestigious law firm', says ___, who left that track in order to stay home with her three children. 'Some people define that as success. I don't' ...
>
> 'I don't want to be famous; I don't want to conquer the world; I don't want that kind of life', says ___, who was a theatre major and teacher and earned her master's degree in English, then stepped out of the work force when her daughter was born. 'Maternity provides an escape hatch that paternity does not. Having a baby provides a graceful and convenient exit'. (ibid.)

Thus, a central question embedded in this analysis is as follows: Is it possible that female achievement has a bifocal component: on the one hand, the structurally induced competing to lose that is the inevitable component of female enculturation in which losing is tantamount to winning; and on the other, achievement is itself experienced as a form of 'losing'? It seems to me that bifocality of this kind, and the conditions of its production, must play a central role in anthropological analyses of achievement.

For women who are not part of the social elite and who, moreover, are racially stigmatised – that is, Black – the social dynamics that support or inhibit achievement are even more complex. As I have shown in my previous work (Fordham 1993, 1996), which focused specifically on high-achieving Black students, those who manage to exceed the limited expectations of the dominant society pay a high price, not only for their defiance of racialised standards but also for their difference from their Black peers. Gender exacerbates this problem.

Social scientists, policy makers and ordinary Americans are well aware that in school the strictures of gender are looser than elsewhere in society, enabling girls to earn excellent grades, score high on standardised tests, and graduate at rates that mimic and often exceed those of their male peers. But, once females advance past entry-level jobs, these academic achievements fail to produce the same outcomes. Girls' comparable or higher performance does not automatically entitle them to a preferred or winner status. Their (White) male peers, despite their lower scores on achievement tests and lower grade-point averages, are generally preferred in hiring, and advance more rapidly than equally or better qualified women in corporations and male-dominated professions. Gender is so salient in the workplace that female achievers are not fully accepted in the areas of their professional expertise and, at the same time, lose their connections to other women.

In addition, Black women often must forfeit their ties to the Black community from which they came. In my previous work, I identified this process among Black high-school students as 'the burden of "acting White"' (Fordham 1988, 1996, 1998, 2008, 2009, 2010; Fordham and Ogbu 1986). The predicaments faced by all Black students are significantly intensified for Black girls, and the accommodations that successful Black male students can make are seldom open to Black female students (Fordham 1993). Being Black and female is a particularly powerful and potentially damaging combination.

It is in this context that achievement may become a pyrrhic victory for North American and especially African American girls. Are girls who act assertive and independent and who display self-confidence and promote their own accomplishments rewarded in the same ways as their male peers? I argue that achievement is differentially rewarded in males and females throughout the life course, but especially during adolescence and early adulthood. Moreover, Black females who exhibit attributes that are socially assigned to males are doubly stigmatised for their deviance from gender prescriptions, especially when they act in ways that would be valued in White males; their behaviour is treated as a challenge to both the racial and the gender order.

The 'social destinies' of both men and women are perpetuated, albeit often on a subconscious level, by what Pierre Bourdieu (2004) terms 'symbolic force'. This notion is supported by a plethora of researchers and social theorists, such as Michel Foucault and Loïc Wacquant, as well as anthropologists including

Paul Farmer, Philippe Bourgois, Veena Das and Nancy Scheper-Hughes. The common theme in their findings is that the kind of violence most prevalent when nations or individuals are not in armed combat (and sometimes even when they are) can be accurately defined as 'symbolic' violence, which takes many forms, including gender-specific relational aggression, imagery and language, and holds numerous meanings. This symbolic domination is brought about not through conscious behaviour but through habit and social normalcy.[7]

Analysing the predicaments and self-conceptions of Black girls and their interactions with White girls, as well as Black and White boys, will help us to tease out the entangled threads of race and gender in Black girls' academic achievement – and to sort out the benefits and costs of Black girls' inadvertent and/or deliberate penchant for transgressing socially approved gender-specific roles. In fact, the issues confronting White girls are greatly exacerbated in the lives of African American girls, who are at greater risk both academically and socially because of their lack of fit with the dominant society's norms of femininity and their reluctance to embrace this way of being female. The question then becomes: How do Black females use competition to negotiate achievement, since loss looms so large in their lives? How do they compete with one another and with White girls when success is penalised because of their race and gender? What effects do the social dynamics among and between Black and White females have on their academic performance?

While both the Black/White and the male/female achievement gaps are the subject of a substantial body of scholarship, social scientists have seldom paid attention to the achievement gaps among females who belong to different racial-ethnic groups and class positions. At best, White feminist scholars have masked those differentials by the claim of a one-dimensional sisterhood. Researchers repeatedly generalise about girls' academic performance as though it were undifferentiated by race, ethnicity and class. Even studies that include both males and females, and/or include both White females and females who self-identify and are identified as belonging to different racial-ethnic and social groups, have fallen into this error (AAUW 1991; Brown 1998, 2003; Rimm 1999; Lamb 2002). The intra-gender achievement gap, especially between girls who do and do not belong to the dominant group, should be at the heart of our understanding of how girls perform in school, even though it is the male/female achievement images that insinuate the value of competing to lose.

None of the academic studies and popular books that have tried to explain what happens to girls' intellectual development when they reach adolescence has dealt adequately with female aggression and cross-cultural bullying.[8] Instead, most have concluded that female-specific modes of interaction induce girls to view those who exercise power or are successful competitors as 'mean' and unfeminine. According to these authors, girls who lead all-female cliques, who may be known as 'queen bees' (Weisman 2000) or 'the CEOs' (Milner 2006; Kochman and Mavrelis 2009), are both feared and hated by not only the girls/women who are within their cliques but also by those who are not. Demonstrating leadership potential in arenas commonly identified with masculinity is threatening, and their peers' negative responses often prompt these girls to avoid showing such hubris. These scholars fail to recognise that these dynamics are especially marked for Black girls, who are often singled out as the 'queens of mean' (Boo 1995). How Black and White girls compete with one another, and the consequences of that inter-racial, intra-gender competition, are woefully understudied.

Underground at an 'Integrated' High School

In order to explore these questions through ethnographic methods, I spent two-and-a-half years from January 2004 to October 2006 observing and interviewing twenty-two female students at a suburban, predominantly White, senior high school. After enduring a convoluted and frustrating institutional review process and obtaining permission from the girls' parents, I observed the students in class, in the lunchroom and hallways, during their extracurricular activities, and, where possible, at home, at work and in other situations. During this process, information was often gained from parents and other relatives, teachers, counsellors and school officials. The interviews included both free-ranging, informal discussion, in keeping with the ethnological tradition of discussing topics brought up by the individual and/or suggested by their particular physical, family, school and relationship situations, as well as formal interviews utilising specific questions designed for more systematic analysis concerning such topics as: aggression, competition and relationships among Blacks and Whites, males and females, family members and friends; schooling history and academic achievement; and specific fights and other conflicts that took place in and out of school. I kept voluminous field notes and tape-recorded and transcribed the formal interviews for analysis. In addition, the students were asked to record their weekly interactions with their female peers, teachers and parents in diaries. These young women often failed to keep their appointments, which required me to track them down; they had to be convinced to write and submit the diaries in exchange for 'movie money'. Most important, some girls – both Black and White – were reluctant to consider the issue of aggression and fighting among girls and to discuss topics related to race and racism (this was especially true for the White girls) at the school and in the community at large.

What I call Underground Railroad High School (UGRH) is located in a predominantly White, lower-middle- to solidly middle-class suburb in upstate New York, which I call Rodman. A former 'sundown town' (Loweon 2006) – a place where Whites lived and Blacks might work but could not reside – adjacent to a major city in upstate New York, Rodman retains vestiges of that racially segregated past. It is now a marginally integrated community, meaning that Black and Brown people are able to work, buy homes, shop and go to school there. But people of colour remain concentrated in the city centre, and around

85 per cent of Rodman's residents are White. Black youth comprise just over 10 per cent of the school's 1,500 students.

Most of the Black students' parents came from the city to this close-in suburb in search of a better environment in which to raise their children, and with the conviction that Rodman would offer their children a superior education. Black parents in particular believed that inner-city schools do not provide Black children with an education comparable to that of White children, so they moved to this predominantly White suburb in order to enable their children to compete more effectively for college admission and employment, the first steps to success.

The community in which UGRH is located is best defined by its residents' hunger for status and by its 'shades of white' demographic composition 'on the precipice' of becoming racially integrated and culturally diverse (Perry 2002). Whites in Rodman appear to loathe this prospect and to work diligently to deny social acceptance to non-White residents. This issue intensifies the achievement problem for all Black and Brown students at the school, especially Black female students. Rodman is 'on the precipice' economically as well as demographically, for the suburb owes its existence to the nearby industrial city. With the decline of manufacturing, the urban economy has undergone a structural transformation and near collapse. The major employers have downsized and laid off substantial numbers of employees, generating economic insecurity. The anxiety this situation produces is compounded by Rodman parents' commitment to giving their children the economic, educational and social advantages they did not have when they were growing up, and to protecting them at all costs.[9]

In striking contrast, the Black and other students of colour[10] at UGRH differ in their approach to academic achievement, seeking not to stand out from their peers but to be smothered in the womb of the collective. Their body language, especially in classrooms, suggests an aversion to visibility. They appear to be afraid of achievement as it is narrowly defined in this context, and they avoid competing with White students in the classroom. Outside the classroom, they are much more confident, even ebullient, more willing to compete with one another and with their White peers, and more likely to take risks that stretch their social, emotional and economic capacities. The Whiteness of the classroom space and the salience of what Claude Steele (2010) labels the 'stereotype threat' appear to stifle their freedom to create the kind of improvised life that they exhibit in the hallways, the cafeteria, the gym and other non-classroom spaces. School officials are not as successful in their efforts to keep all Others' cultural behaviours and practices at bay in these non-classroom spaces, and, ironically, the students who do not excel academically enjoyed higher status among their peers (see Dickar 2008). The classroom represents the core of the educational system, a space where Setha Low's (2003) concept of gated communities seems apposite.

Significantly, racial segregation exists within UGRH primarily in the tracking system (see Rosenbaum 1976; Oakes 1985; Barlow and Dunbar 2010) that separates 'high-achieving' students from 'ordinary' students by placing them in 'gifted and talented' programmes, Advanced Placement (AP) courses, and a variety of courses with 'accelerated' and 'enriched' curricula. Academic tracking imposes and reinforces White privilege (Harris 1993), racial exclusion and invidious expectations of Black students. Access to the most highly valued and best-rewarded aspects of our culture is offered primarily to students who are socially defined as White, regardless of gender or class.

This pattern is evident at many American high schools. Since my research at Capital High is relatively well known (Fordham 1988, 1993, 1996, 1999; Fordham and Ogbu 1986), suffice it to note here that, although the school was overwhelmingly Black, its 'magnet' component was the most achievement-oriented and its curriculum was the least inclusive of diverse racial-ethnic and gendered perspectives. As at UGRH, the elite programme at Capital High was deeply infused with the values and norms of the dominant society.

At UGRH, Black and other racial-ethnic minority students compete and seek achievement primarily in non-classroom settings. Black males and females achieve in the gym by playing basketball and by running on the track; Black males compete and achieve on the football field and baseball diamond. The Black males at UGRH are the 'It' people, the school's most prominent 'human mascots'.[11] As sports stars, they epitomise masculinity and are rewarded and appreciated for their 'public service to the school community', and for their presumed subordination of a selfish or myopic preoccupation with individual academic achievement. This positioning of Black males means that they are rewarded for not competing with White males for dominance in academic achievement; they are rewarded primarily for competing with other Black males to win at sports. Black males' status as the school's sports stars, combined with their imagined hyper-masculinity, makes them magnets for females. The vast majority of females at the school, regardless of race or ethnicity, want to date Black males, despite and sometimes because of their parents' disapproval.[12]

Although Black students at UGRH insist that race and gender relations are now more equal and flexible than they were in previous generations, they also lament the continuing lack of racial and gender equality in their school. Pervasive inequalities continue to limit not only their academic opportunities but also their options for dating and mating. Although Black students' dating practices are less constrained and much more nuanced than they were when their parents were young, they are still marked by a clear gender imbalance. Black males at UGRH are freer to date outside their race than Black girls; Black girls can date White boys only if they and the males involved are willing to withstand social disapproval. In order to avoid even greater social isolation at school, Black girls seek relationships with Black males in the nearby urban area in the city, where there are fewer non-Black people and the cultural rules are widely understood, even if these suburban Black girls do not know them all. The 'dual citizenship' issues (Fordham 2009) they confront everyday at UGRH are not as critical among their primarily Black peers in non-school contexts.

De facto segregation and the existence of a two-tiered status mobility system within UGRH are reflected in the continuing existence of the 'Black table' in the cafeteria (Tatum 1997).[13] This male-dominated space is highly desired by the Black females, especially since most of the Black girls consciously choose to limit their dating to Black males. Both the Black table and a White male teacher's classroom where Black students feel comfortable eating lunch together afford Black students a space to have a daily [s]kinship reunion.[14]

Say My Name: Nadine and Keyshia

Nadine, nicknamed Dee-Dee, is a seventeen-year-old, self-identified Black student. In the last semester of her senior year, she is looking forward with ambivalent excitement and anxiety to graduation and her new life after high school. At just over five feet tall, weighing less than a hundred pounds soaking wet, and speaking in an exceedingly soft voice, she exudes hegemonic femininity – except for her brown face. Her shoulder-length hair, the primary visible marker of idealised femininity, is permed and carefully coiffed.

Nadine has always lived in upstate New York. She was born in the nearby city and went to elementary (primary) school there for a year. But her parents believed that their four children would receive a better education in the suburbs. So Nadine's mother, who works in health care at a job that pays just above the minimum wage, moved the family into an apartment in Rodman. Her father, who is separated from her mother, lives nearby. Although her parents never married, they have a very civil relationship and he remains an important person in her life. Nadine is growing up in a two-bedroom apartment with a younger sister and two younger brothers. Her life is filled with happiness, but it is also chaotic and largely improvised. In an effort to be like her best friend's family and society at large, she focuses on the ways it does not conform to what is seen as normal.

Nadine virtually lived at Keyshia's house before discovering that her best friend was secretly dating her then boyfriend, Kyle. She was Keyshia's 'roommate' mostly because she had such an unstable family life. Her mother was currently dating a man whom Nadine did not like; her father was living with a woman who did not like her; and she and her siblings were competing for the little love and attention that her parents were able to give them.

Keyshia, who is also a seventeen-year-old, self-identified Black student, belongs to a family that epitomises the newly arrived, yet relatively secure, Black middle class. Her parents moved from the Washington, D.C., area to Rodman about one and a half years ago. Although Keyshia excels in school, getting married and raising children is her greatest ambition – indeed, her only ambition. She cannot think of anything more important. This desire helped precipitate the feud that erupted when she started dating her best friend's boyfriend the previous year. The only downside to Keyshia's dream is her parents' insistence that she continue in higher education. She takes advanced classes but does not really care about schoolwork. This attitude has led to enormous tension and conflicts with her parents, especially her mother.

Keyshia lives with both her parents and a younger brother in a four-bedroom, three-bathroom house with a family room, near the village of Rodman. This house is her parents' pride and joy, and they work hard to make it comfortable. Keyshia's parents are professionals and both have always been employed, even when the children were young. Yet they have clearly defined gender roles, and her father seems to think that his work is more demanding and more important than her mother's. As one of only two Black scientists employed by a large corporation, he is in many ways a pioneer. Her mother, a science teacher in a city high school, is in charge of the household, and everyone, including her father, acquiesces to her rules and expectations. Keyshia remembers the gut-wrenching conversations her mum and dad engaged in around the dinner table on a nightly basis that focused on race and, to a lesser extent, gender, and how it shaped their professional lives. Keyshia has attended both private and state schools. She is really good at taking exams and could get straight As in her classes if she were willing to do her homework consistently and stay focused in class – but she is not. Moreover, since she treats academic achievement as a game she can win with little effort, she wonders why she does so much better in school than her Black peers. Indeed, she worries that she is a fluke, and harbours enormous insecurities regarding her Black identity, though not her intellectual ability.

When Keyshia and Nadine became friends, Nadine assumed that she needed Keyshia because she was a lower-class Black girl in a predominately White suburban school. What she did not even begin to appreciate is that Keyshia, as a middle-class Black girl, feels keenly the inadequacy of 'not being Black enough' in this environment (Boyd 1997; Baszile 2009). Among the Black students at UGRH, and perhaps in many other predominantly White schools, being what is perceived as authentically Black trumps a person's class position. Performing a Black identity, not succeeding in AP courses, confers status. It was painful for Keyshia to come to that conclusion. The realisation led her to revisit her memories of a brief time at a private school in suburban Maryland and then a longer time in the state schools in Columbia, Maryland. She cannot forget the alienation and isolation she endured there. Most of the Black kids avoided her, primarily because of her strong affiliation with the White kids, especially White girls. The situation got so bad that her mother bought her a book by a successful Black journalist called *My First White Friend* (Raybon 1997). Reading about the racial struggles of this young woman in an elite, predominantly White, suburban school was like looking in a broken mirror; the person Keyshia saw was herself. Nadine still does not know that Keyshia needs her as a friend more than Nadine needs Keyshia. Her friendship and support shore up Keyshia's connection to the Black students at UGRH and erase the feelings of inadequacy that arise from her class and cultural differences from her Black peers.

Keyshia earned 1450 on the SAT (formerly the Scholastic Aptitude Test),[15] which she took at a school out of state, thanks to the help of one of her father's friends, but she made her parents swear not to tell anyone about her high scores. Like most parents, they want to and do tell their friends how smart their daughter is as a way of affirming their superior parenting practices and the inherited intelligence they pass on to her. Using teenage logic, Keyshia assumed that if she told only selected friends and made them promise not to tell, that she could control who knew about her superior performance. She is hoping that she will not have to take more boring AP classes with the nerdy White kids while all of her Black friends are consigned to the regular curriculum. She wants to avoid being envied by her White peers, who she fears will inevitably insist that her exam was scored by an affirmative-action officer, and being derided by her Black peers, who she is afraid will accuse her of 'acting White' (Fordham and Ogbu 1986). She is sick of this never-ending conflict, of having to juggle everyone else's expectations in order to be acceptable, but being accepted by no one. This response is a clear example of the bifocal reality that shapes the lives of most of the Black girls at UGRH: seeking to pacify their parents' expectation of academic achievement and, at the same time, experiencing achievement as loss vis-à-vis their peers.

Keyshia is looking forward to graduation, when she can start a new life for herself. She thinks that her parents still treat her like a baby. What she anticipates most is having more time to date after she is done with school. Much to her parents' dismay, she sees finding a husband as central to her future. Nadine would have something to say about how boy-crazy Keyshia is. Even though – or maybe because – she and Keyshia are best friends, they got into a physical fight last year after Keyshia started hooking up with Nadine's boyfriend without her knowledge. Keyshia knew they were still dating, but he was 'hot' and she really liked him, and he didn't seem to be really into Nadine that much anymore – but that was her assessment, not Nadine's.

Goldilocks and the Girls Who Are Not

On this beautiful May day, Nadine and her former BFF ('best friend forever'), Keyshia, have agreed to meet for lunch in order to try and mend their broken friendship.[16] They enter the cafeteria together and put their backpacks on the chairs at a table in the middle of the room, close to the two major serving lines on opposite ends of the room near the kitchen. They decide to take a pass on the full, heavy-duty lunch and go to the shorter line selling packaged snacks and sodas. Each girl purchases what she likes and returns to the table where they left their backpacks.

As they round the corner and see the table they have chosen, they become aware that a group of White girls is sitting there. It slowly dawns on them that the group is comprised primarily of the school's cheerleaders, though they are not in uniform; Keyshia recognises them before Nadine does. This group argues that they have prior claim to the seats at the table and all the other chairs there.

Both Nadine and Keyshia insist that they had the seats first and they are not going to move. The disagreement escalates. The hegemonic discourse practice of turn-taking-when-speaking falls by the wayside as the White girls all chime in to say that these two girls are out of place in seeking to occupy two of the chairs at this long table, and that this entire table belongs to them because they sit there every day. In the more familiar female discourse style, everyone begins talking at the same time, words cascading like water and bumping into each other, creating an unfathomable flood of speech, littered with the gender-specific racial and cultural debris these young women have mastered in their sixteen, seventeen and eighteen years.

Nadine tries to argue that no one can claim proprietary rights to a seat or a table in the school's cafeteria; this is public, communal space, she contends. She doubts that anyone hears her because everyone is talking at the same time. Nevertheless, the moment the tall, willowy, blonde (a euphemism for White) girl calls Nadine 'nigger bitch', everybody hears it; it is as if the speaker threw a stink bomb on the table, and everyone is suddenly immobilised, holding her nose, waiting to see what happens next. The words echo amid a profound silence. Nadine's heart pounds. The blood rushes to her face, but because her skin is dark no one notices. She is suddenly, inexplicably chilled to the bone. Her sense of shame and humiliation is too much to bear. With her right hand, she reaches up (the girl who uttered the slur is taller than she) and, with every ounce of strength she can muster, she slaps the White girl full across the face. Her hand stings, the force is so great. She notices her handprint on both sides of the White girl's face, which slowly turns from pink to beetroot red to splotchy purple in anger and dismay. Tears well up in Kristen's eyes and she begins to cry, silently at first; then she is convulsed by sobs. Her friends push Nadine away with great force as they gather around her, forming a protective wall. Adults arrive, including an assistant principal who takes Nadine immediately to his office, hurling her flimsy young body before him as he assumes command.

This assistant principal, a youngish-looking White American male, knows her; students at the school are assigned to these officials by gender and/or grade level. He has reprimanded her in the past, including the one time she was involved in a physical altercation. He knows she is a senior, scheduled to graduate in less than a month. No matter. He immediately suspends her for a whole week and tells her that she is lucky he is not recommending that she be expelled. Nadine tries to engage him in a conversation that will make him realise that slapping the White girl was warranted; she called Nadine two of the most vile names anyone can call a Black female. He refuses to listen, repeatedly reminding her that violence is not tolerated at this school. He calls her mother at work and tells her that her daughter was just involved in a fight and she must come immediately to take her away. No longer permitted on school grounds, Nadine is denied access to the library and all other academic resources. Her plea regarding her impending exams goes unheeded. He reminds her that she has been in trouble before and that she knows the rules against engaging in violence.

When she tries to argue that she is also a victim of violence, that she was violated by being called a 'nigger bitch', he points out that there is no comparison between her hitting her antagonist and the provocative names the other girl called her. The message conveyed by the professional adults at the school is that the only harm in this dispute was physical.

In striking contrast, the White girl's physical and emotional discomfort is recognised and validated. Crying angry tears, she is immediately escorted by her friends and several adults to the principal's office, both to inform school officials and to call her mother. She is followed by her younger sister and a posse of her friends who vow to 'sue her' – that is, the Black girl, Nadine. What can all this tell us about achievement, gender and race at UGRH?

Complicity and the 'Presence of an Absence'

Underground Railroad High School is the pseudonym by which I identify the site of my two-and-a-half-year study of female violence, including aggression, bullying and competition. I believe this alias is particularly appropriate for three reasons: First, as a nod to the famous Underground Railroad that operated in this area during official enslavement from circa 1810 to circa 1850, the name itself is bloated with symbolic violence. Second, it captures the underground – or hidden – nature of important social practices at the school; that which was official and visible was not what was central or critical in the lives of the females, especially the Black girls. And third, and even more critical to this analysis, is the connection of its name to the contemporary practice of feminists – from the first to the third wave – who have and continue to clamour vigorously, albeit unsuccessfully, for the same opportunities as their male peers, as inscribed in the nation's official documents and embedded in the hegemonic practices of the patriarchy, but whose efforts are repeatedly subverted by what is popularly known as backlash (see Faludi 1991; Coontz 2002, 2005; Bolick 2011). Indeed, we can identify an ongoing, if largely unconscious, complicity – on the part of both females and their male peers – to maintain their carefully choreographed inequality by reproducing the gender-specific female world that has compelled women to be subordinate in the first place.

The notion of symbolic force is most significant in the case of Black girls at UGRH, where the pressure to be carbon copies of the socially dominant (most often White) females is overwhelming. Symbolic gender violence is primarily effective because of its habitual ordinariness or everyday-ness, its culturally prescribed normality and 'naturalness', its disavowal of brute force (with no need for external policing), its ostensible political neutrality, and its unobtrusive presence. As we learn appropriate gender norms, these 'springs' are deeply embedded in our subconscious, shaping the mind so that we are incapable of seeing what was initially learned as one of many options – not the only option. These classifications compel the individual and social group not only to 'misrecognise' what is happening to them, but even to approve of it (Bourdieu and Wacquant 2004: 272–74). Complicity on the part of the victim is inevitable, as evidenced in the daily lives and experiences of the adolescent women discussed here.

Consequently, above ground – that is, at the official level – the insatiable quest for change is palpable, with evidence of 'progress' clearly visible in so many areas of the lives of all women.[17] These include greater female academic achievement, as manifested in the large number of female students graduating from high school, college and graduate school (see, e.g., Coontz 2002, 2005); a spike in later or delayed marriage, and no marriage at all; the profoundly non-traditional idea of giving birth to children much later in life – after a woman has established or at least begun her chosen career path (Coontz 2002; Bolick 2011); and the growing practice of cohabitating and procreating with a same- or opposite-sex partner *sans* marriage.

Underground, however, where the 'rubber meets the road', women, especially the younger generations, are continuing – albeit in different guises – the practices that have historically been affiliated with their gender. It is in light of this conundrum, captured in James Clifford's (1986) notion of the inevitable 'partial truths' of social life (that is, the idea that almost as much is hidden as is revealed in cultural practices), that I seek to capture here the underground lives of the competitive and aggressive practices of the high school girls I studied for two-and-a-half years.

Indeed, I explicitly argue here that it is our failure to recognise (or our tendency to misrecognise) structurally induced violence that activates patterns of shared cultural beliefs that are so powerfully influential in the maintenance of the power differential between all segments of American society, and particularly among Black and White girls. In most Euro-American contexts, this kind of symbolic violence is both pervasive and unacknowledged, concurrently present and invisible. This kind of violence embodies what we tend to think of as progress; it is a powerful form of social control, yet cultures that regularly utilise it, including the United States, are invariably viewed as progressive and civilised, unlike their more barbaric, underdeveloped sibling states that utilise externally imposed physical force, or at least the threat of coercion. Since physical violence, as traditionally defined and identified, is both outlawed and disparaged within 'civilised' societies, the preferred social controls and management of individuals must be enculturated through gender-appropriate methods that disavow such social practices as strong or direct language, spanking, scolding, and so on. The presumed markers of civilisation are the normalised 'soft' rules of engagement promulgated, practised and sanctioned by race- and gender-defined elite persons. For example, instead of spanking a child, a 'time out' is the socially approved form of punishment, where the child spends age-appropriate time in isolation from other humans.

Intriguingly, the most widely used form of symbolic violence is language, in its broadest sense. According to Veena Das (2004), language is the space where suffering is not only recognised but even socially appreciated. As used here, language includes images and logic as well as speech. There are many examples of gender-specific images, but some are more emblematic than others. Kristen, the White cheerleader, was able to humiliate and demean Nadine by using language that both she and Nadine recognised would inflame the contested geographical and social space they both sought to claim.

Competing to Lose as Female Power

Competition is the engine of achievement at, as well as outside, school. It fuels the designation of winners, who are generally considered dominant, and losers, who are seen as subordinate. Losers are deemed ineligible for society's most prestigious awards. In addition, while there is obvious variability (indeed, variance is necessary in order to establish what is normal), winning and losing are gender-differentiated, with achievement and winning assigned primarily to males and losing considered females' rightful place. Males are taught to abhor losing (Pollack 1998; Kimmel 2002), in part because of its connections with femininity (Spender and Sarah 1988; Corbett 2001; Simmons 2002; Pascoe 2007).

Following Michel Foucault (1977) and John Fiske (1993: 74), we can see the way in which relations of power define normalcy in any given society. Power, according to Foucault, is the authority to produce 'docile bodies' that obey culturally prescribed rules. Hence, while a female body is constructed to be docile, it is not without power. On the contrary, its power is achieved precisely through its docility. For a docile female body, losing is winning. Fiske insists that docile bodies, whether male or female, are indicative of the successful school practice that compels individuals to accept the routinisation of social roles and the inculcation of expectations from persons occupying authoritative positions as the norm (Cohen 1971). For females, losing is represented as normal or routine, a prestigious gender-specific status. Analysing 'learning to lose' (Spender and Sarah 1988) involves ascertaining how girls acquire docile, disciplined bodies – that is, become 'good girls' – and in the process come to accept losing as normal. Being taught how not to win is a form of socially approved rape of the female body in America's male-dominated society. Moreover, learning to lose entails inverting the customary meaning of loss, redefining it so that, when attached to a female body, it is more prestigious than winning.

This broader conceptualisation of loss is an important element in the way anthropologists and other social scientists have understood the privileged form of White femininity and its divergent cousin, Black womanhood. In the Euro-American context, anthropologists have repeatedly connected the presence or expression of anger, which is regarded as inappropriate in women (as in the common saying, 'hell hath no fury like a woman scorned'), with female performance and behaviour; but ethnographers and other researchers have failed to adequately document how females' incarceration in a dynamic of loss structures their emotional development and mental well-being. White females are supposed to exhibit a willingness to endure inhumane or extremely undesirable social conditions without being angry, disagreeable or unpleasant; they are socially rewarded for remaining calm and accommodating in all social interactions, no matter how disadvantageous these interactions are to the women themselves. Black females who are unwilling and/or unable to comply with this invidious norm are punished for their deviations. For Black girls, in particular, not only is losing winning, but winning is also losing.

> On the day of the fight between Nadine and the White cheerleader, I was sitting in the office as the White girl's friends and her sister escorted her there, so I observed firsthand the White girl's flushed face, her tears and sobs. The 'victim' went immediately into the principal's office and closed the door. I listened intently as her sister called their mother and told her that her older sister had been physically attacked by a Black girl. Apparently, their mother agreed to come immediately to get them both out of harm's way. I heard the details from the Black girls later. (Field notes, 17 May 2005)

As this scene suggests, crying is an important weapon – a stealth bomber – in female bullying and aggression. It is highly effective because it masks the contempt of the bully.[18] Instead, the White girl has become the victim of the scenario, the 'loser', who, in the inverted logic of female loss, wins the role of social approval. Nadine and the other Black girls at the school understand that if they report being called the N-word or the B-word, the school officials will do nothing; indeed, Nadine is offered no sympathy – not even the respect of being heard – for what happened to her. Thus the Black girls know that they have to defend themselves, even though, in stepping outside the socially prescribed norm of losing gracefully, they risk a punishment that affects their ability to achieve academically and to be viewed as winners.

On the day of the fight with the White girl, Nadine and Keyshia were trying to repair their badly damaged relationship, attempting to bridge the gap between their sense of betrayal and the friendship they had enjoyed before the breach. The fight with the White girl added an additional layer of complexity to a situation that was already loaded with loss. The two Black girls were fighting with each other over who won and who lost in the 'boys are my only achievement' syndrome. Though ostensibly Keyshia had been the 'winner' in this situation (winning the boyfriend away from Nadine), the winning had resulted in loss of social capital (she had violated social norms) and loss of her best friend besides. The fight between Nadine and the White cheerleader had its origins, too, in the competition for boys and the social codes defining acceptable and unacceptable behaviours in that competition: Nadine was currently dating a White guy who, although not a student at UGRH, was deemed an inappropriate suitor; and the White girl was dating a Black guy who was a student at UGRH. Nadine's behaviour was unacceptable to both the Black and the White communities at the school. The White girl's higher status made it possible for her to ignore the disapproval of the Black female students who were essentially the only segment of the student population that overtly disapproved.

Conclusion

The social life of achievement is the Gordian knot in American high schools. It is particularly problematic for females, especially Black females, because its underbelly – that is, losing – generates pain, which fuels female-specific bonding. Both the insatiable quest for status and prestige within the racially defined world of state education and the professional adults' inability to penetrate it (Milner 2006) make altering its structural constraints extremely difficult. With the completion of this study at UGRH, I have come to understand the female-specific status mobility system and how it privileges losing. While losing looms large in women's professional and personal lives, in the school setting most young women attempt to create a kind of achievement that allows them to blend winning and losing in the eyes of their peers and, secondarily, in their own self-conceptions. They are willing to embrace a patriarchal ideology that valorises masculinity, adopt a discourse style that emphasises their own uncertainty and defers to others' opinions, and practise a leadership style that promotes working collaboratively in groups rather than individually.

Following Martha Ward and Monica Edelstein (1996), I argue that while this analysis may be applicable to women cross-culturally, the situation of African American women is particularly acute. Black women are understandably reluctant to embrace the hegemonic system, not only because it doubly disadvantages them but also because they are socialised into an alternative mode of womanhood that prioritises taking care of themselves and of those who depend on them as against relying on, or deferring to, any male, or, for that matter, the dominant society (Collins 1991). As Angela Davis (1971) notes, the historically generated 'deformed equality' between Black males and Black females has required Black females to develop and hold fiercely to whatever independence they are able to achieve. At the same time, they pay a very high price for that form of achievement. Although their academic and professional success may be positively valued by the dominant society, even though it threatens the hegemonic model of White femininity, it imposes other burdens on Black women. They feel the pain of losing at what they and their community value most: motherhood, a core value of Black women themselves, and partnership with a man, as well as their sisters and kin, in facing life's challenges. African American females' academic achievement is drenched in loss, freighted with deprivation, and marked by a steely resolve to survive.

When we consider not only those Black women who achieve against the odds and at any cost but also young Black women in high school, we find an even more discouraging situation. The exclusion of Black females from the highest-ranked academic programmes (see Barlow and Dunbar 2010), buttressed by the stereotype threat (Steele 1992, 2010), compels them to alter the social meaning of achievement in potentially fatal ways. Black students, especially Black girls, redirect their ambitions toward non-academic arenas. 'Good girls' (Tolman and Higgins 1996) are represented as disciplined bodies that win by losing, but Black girls are not eligible for that status. The ways they defend themselves against other girls further marginalises and penalises them, as we can see in the fight between the White cheerleader and Nadine.

White girls are the holy grail of gender-specific achievement, while Black girls are the third rail. Black women are often guilty of exceeding limited expectations and, indeed, it is their ability to prevail (Parks 2010) that is responsible for their loss. The African American female body is a vulnerable colonised terrain, an unprotected site of resistance to dominant notions of femininity. The young Black female is wantonly raped of her power and deprived of either her winning practices or her claim to womanhood. Indeed, Black girls' reluctance and sometimes downright refusal to 'learn to lose' is translated into both higher academic performance and social marginalisation relative to Black males and White females. The findings reported here highlight the ways in which Black girls' perceived deficiencies compel them to achieve and, despite or because of their accomplishments, to lose.

The experience of achievement as loss is both structurally induced and gender-specific: women's gendered enculturation is not just different – learning to compete to lose – but designed to assure and reward their subordination, or loss. This is uncomfortable to acknowledge; it is even more uncomfortable to live. In American high schools, Black girls are compelled to reconcile multiple different, even contradictory, discourses of achievement, of winning and losing: witness Keyshia's sense of having to juggle everyone else's expectations in order to be acceptable, but being accepted by no one. If we wish to begin to unravel this tangled pattern, memory, which defies the fiction of a totally new beginning (see Miliani 1996), is our enemy, primarily because it subverts our efforts to reinvent ourselves and transform our society. Nevertheless, we must keep trying. Only in re-imaging womanhood and de-privileging female loss will we be able to accurately delineate the African American female in a way that shows her winning, not as a subverted version of the dominant White pattern of female loss or as a deviation from solidarity with Black males, but as a matter of Black women naming and defining themselves. Our continued failure to follow this course of action will produce and perpetuate what Weitz and Gordon deplored: a perception that Black girls' 'achievements either are not rewarded or are even held against them by whites as signs that these black women are stepping out of their "place"' (Weitz and Gordon 1993: 32). It is this racialised, gendered problem that renders Black female achievement a pyrrhic victory, and by extension, the penultimate loss.

Notes

1. As a metaphor, a third rail is any emotionally charged issue that is so controversial that anyone who dares to challenge the extant meaning/understanding will suffer extreme harm. Here I argue that the hegemonic definition of achievement meets this requirement.

2. While the focus in this analysis is on African American girls ('Black' and 'African American' are used here interchangeably), competing to lose as a component of loss, I argue, is a reality in the lives of most women and girls cross-culturally.
3. As this volume goes to press, Sheryl Sandberg's (2013) book, *Lean In: Women, Work and Leadership*, is one of the most talked about books in America, at least among women. The former Google executive and the current chief operating officer of Facebook argues that in the corporate world, women are probably their own worst enemies in that we fail to be present in our own professional lives: we fail to negotiate, and we fail to ask for promotions and other things that will enhance our careers and working lives. This book has produced a greater firestorm than earlier books in this genre in part, I think, because she is such a successful woman.
4. Obviously, these concepts – 'competing to lose' and 'competing to win' – are opposite in meaning, in that the latter suggests dominance or accomplishment while the former suggests subordination or less than success. While this is open to debate, that will have to take place in another context. The central point I am attempting to make explicitly clear in this analysis is the following: according to the vast majority of anthropological research, in most of the world's cultures, individuals gendered female have less access to public power and, ironically, they learn to see lack of power as gender-appropriate – a central component of who they are – and then compete to reproduce the world they have inherited and by extension their loss or subordination.
5. Following anthropologists Martha Ward and Monica Edelstein (1996) and historian Gerda Lerner (1986), I use the term 'loss' to highlight the cross-cultural estrangement between men and women, and among women, that has its origins in the construction and performance of gender-specific practices, expectations and norms. Arguing that loss is a female-centred norm, I show how the imposition of achievement as a gender-neutral norm in social spaces that once excluded women and today remain male-dominated compels females to adapt by embracing the idea of competing – but primarily in order to lose rather than to win in the sense that is open to males.
6. Idleness – as in leisure or unencumbered time, also known as 'flex time' – is not to be equated with and/or interpreted as meaning either laziness or the lack of a desire for achievement. It is, instead, both a rejection of the hegemonic practice of working – non-stop – in a designated space, 9 to 5, Monday to Friday, and a strong desire to have work fit more into the needs and practices of a family and recreational life. Belkin's article (2003; see also Anon. 2004) was the spark that set the gender wars on fire and kept them burning for years, with a plethora of respondents reacting to the thesis set forth in her essay – some in support, others in passionate disagreement, and still others on the proverbial fence. Stay-at-home mothers are celebrated as the embodiment of the appropriate wife and mother; there is virtually no claim made that an adult gendered female is behaving in ways that violate a central feature of her gendered self if she is un- or under-employed; no voiced disappointment that an adult woman, even one who is married, is not gainfully employed outside her home. Ironically, the reverse is a critical feature of the debate: Should an adult female who is also a mother be expected to be employed once she becomes a mother? The ability to be idle and female has been raised to new heights now that the stigmatised welfare system that enabled poor Black women to remain at home in order to rear their children has been socially eviscerated. In today's economic environment, for an adult female to be able to take advantage of this option, she has to have a partner whose income is sufficient to support the family she (or in the case of gay couples, he or she) has created. Consequently, in this context, idleness (or partial employment) means lack of explicit remuneration – a pay cheque – for one's reproductive and household labour. Tokens, the most important of which is labelled 'love', are considered more than adequate, gladly and widely accepted.
7. The most accessible and meaningful definition of this concept is offered in Bourdieu and Wacquant (2004). It is important to acknowledge that they do not intend to negate the

existence of other, more recognizable forms of violence as they relate to gender. It is sometimes assumed, they note, that symbolic violence 'minimize[s] the role of physical violence, ... make[s] people forget that there are battered, raped and exploited women, or worse, [seeks] to exculpate men from that form of violence' – which is obviously not the caseIt is sometimes assumed, they note, that symbolic violence 'minimizes the role of physical violence ... makes people forget ... that there are battered, raped and exploited women, or worse, to seek to exculpate men from that form of violence – which is obviously not the case. Understanding "symbolic" as the opposite of "real, actual", people suppose that symbolic violence is a purely "spiritual" violence, which ultimately has no real effects (ibid.: 339).

8. See, e.g., Holland and Eisenhart (1990), Pipher (1994), Merten (1996, 1997), Brown (1998, 2003), Weisman (2000), Lamb (2002), Simmons (2002) and Talbot (2002).
9. For similar material situations and parenting styles elsewhere, see Lareau (2000), Robbins (2006) and Demerath (2009).
10. Academic competition with Asian Americans is a deeply fraught issue for White students and their parents. For an in-depth discussion of how the White parents at a highly competitive high school in California with a large Asian American population reacted to these students' tendency to outperform their children academically by moving their children to schools with fewer Asian American students, see Hwang (2005).
11. Expression used by Faye Harrison (personal communication, 2008).
12. Kristen, the White cheerleader who was involved in the fight with Nadine and discussed in the case study presented in this analysis, is a case in point. Unlike most of the other parents whose permission I sought in order to include their child or children in the study, Kristen's parents desperately wanted her to be involved in my research project. It was not until much later that I understood why they were so different from most of the White parents: they thought her participation in the study would be influential in dissolving her relationship with her Black boyfriend. Ironically, she would not agree to participate in the study because she feared that I would learn too much about her relationship with her lover and share that information with her parents. My insistence that I was professionally obligated to keep all information confidential was not convincing.
13. Beverly Tatum's (1997) book is widely cited as evidence of the fact that Black students are guilty of self-segregation. My research at UGRH challenges that conventional wisdom. I argue that the Black table at UGRH was almost totally Black (with the exception being females from other racial-ethnic groups who were dating or trying to date the Black males at the school) primarily in response to the conventional wisdom that, like sex, with whom one eats is evidence of intimacy and acceptance. The exception to this is when eating serves an instrumental purpose (see Milner 2006). Moreover, as the ethnographic data presented here documents, it was the White girls who excluded the Black girls from the table in the cafeteria that was *not* defined as the Black table, and was also big enough to seat both groups without contact or interaction.
14. I use the term '[s]kinship' to capture the practice of racial haemorrhaging that is supplanting the once-impenetrable wall between Black and White racial categories. It acknowledges the emergence of a form of kinship that defies the binaries that White Americans have imposed on others since enslavement, which define every person with any visible African ancestry as ineligible for any social category other than Black regardless of their ancestry or paternity. African Americans have constructed an inclusive form of kinship, accepting every mother's child and extending mutuality to people unrelated by descent or marriage. The term '[s]kinship' describes the concurrent merging and dissolution of Black and White racial categories once the distinction between them is recognised as fictional, and highlights the saliency of skin colour and the emergence of an identity that is neither Black nor White. At UGRH, [s]kinship was evident as students who self-identified or were perceived by others as bi-racial or some identity other than African American rarely sat at the Black table, interacted with Black students or had sustained

relationships with them – except for some instances when a bi-racial (or a White, Asian or Hispanic) female opted to date a Black male classmate. This structurally supported intra-racial divide fuelled the existing stigmatisation and marginalisation of students racially defined as Black, leading to a Black table that was dark in skin colour, especially with regard to the female participants. For a more detailed explication, see Fordham (2010).

15. I did not have access to the students' files and I was unable to independently verify this claim, although one of Keyshia's teachers and several of her friends repeated this story.
16. This ethnographic vignette is drawn from Fordham (forthcoming).
17. Because Euro-Americans idealise 'progress' as the act of becoming – that is, a linear rather than a non-linear process (see Lee 1987) – it is erroneously assumed that if laws are passed (e.g., the Thirteenth Amendment to the U.S. Constitution) and other social remedies are put in place (e.g., Fair Housing legislation), using unquestionably efficacious mathematical formulae, we cannot explain or understand the messy, non-linear reality that is our daily reality. The failure of social legislation to produce the desired outcome is blamed on the inadequacy of the rules, legislation and so on, rather than the instrument(s) used to validate them and, by extension, the potentially inherent messiness of social life.
18. In her popular book, *The Bully, the Bullied and the Bystander*, Barbara Coloroso insists that bullying is not about anger but contempt: 'a powerful feeling of dislike toward somebody considered to be worthless, inferior or undeserving of respect' (Coloroso 2003: 20).

References

Anon. 2004. Staying at Home: Career Women Deciding to Stay at Home to Raise Their Kids, *60 Minutes*. CBS News, 10 October.

AAUW. 1991. *Shortchanging Girls, Shortchanging America*. Washington, DC: American Association of University Women.

Barlow, K., and C.E. Dunbar. 2010. Race, Class, and Whiteness in Gifted and Talented Identification: A Case Study. *Berkeley Review of Education* 1, no. 1: 63–85.

Baszile, J. 2009. *The Black Girl Next Door: A Memoir*. Clearwater, FL: Touchstone Books.

Belkin, L. 2003. The Opt-Out Revolution: Q: Why Don't More Women Get to the Top? A: They Choose Not To. *New York Times Magazine*, 26 October.

Benedict, R. 1934. *Patterns of Culture*. New York: Houghton Mifflin.

Bolick, K. 2011. All the Single Ladies. *Atlantic Monthly* 308, no. 4: 116–136.

Boo, K. 1995. The Tower Girls: At D.C. Home, Teen Girls Struggle to Recover the Futures They Left Behind. *Washington Post*, 12 February.

Bourdieu, P. 2004. Gender and Symbolic Violence. In *Violence in War and Peace: An Anthology* (eds) N. Scheper-Hughes and P. Bourgois, 339–342. Malden, MA: Blackwell.

Bourdieu, P., and L. Wacquant. 2004. Symbolic Violence. In *Violence in War and Peace: An Anthology* (eds) N. Scheper-Hughes and P. Bourgois, 272–274. Malden, MA: Blackwell.

Boyd, T. 1997. *Am I Black Enough For You? Popular Culture from the 'Hood and Beyond*. Bloomington: Indiana University Press.

Brown, L.M. 1998. *Raising Their Voices: The Politics of Girls' Anger*. Cambridge, MA: Harvard University Press.

——— 2003. *Girlfighting: Betrayal and Rejection among Girls*. New York: New York University Press.

Clifford, J. 1986. Introduction: Partial Truths. In *Writing Culture: The Poetics and Politics of Ethnography* (eds) J. Clifford and G.F. Marcus, 1–26. Berkeley: University of California Press.

Cohen, Y. 1971. The Shaping of Men's Minds: Adaptations to the Imperatives of Culture. In *Anthropological Perspectives on Education* (eds) M.L. Wax, S. Diamond and F.I. Gearing, 19–50. New York: Basic Books.

Collins, P.H. 1991. *Black Feminist Thought: Knowledge, Consciousness, and the Politics of Empowerment.* New York: Routledge.

Coloroso, B. 2003. *The Bully, the Bullied, and the Bystander.* New York: HarperCollins.

Coontz, S. [1992] 2002. *The Way We Never Were: American Families and the Nostalgia Trap.* New York: Basic Books.

—— 2005. *Marriage, a History: From Obedience to Intimacy, or How Love Conquered Marriage.* New York: Viking.

Corbett, K. 2001. Faggot=Loser. *Studies in Gender and Sexuality* 2, no. 1: 3–28.

Das, V. 2004. Language and Body: Transactions in the Construction of Pain. In *Violence in War and Peace: An Anthology* (eds) N. Scheper-Hughes and P. Bourgois, 327–333. Malden, MA: Blackwell.

Davis, A.Y. 1971. Reflections on the Black Woman's Role in the Community of Slaves. *Black Scholar* 12, no. 6: 2–15.

Demerath, P. 2009. *Producing Success: The Culture of Personal Advancement in an American High School.* Chicago: University of Chicago Press.

Dickar, M. 2008. *Corridor Cultures: Mapping Student Resistance at an Urban High School.* New York: New York University Press.

DiSesa, N. 2006. *Seducing the Boys' Club: Uncensored Tactics from a Woman at the Top.* New York: Ballantine Books.

Faludi, S. 1991. *Backlash: The Undeclared War Against American Women.* New York: Three Rivers Press.

Fiske, J. 1993. *Power Plays, Power Works.* London: Verso.

Fordham, S. 1988. Racelessness as a Factor in Black Students' School Success: Pragmatic Strategy or pyrrhic Victory? *Harvard Educational Review* 58, no. 1: 54–84.

—— 1993. 'Those Loud Black Girls': (Black) Women, Silence and Gender 'Passing' in the Academy. *Anthropology and Education Quarterly* 24, no. 1: 3–32.

—— 1996. *Blacked Out: Dilemmas of Race, Identity and Success at Capital High.* Chicago: University of Chicago Press.

—— 1998. Speaking Standard English From Nine to Three: Language as Guerrilla Warfare at Capital High. In *Kids Talk: Strategic Language Use in Later Childhood* (eds) C. Adger and S. Hoyle, 205–216. New York: Oxford University Press.

—— 1999. Dissin' 'the Standard': Ebonics as Guerrilla Warfare at Capital High. *Anthropology and Education Quarterly* 30, no. 3: 272–293.

—— 2008. Beyond Capital High: The Strange Career of 'Acting White'. *Anthropology and Education Quarterly* 39, no. 3: 227–246.

—— 2009. Write-ous Indignation: Black Girls, Dilemmas of Cultural Domination and the Struggle to Speak the Skin We Are In. In *Anthropology Off the Shelf: Anthropologists on Writing* (eds) A. Waterston and M.D. Vesperi, 79–92. New York: Wiley.

—— 2010. Passin' for Black: Race, Identity, and Bone Memory in Postracial America. *Harvard Educational Review* 80, no. 1: 4–30.

—— forthcoming. *Downed by Friendly Fire: Black Girls, White Girls and Female Competition at Underground Railroad High.* Minneapolis: University of Minnesota Press.

Fordham, S., and J.U. Ogbu. 1986. Black Students' School Success: Coping with the 'Burden of "Acting White"'. *Urban Review* 18, no. 3: 176–206.

Foucault, M. 1977. *Discipline and Punish: The Birth of the Prison* (trans. A. Sheridan). New York: Random House.

Harris, C.I. 1993. Whiteness as Property. *Harvard Law Review* 106, no. 8: 1707–1795.

Holland, D.C., and M.A. Eisenhart. 1990. *Educated in Romance: Women, Achievement, and College Culture*. Chicago: University of Chicago Press.

Hwang, S. 2005. The New White Flight. *Wall Street Journal*, 19 November.

Kimmel, M. 2002. Toward a Pedagogy of the Oppressor. *Tikkun* 17, no. 6: 42–48.

Kochman, T., and J. Mavrelis. 2009. *Corporate Tribalism: White Men/White Women and Cultural Diversity at Work.* Chicago: University of Chicago Press.

Lamb, S. 2002. *The Secret Lives of Girls: What Good Girls Really Do – Sex Play, Aggression, and Their Guilt.* New York: Free Press.

Lareau, A. 2000. *Unequal Childhoods: Class, Race, and Family Life*. Berkeley: University of California Press.

Lee, D.D. [1959] 1987. *Freedom and Culture.* Long Grove, IL: Waveland Press.

Lerner, G. 1986. *The Creation of Patriarchy*. Oxford: Oxford University Press.

Low, S. 2003. *Behind the Gates: Life, Security, and the Pursuit of Happiness in Fortress America*. New York: Routledge.

Loweon, J.W. 2006. *Sundown Towns: A Hidden Dimension of American Racism*. New York: Touchstone.

Merten, D.E. 1996. Burnout as Cheerleader: The Cultural Basis for Prestige and Privilege in Junior High School. *Anthropology and Education Quarterly* 27, no. 1: 51–70.

——— 1997. The Meaning of Meanness: Popularity, Competition, and Conflict among Junior High School Girls. *Sociology of Education* 70: 175–191.

Miliani, A. 1996. *Tales of Two Cities: A Persian Memoir*. Washington, DC: Mage Publishers.

Milner, M. 2006. *Freaks, Geeks, and Cool Kids: American Teenagers, Schools and the Culture of Consumption*. New York: Routledge.

Oakes, J. 1985. *Keeping Track: How Schools Structure Inequality.* New Haven: Yale University Press.

Parks, S. 2010. *Fierce Angels: The Strong Black Woman in American Life and Culture*. New York: One World Books.

Pascoe, C.J. 2007. *Dude, You're a Fag: Masculinity and Sexuality in High School*. Berkeley: University of California Press.

Perry, P. 2002. *Shades of White: White Kids and Racial Identity in High School*. Durham, NC: Duke University Press.

Pipher, M. 1994. *Reviving Ophelia: Saving the Selves of Adolescent Girls*. New York: Ballantine Books.

Pollack, W.S. 1998. *Real Boys: Rescuing our Sons from the Myths of Boyhood*. New York: Henry Holt.

Raybon, P. 1997. *My First White Friend: Confessions on Race, Love, and Forgiveness*. New York: Penguin.

Rimm, S. 1999. *See Jane Win: The Rimm Report on How 1,000 Girls Became Successful Women*. New York: Three Rivers Press.

Robbins, A. 2006. *The Overachievers: The Secret Lives of Driven Kids.* New York: Hyperion.

Rosenbaum, J. 1976. *Making Inequality: The Hidden Curriculum of High School Tracking.* New York: Wiley.

Sandberg, S. 2013. *Lean In: Women, Work and the Will to Lead.* New York: Alfred A. Knopf.

Simmons, R. 2002. *Odd Girl Out.* New York: Harcourt.
Spender, D., and E. Sarah (eds). 1988. *Learning to Lose: Sexism and Education* (rev. edn). London: Women's Press.
Steele, C. 1992. Race and Schooling of African Americans. *Atlantic Monthly* 269, no. 4: 68–78.
——— 2010. *Whistling Vivaldi and Other Clues to How Stereotypes Affect Us.* New York: Norton.
Talbot, M. 2002. Mean Girls and the New Movement to Tame Them. *New York Times Magazine*, 24 February.
Tatum, B.D. 1997. *'Why Are All the Black Kids Sitting Together in the Cafeteria?' A Psychologist Explains the Development of Racial Identity.* New York: Basic Books.
Tolman, D.L., and T.E. Higgins. 1996. How Being a Good Girl Can Be Bad for Girls. In *'Bad Girls'/'Good Girls': Women, Sex and Power in the Nineties* (eds) N.B. Maglin and D. Perry, 205–225. New Brunswick, NJ: Rutgers University Press.
Ward, M., and M. Edelstein. 1996. *A World Full of Women* (4th edn). Boston: Pearson.
Weisman, R. 2000. *Queen Bees and Wannabees.* New York: Crown.
Weitz, R., and L. Gordon. 1993. Images of Black Women among Anglo College Students. *Sex Roles* 28, nos. 1/2: 19–33.

Notes on Contributors

Susan Bayly is Reader in Historical Anthropology at the University of Cambridge. Her publications include *Saints, Goddesses and Kings: Muslims and Christians in South Indian Society 1700–1900* (Cambridge University Press, 1989), *Caste, Society and Politics in India from the Eighteenth Century to the Modern Age* (Cambridge University Press, 1999) and *Asian Voices in a Postcolonial Age: Vietnam, India and Beyond* (Cambridge University Press, 2007).

Rebecca Cassidy is Professor of Anthropology at Goldsmiths, University of London. Her publications include *The Sport of Kings: Kinship, Class and Thoroughbred Breeding in Newmarket* (Cambridge University Press, 2002) and *Horse People: Thoroughbred Culture in Lexington and Newmarket* (Johns Hopkins University Press, 2007); she also co-edited (with M. Mullin) *Where the Wild Things Are Now: Domestication Reconsidered* (Berg, 2006). She is currently the Principal Investigator of GAMSOC, a European Research Council funded project on gambling in Europe.

Joanna Cook is Lecturer in Medical Anthropology at University College London. She is the author of *Meditation in Modern Buddhism: Renunciation and Change in Thai Monastic Life* (Cambridge University Press, 2010) and co-editor of *Southeast Asian Perspectives on Power* (Routledge, 2012).

Peter Demerath is Associate Professor in the Department of Organizational Leadership, Policy, and Development at the University of Minnesota. A trained anthropologist, he is the author of *Producing Success: The Culture of Personal Advancement in an American High School* (University of Chicago Press, 2009) and numerous articles on achievement and education in both the U.S.A. and Papua New Guinea.

Signithia Fordham is Associate Professor of Anthropology at the University of Rochester. She is the author of *Blacked Out: Dilemmas of Race, Identity and Success at Capital High* (University of Chicago Press, 1996) and *Downed by Friendly Fire: Black Girls, White Girls and Female Competition at Underground Railroad High* (University of Minnesota Press, forthcoming).

Sarah F. Green is Professor of Social and Cultural Anthropology at the University of Helsinki. Her publications include *Urban Amazons: Lesbian Feminism and Beyond in the Gender, Sexuality and Identity Battles of London* (Macmillan, 1997) and *Notes From the Balkans: Locating Marginality and Ambiguity on the Greek–Albanian Border* (Princeton University Press, 2005).

Nicholas J. Long is Assistant Professor of Anthropology at the London School of Economics and Political Science. He is the co-editor of *Southeast Asian Perspectives on Power* (Routledge, 2012) and *Sociality: New Directions* (Berghahn, 2013) and author of *Being Malay in Indonesia: Hopes, Histories and Citizenship in the Riau Archipelago* (NUS/NIAS/University of Hawai'i Press, 2013).

Laura Mentore is Assistant Professor of Anthropology at the University of Mary Washington. She received her Ph.D. in social anthropology from the University of Cambridge. Her research is based in Amazonia and the Caribbean. Her primary areas of specialization include the anthropology of the environment, critical theories of development, indigenous cosmologies and indigenous social movements. Other teaching and research interests include economic anthropology and the anthropology of race and gender.

Henrietta L. Moore is Director of the Institute for Global Prosperity, and Chair of Culture, Philosophy and Design at University College London. She is the co-editor of *Understanding Global Sexualities* (Routledge, 2012) and *Sociality: New Directions* (Berghahn Books, 2013). Her most recent monograph is *Still Life: Hopes, Desires and Satisfactions* (Polity Press, 2011).

Olga Solomon is Assistant Professor of Occupational Science and Occupational Therapy at the University of Southern California. An applied linguist with a background in clinical psychology and linguistic anthropology, she is interested in the mutually constitutive relation of activity, experience and meaning, and in ways in which engagement and participation in everyday activities intersect with both personal experience and family life. Her research examines the socio-cultural, psycho-social and structural phenomena that support engagement and participation with an eye for mediating potentialities of social practices, innovations and technologies.

Kathleen C. Stewart is Professor and Chair of Anthropology at the University of Texas at Austin. She writes and teaches on affect, the ordinary, the senses and modes of ethnographic engagement based on curiosity and attachment. She is author of *A Space on the Side of the Road: Cultural Poetics in an 'Other' America* (Princeton University Press, 1996) and *Ordinary Affects* (Duke University Press, 2007).

Index

www.ingramcontent.com/pod-product-compliance
Lightning Source LLC
Chambersburg PA
CBHW060034030426
42334CB00019B/2319
9781785332159